on your side

The Story

of the

Nationwide Insurance Enterprise

By

Peter D. Franklin

Nationwide Insurance Enterprise

Columbus, Ohio

Dedicated to

Our Customers

and

Those Who Serve Them

CONTENTS

Foreword

This is a book about the future.

That's so of the history of any successful institution. It is constantly becoming what it will be. You can write but you can never finish its history for there are exciting new chapters to come.

On the following pages are exciting chapters that tell the story, so far, of the Nationwide Insurance Enterprise. While our founders thought far ahead in seeking to provide broad financial security, there were few clues of what the Nationwide Insurance Enterprise might be in the 21st century from what it began to become in the early part of the 20th: A group of farmers organizes the Ohio Farm Bureau Federation. Next thing they're setting up an insurance company. Fast-forward and that company is a multi-billion-dollar business complex with national reach and even global. How it got from there to here is the stuff of this book. So is a follow-through look at tomorrow.

Early on you'll read how an enduring Enterprise heritage was created, of the beliefs and values that still define what Nationwide has been, is, and always will be. The founders were good cooperators and the Nationwide heritage is steeped in that philosophy. For almost seven decades it has been the steady check and balance as decisions were made, changes shaped and progress forged.

To assure the ongoing success of Nationwide we will see in moving forward that all we do continues to be true to our founding beliefs and values. There's more about that in chapter 18, but please don't turn back and read it just yet. Savor the rest of the story first. In due course you'll discover that last chapter of this book is also the first of those future ones yet to be written.

The underlying theme of those future chapters will flow from action taken November 4, 1993, by the Nationwide Board of Directors. I presented to them and they approved a new Enterprise Vision. It is a Vision that reaffirms our founding doctrines while setting a common direction for the future. It is being shared by all of our Nationwide companies including affiliates and subsidiaries and by all Nationwide people. As this book is published we are deeply immersed in developing our collective understanding of the Enterprise Vision, and our unified dedication to it.

The past as chronicled herein is essential prologue to our Vision for the future. I know you'll enjoy this fascinating Nationwide story. The author has constructed it in rich detail and a readable and entertaining style. If you like a story with a plot that's good enough to be true, you'll want to read on.

D. Richard McFerson
President and Chief Executive Officer
Nationwide Insurance Enterprise

Introduction

This project began as an assignment to me from the Nationwide Board of Directors. They initially asked me to weave some of my observations into a history. Arden Shisler, our parent company board chairman, said, "John, you've got 40-plus years here; you can dictate it from memory." Arden can put a complex issue into very simple terms!

The book idea was timely, however. There's a little of our early story in *Vice President in Charge of Revolution.* That's the 1960 autobiography of our longtime President Murray Lincoln. But no real corporate history has been done otherwise or since.

We decided we should take a broader approach to this book than just my personal perspectives. We would capture the important subject matter while we still had good recollection by a number of key people. It would also be timely to cap off with a prospective glimpse toward Nationwide in the 21st century.

We further decided this book should not be a ponderous historical recitation but rather a people story. Show the spirit and progress of Nationwide. Look with some candor at learning from our mistakes as well as successes. Make it honest, accurate, interesting — and fun to read.

I wanted to be sure our story would make it clear that from the beginning, Nationwide has had a worthy social purpose. That includes helping people through insurance and financial services, through other activities such as communications, through cooperatives, and through charitable works of all kinds. If it is a meaningful cause, Nationwide people get behind it. Over the years Nationwiders have tried to respond to things that will really make a positive difference in other people's lives.

Nationwide has always been an organization based on a strong underlying philosophy and mission. It is more than a business.

(I had even thought "More Than a Business" would be another good title to consider for this book.) It was that broader humanitarian role that first attracted me to the company and was a great point of satisfaction throughout my career.

We were fortunate to commission an award-winning writer to author our history. Peter D. Franklin knew just enough about Nationwide beforehand to know what he didn't know. I think this helped him in being the thorough researcher and interviewer he was and asking the insightful and incisive questions.

My own involvement with this project has been a great chance to reflect on my sincere appreciation for the privilege of having been associated almost all of my working life with what is now the Nationwide Insurance Enterprise. This is an important book and it was high time for it. I am immensely grateful to those on the Nationwide board who thought it should be done and I trust you will come to share that feeling.

John E. Fisher
General Chairman and Chief Executive Officer, Retired
Nationwide Insurance Enterprise

Acknowledgments

Perhaps you have wondered who are all the people authors list in their acknowledgments. In my case the list begins with Ed Bley, to whom I owe so much for showing me the way so many years ago. Most recently added to the list are those on whom I heavily relied to flesh out this story, check for the accuracy of the most minute, and seemingly insignificant, details, cut through red tape, lend support in my darkest hours, and otherwise try to make my task easier.

Although he had been dead for 27 years at the time I started this project in the summer of 1993, Murray D. Lincoln was of invaluable assistance. Lincoln's papers, on file in Nationwide's archives, provided a wealth of information and often devastating insight to the decision-making process between 1926 and 1964, when he retired. Most of his speeches to the board were taped, transcribed and filed: That is why today we have so many of his thoughts, word for word.

Beyond the documents on file, I conducted more than 150 hours of interviews with executives, agents, directors and retirees, as well as others outside the Nationwide Insurance Enterprise. I can't single out all of them for praise, but I think each knows how much I enjoyed learning from them.

Stephen A. Rish, vice president–public relations, and his entire public relations and corporate communications staff get special mention, including Louis V. Fabro, director–media relations; Mark A. Mills, communication services manager, and Bea Hahne, secretary to William C. Lamneck, director–enterprise communication services. He served as coordinator of the book project and as chief whip-cracker.

I owe retired General Chairman John E. Fisher and President and Chief Executive Officer D. Richard McFerson a big dose of thanks. They put in many more hours before the tape recorder than anyone. Charlotte Glenn, secretary to Mr. Fisher, and

Fran Higgins, executive secretary to the enterprise secretary, were so very helpful, as were Robert A. Bober, manager-records administration and corporate archivist; his associate in the archives, Matthew Ardrey, and Vicki F. Blackford, chief Nationwide librarian, and her staff.

Others who helped immeasurably include: Mary Dabner, administrative assistant to the president, and Brad Zweck, manager, public relations, Wausau Insurance Companies. Robert L. Chapman, president, Proliance Insurance Co., Columbus, who shared his boyhood memories of his neighbor, Lincoln; Dr. Jerry C. Doss of Neenah, WI; James C. Bradford Jr. of Louisville, KY.; Dan Barringer, records specialist, company history unit, State Farm Insurance Companies, Bloomington, IL.; Robert A. Lincoln of Wrentham, MA., the only surviving Lincoln brother; the Columbus Metropolitan Library; Diane McGuire of the Raynham Historical Commission, Raynham, MA; Cindy Hollingshead, secretary to C. William Swank at the Ohio Farm Bureau; Thomas C. Thomsen of Waccabuc, NY; Mrs. Robert Acton, of Wellston, OH; Robert W. Gunderson, retired vice president, advertising, Wausau Insurance Companies; Lou T. Zellner, senior vice president, corporate planning, Mortgage Guaranty Insurance Corp., Milwaukee; Terri Leist, chief of public information, Ohio Department of Insurance, and Sheldon Goldberg, historian, Center for Air Force History, Bolling Air Force Base, DC.

Finally, it is most important that everyone know that this book could not have been written without the incredible support of Eleanor, my wife of more than 39 years. To have her on my side through the years has meant so much, especially in the most difficult of times. Never will I be able to adequately express to her my deepest appreciation — and love.

Peter D. Franklin
October 1994

What's in a title?

The title for this book comes from an advertising slogan Nationwide has used since 1973 — *Nationwide is on your side!* The company's New York advertising agency, Ogilvy-Mather, created the slogan. It was intended to reflect Nationwide's tradition and intention to be customer-oriented.

The Nationwide "N-and-Eagle" trademark has been in use since September 1, 1955, the date the company changed its name to Nationwide. It was born of the combined efforts of a corporate task force, two design firms and 25 designers.

The "N-and-Eagle" served to reflect the national scope of Nationwide's expanding operations. The eagle has long been an accepted symbol of strength and national protection, a bird that stands alert and proud on a lofty perch, capable of soaring to great heights. The record of the Nationwide Insurance Enterprise seems worthy of its trademark.

1

THE START OF SOMETHING BIG

The practiced and firm hand crafted the signature, "Ezra C. Anstaett," at the bottom of the simple form. As he began to put the pen down, the photographer asked for "just one more" opportunity to record the scene.

"Now, Mr. Lincoln; if you would just move in a little closer to Mr. Anstaett this time. And you, too, Mr. Palmer; just a little closer. And gentlemen, let's try one this time with both of you looking at the paper Mr. Anstaett is signing. Good, good. That's good."

Murray D. Lincoln, a tall, almost gaunt, figure, quickly ran his hand over the few locks that fell across an otherwise bald head. Lincoln was the executive secretary of the Ohio Farm Bureau Federation, and the cherub-faced Lee B. Palmer, a sheep breeder from Licking County, was in his third term as president.

Both looked down at the seated Anstaett and stared, as requested, at the first auto insurance policy issued by the Farm Bureau Mutual Automobile Insurance Company. Although none present knew it, it was the start of something big.

The issuance of the initial policy to Anstaett was largely

ceremonial. After all, it was only four days earlier, on April 10, 1926, that the insurance company obtained a license to do business in Ohio. Two days later it acquired its financing, a $10,000 loan drawn from the membership dues of the Ohio Farm Bureau Federation and secured by the Society for Savings Bank in Cleveland.

The sole public notice of the new company appeared in the *Ohio State Journal* April 14, 1926. The headline over the two-paragraph story noted "Farm Insurance Company Gets Issuing Permit."

The policy to which Anstaett affixed his signature insured his 1924, four-cylinder, "Tudor" Ford sedan valued at $690. For $300 worth of insurance, he agreed to pay $7.82 every six months: 58 cents for fire, $1.74 for theft, $2.50 for collision, $1 for property damage and $2 for personal injury.

Not only was Anstaett the first customer of Farm Bureau Mutual, he was its first employee and first general agent.

As a young firebrand out of Clermont County Anstaett made his mark by successfully recruiting members for the Farm Bureau there. The direct result of his pioneering work was an invitation from Lincoln to join the organization's home office in Columbus. The salary: $250 a month. Anstaett accepted and brought with him "a profound talent for organization and sales promotion and a wellspring of personal enthusiasm."[1]

Anstaett arrived at the Farm Bureau's two-room office in the Southern Hotel on a chilly, gray day in December 1920. There he found the 29-year-old Lincoln, who had been on the job since March 15, buried in his work. What, the eager Anstaett asked, would the executive secretary like him to do?

"Sit over there and keep busy," replied Lincoln, pointing to a desk. Many were to comment in later years that Lincoln's oft-abrupt manner sometimes stomped on the social graces.

Although somewhat dismayed by the lack of direction, Anstaett plowed into menial tasks. After three months Lincoln asked Anstaett to check out stories emanating from the Cleveland Better Business Bureau that strong-armed shysters were operating in the corn fields.

Anstaett established the bureau's investigative department after confirming that farmers were indeed being fleeced by dishonest securities salesmen. Not only did he put the skids to much of the fraudulent activity under the watchful eye of the bureau's investigative department, established in 1921, but Anstaett's work also led to the rewriting in 1923 of Ohio's Blue Sky law requiring all investment companies to register with the state.[2] That year the state recorded nearly 2,400 license rejections or revocations, or about 50 times the number posted in 1921, the year Anstaett began his investigation.

Con artists were the least of the farmers' problems in the 1920s, though. Their "crash" came at the beginning of the decade, not at the end.

Many farmers prospered before and during World War I. As quickly as the money rolled in, it rolled out again to buy more land and more machinery. When government and overseas orders dried up after "the war to end war,"* the bottom fell out, ending 25 years of unprecedented agricultural abundance.

With only a brief respite in 1923, farm prices plunged. At the turn of the decade, for example, the price of wheat went from $2.50 a bushel to 32 cents a bushel. Corn prices fared no better, dropping more than 75 percent to almost 30 cents a bushel. Beef sold for slightly more than 5 cents a pound at the Chicago stockyards. Sheep growers felt lucky to get 20 cents a pound for their wool, less than a third the price it had been. Crops became fuel for the kitchen stove or rotted in the field, not worth the harvest.

---

* In 1914 H.G. Wells wrote a book *The War That Will End War.* Although many after World War I used the phrase in altered forms, such as "the war to end all war," Wells claimed authorship of "the war to end war" in an article in *Liberty,* December 29, 1934, p. 4.

Foreclosure after foreclosure followed. Even if a farmer held on to his land, the rising costs for fuel, fertilizer, seed and transportation left little for anything else. "They (the farmers) were, for all practical purposes, nonconsumers in the nation's consumer society."[3]

The "consumer society" hardly noticed. It was too busy roaring through the decade. The White House inhabitant, President Calvin Coolidge, told the nation, "The business of America is business." Al Capone and other mobsters listened and did their part, bolstered by Prohibition. Charles "Lucky" Lindbergh flew the Atlantic Ocean, Gertrude Ederle swam the English Channel and Red Grange crossed everybody's goal line. Al Jolson dropped to one knee in *The Jazz Singer* but Babe Ruth brought him to his feet again with 60 big ones.

An Ohio State University professor, R.F. Taber of the Department of Rural Economics, saw different and disturbing numbers developing down on the farm, however. "An analysis of farmers' accounts," he said, "showed a decrease of income of 40 percent and an increase of expense of 13 percent in 1920 as compared to 1919."[4] In 1921 and 1922, it got even worse.

In his unpublished early history of the Ohio Farm Bureau Federation, Perry L. Green also noted the "desperate" economic straits farmers faced. Green was president of the organization from 1933 to 1948 and a close Lincoln confidant. He also served as an Ohio legislator from Portage County and as director of the Ohio Department of Agriculture. He wrote of the farmer:

"Because of his over-expansion in real estate and the increasing capital needs for power equipment, he had built up a debt structure that was in great disparity with farm prices. All this created a chronic economic illness with which he struggled until another war finally came to his relief."[5]

Lincoln and the Ohio Farm Bureau Federation struggled with the times, too, although initially the task seemed almost as easy as plowing a rockless field. Farmers were looking for help.

The Farm Bureau's growth immediately following its founding January 27, 1919, in the Botany and Zoology Building at The Ohio State University was as rapid as any state farm organization in the land. By early 1921, a total of 92,901 farmers had invested in a membership at fees ranging from $10 in 13 Ohio counties to $1 in 69 others.*

One of the early volunteers to travel the rural back roads in search of members was Lincoln, even though in 1919 he still worked as the agricultural representative of the Society for Savings Bank in Cleveland. His efforts as a salesman surely made him the butt of a joke or two among the wags at the Farm Bureau: Green reports that Lincoln made 18 calls in one day and failed to make a single sale.[6]

"I used to shrink from … (going) up and down the roads, asking other farmers" to join the Farm Bureau, Lincoln recalled many years later. To him it was "literally begging; that's what we were doing … "

Other farmer-salesmen had much greater success, as did their counterparts across the nation. Like crocus in the spring, state farm organizations popped up, one after the other, gaining not only members but economic and political strength. The Ohio group, one of the largest, also was an early supporter of the American Farm Bureau Federation, which also quickly grew to more than 1.5 million in national membership.

As the farmers' Depression took hold, however, membership dwindled as quickly as it had grown. In Ohio, farmers either couldn't spare the money for the fee or they didn't see the organization helping them through their crisis. Within five years Ohio Farm Bureau membership declined by two-thirds.

Lincoln remained confident. "Farmers of Ohio are solving and can continue to solve their economic problems by the

---

* Only six of the 88 Ohio counties were without any Farm Bureau members, according to Murray D. Lincoln, "A Year's Achievement of the Ohio Farm Bureau Federation," June 1, 1921.

application of self-help. ... In the main, the problems recently faced by farmers have been economic, and our hope lies in economic remedies rather than in looking to Congress or the Legislature for those things which we have within our power to do."

Green recorded that this was the early formulation of a philosophical statement that Lincoln was to make repeatedly: "People have within their own hands the tools to fashion their own destiny."[7]

Then as today, the primary goal of the national and state farm organizations was to influence legislation and make the system more equitable for the farmer. Under President Coolidge big business enjoyed a postwar utopia, what with loose regulation, easy money and low taxes. Agriculture carried an estimated 75 percent of the tax load.

"Business should be unhampered and free," Silent Cal told the New York State Chamber of Commerce. He believed the country had enough laws, "and we would be better off if we did not have any more," he said on another occasion.[8]

Lincoln understood the need for legislative action when he quit the Cleveland bank and accepted the job as the Ohio Farm Bureau's chief executive officer, but his interests clearly lay in discovering and developing the "economic remedies." To reach his goals and uphold his ideals, he willingly would fight for them.

One of the early battles in which he became embroiled involved the price of fertilizer. In the early 1920s the Ohio Farm Bureau and virtually every other farm organization fought on national and local levels against the large industry cartels that had jacked up fertilizer prices to near wartime levels.

On the national scene the battleground centered on the giant Muscle Shoals hydroelectric dam and nitrate plant on the Tennessee River in Alabama. It was to have produced nitrates for the war effort, but the plant was completed only after World

War I. Then the federal government had to decide what to do with it.

All manner of political animals teamed up to gain control of the project, among them Henry Ford and Thomas Edison. These giants of American ingenuity saw in Muscle Shoals an opportunity to create a wellspring for industry and agriculture. Muscle Shoals would provide the power for huge factories — including those to make Ford parts — thousands of homes and for low-cost fertilizer.

"It has been his dream," said one of Ford's top engineers, "to make fertilizers so low (in cost) that everybody can use all he wants."[9]

That attracted the attention of many farm groups who supported Ford and Edison. In the main, however, the farmer bloc favored public ownership as the best path to inexpensive fertilizer over the long haul. Lined up solidly on the side of privatization were the power companies and the large chemical concerns whose interests were to maintain control of their industries.

A long and bitter fight in the Congress ensued. Legislation that would have put the development in the hands of the people was vetoed by President Coolidge and President Herbert C. Hoover, both of whom wanted to avoid any semblance of government competition with private interests. It was not until the first administration of President Franklin D. Roosevelt that the public interest won out with the creation of the Tennessee Valley Authority for the benefit of the people of the region.

Farm organizations claimed victory and a sense of new political power, but Lincoln was not impressed. He always had a bigger idea in mind.

"My interests lay in a different direction. I wanted to see the Farm Bureau used to persuade farmers to create economic organizations through which they could acquire the power to solve their own problems."[10]

Again, the theme: "People have within their own hands the tools to fashion their own destiny."

Even before the protracted fray over Muscle Shoals began in Washington, Lincoln and the Farm Bureau "launched what has been termed 'the revolution in burlap.' The Ohio Farm Bureau members pooled their orders and went shopping for better prices."[11]

The combines monopolizing fertilizer products in Ohio rejected the bureau's business. They would not lower the price nor would they sell to any cooperative.

"These men ... added insult to injury by flatly declaring that they were not going to ruin their business for 'any bunch of scab farmers.' At that moment the revolution in burlap really got under way."[12]

Little did the fertilizer kings realize that Lincoln had an ace of sorts up his sleeve. It came in the guise of a tip: Henry Ford was preparing to cut the price of his automobiles.

Lincoln soon found a way to use the inside information. The National Fertilizer Association, concerned about the aggressive activity of the Ohio farm group, convened a special meeting in Columbus and summoned Lincoln to appear before the board at the Deshler Hotel. J.T. Welch, president of the Welch Chemical Company, led the questioning why Lincoln had advised farmers to hold off buying fertilizer.

"I've been told the price of Ford cars is going to come down," Lincoln replied, "and when that happens other things are going to have to come down, too, including fertilizer. I think farmers ought to know about it."

"We don't think you have any right as a government agent to be telling farmers what to buy or what not to buy, or when to do either," Welch said, bristling.

"Oops! Who told you I was a government agent?"

"Aren't you?"

"No, sir."

"Who does employ you then?"

"A bunch of independent farmers," Lincoln said. The meeting came to an abrupt end.[13]

The "revolution in burlap" continued as the Farm Bureau sought new, stable and less costly supplies of fertilizer. Forrest Ketner, a former Delaware county agent and the first man hired by Lincoln in the Farm Bureau, searched far and wide before finding a provider in Atlanta. Shipments began out of the South but the first of them never arrived in Ohio.

Chester A. Dyer, a state lobbyist for various farm interests, including the Farm Bureau, was dispatched to track down the missing shipment. He found the railroad freight sitting on a siding in Harrisburg, PA, and a sticker on the side of each boxcar: "Scab fertilizer. Kill it."[14]

Eventually the fertilizer began to flow in at lower prices, saving Ohio farmers between $7 and $12 per ton, according to Lincoln. Flushed with success he then moved toward establishing similar arrangements to purchase and market dairy products, poultry and eggs, fruits and vegetables and livestock. The extra activity led to the establishment January 9, 1923, of the Ohio Farm Bureau Service Company.

Ohio farmers also were having a problem with the feed they bought. It was not the price in this instance as much as what Lincoln described as the "pure rubbish" purveyors put in it. The service company gathered up the experts, who advised the Farm Bureau how to combine nutritious feed for the best results for the different livestock.

Like the fertilizer the Farm Bureau marketed, an analysis of the ingredients went on each bag of feed. Both were innovations in their time. Also among the recommendations from the assembled experts was for chick feed to include cod-liver oil, otherwise known as "barreled sunlight." It was a big success.

Lincoln loved to tell the story of Joe Horchow, a friend who inquired about the workings of the Farm Bureau. It also gave

Lincoln the germ of an idea.

"We set up the Farm Bureau, you pay $10 and that's the chamber of commerce: We work on legislation and education," Lincoln explained. "Then we market your livestock, and grain, and you buy your feed through the service company. You got a finance company to finance you, and … "

Horchow wiggled in his chair and interrupted.

"Now, let me see if I can tell this story right. I pay you $10 and that's gone. And you use that for educational purposes. Then you take my livestock and you sell it for me, and you make a little money on it. And my wheat. And my poultry and eggs. And you buy my feed and fertilizer, and you make a little money on it. And you lend me money, and you make some money on that."

"Yeh, supposed to," Lincoln said.

"What the hell do I pay you $10 for?" Horchow asked. "If you did that much business with *me*, I'd pay *you* $10!"[15]

In the early days of the Farm Bureau, most farmers thought like Horchow: When times were hard, it didn't make any difference how much service was offered. "Literally begging" for memberships often was not enough.

Lincoln said to himself, "By gum, I think that guy's got something." Others were taking from the farmer and not giving enough in return. "And that's where we started to think of what finally resolved into the sponsoring idea," whereby the selling of insurance is tied to membership in the Farm Bureau.

To this day organizations such as the Ohio, Pennsylvania and Maryland farm bureaus that sponsor, or endorse, the Nationwide Insurance Enterprise, receive from the insurance companies fees in return for assisting Nationwide's marketing efforts within the sponsor's membership. Nationwide provides products and services that will serve the interests of the sponsor's members.

The Great Depression for the nation was still in the womb.

The farmer would struggle for economic survival for six more years before millions of the "consumer society" would experience much the same pain of economic deprivation. For the Ohio Farm Bureau Federation, however, it had survived its infancy and had held its own against the odds. By 1923, the four-year-old organization had successfully taken up the tools to fashion its own destiny.

2

THE MAN FROM MASSACHUSETTS

When Ralph Waldo Emerson observed that "an institution is the lengthened shadow of one man," he might well have been thinking of Murray Danforth Lincoln. No one cast a greater shadow over the Nationwide enterprise than he.

Emerson and Lincoln were not contemporaries, of course: Almost 90 years separated them, but both could lay claim to a sturdy Massachusetts heritage. Emerson was born in Boston; Lincoln about 40 miles to the south, in Raynham.

Raynham was a rural, Protestant and hard-rock Republican community in the waning years of the 19th century. It also was a poor community, made more so after Zeno Kelly filed for bankruptcy and closed his shoe plant. That was in 1893. He was a victim of the industrial revolution that passed Raynham by. The manufacture of shoes went to nearby communities, such as Fall River and Brockton.

Others in Raynham were victims, too. Many farm families had supplemented their incomes by stitching leather and affixing heels and soles for Zeno Kelly. When those earnings vanished, the meager harvest from the unyielding, rocky land could not support growing families. Some gave up and followed the shoe industry into larger communities. In their flight they often left behind their debts.

As a result Lincoln's grandfather, Edward, became a casualty, too. He was a farmer, but attached to the front of his large, white home on Broadway near Shaw's Corner was a small country store that served for many years as Raynham's council hall and community center. Farmers would buy dry goods, tools and provisions and pay for them after the harvest of mostly potatoes and berries. The store hadn't been there always; it originally was in nearby Easton. In 1823 it was towed by six yoke of oxen and moved to Raynham on rollers.[1]

Minot J. Lincoln, father of Murray, four other sons and a daughter, also worked at the store when not on the family's 38-acre farm and ran both after his father died in 1913. Minot, who was given the name of an uncle for whom Minot's Lighthouse in Boston's harbor is named, also was a musician, actor and a member of the state legislature in 1908.

The Lincolns traced their heritage to 17th century immigrants from Norfolkshire, England, who first settled in Hingham, MA., now a southern suburb of burgeoning Boston. Among that first wave of Lincolns to immigrate was Thomas, a miller who moved to Taunton, just a few miles from Raynham. It is from his family that Murray Lincoln descended.

Hingham is also the name of a small town in Norfolk, England. It is the ancestral home of Abraham Lincoln, a bust of whom is in the community's parish church. Not too far from Hingham are the towns of East, South and West Raynham. The relationship between Thomas, the miller, and the 16th president of the United States is hazy at best.

Helen Sampson (nee Andrews) Lincoln gave birth to her second son, Murray, on April 18, 1892, in the family's home, Trow House. His middle name, Danforth, was his grandmother's maiden name.

Trow House was a large and beautiful farmhouse, shaded by three large chestnut trees and surrounded by beds of flowers and vegetables. A latticework of wire spread between the barn and the house to support the sturdy vines of Concord grapes that the Lincoln women made into jelly and juice. Scores of cherry, apple, plum and pear trees dotted the property.

"Grandfather Edward (a friend of the renowned American horticulturist Luther Burbank) even developed an apple that he called the Lincoln Seedling," recalled his grandson and Murray Lincoln's brother, Robert.* "It was as big as a grapefruit, deep red, and even when ripe was as hard as a rock, but when you took a bite it was sweet and juicy."

The year Murray Lincoln was born was the eve of hard times, however. The nation didn't know it yet, but just 12 months away was a Depression that would see the lowest wholesale prices in 120 years and the failure of nearly 500 banks and 15,000 businesses. Grandfather Lincoln's store almost folded.

"Grandfather began to incur indebtedness — indebtedness that he was never able to pay off," Lincoln wrote more than 60 years later.[2] His grandfather was too proud to file for bankruptcy; the same could be said for his son and Murray's father, Minot. He also struggled with the store. The burden of paying off debts fell on the family.

"For my own part, it wasn't until 1926 that I was able to pay off some of the debts that the industrial revolution had inflicted upon our family," Lincoln wrote. Nevertheless, the family saved the farm, which Murray's brother, Arthur Howard, continued to operate for many years. Today Interstate 495 runs through the property.

---

* Of the five Lincoln brothers, Robert Sampson Lincoln was in 1994 the sole surviving child of Minot and Helen Lincoln. He was born in 1908, the youngest son, and some 16 years the junior of Murray. Robert Lincoln, a retired laboratory technician for General Electric, lived with his wife, Thelma Mae, in Wrentham, Mass.

Murray Lincoln enjoyed working on the farm "because farming was such hard work." He had little interest in school, yet realized it was a necessary evil if he wanted to attend an agricultural college, which he did.

He was an excellent student at North Raynham Grammar School and later, as a gawky, growing teenager, at the Oliver Ames High School at North Easton 10 miles away. There he played saxophone in the band and competed for top honors in typing class with his future bride, Anne S. Hurst, a North Easton resident and "the best-looking girl in the class."

There couldn't have been too many dates inasmuch as Lincoln had a business that occupied much of his time. Each morning during his high school years he would demand the assistance of his two younger brothers, Warren and Arthur, to load a horse-drawn wagon with a ton of stone taken from the farm. After school Murray drove the load to the stone-crushing plant in Raynham and unloaded it. On Saturdays he sometimes would haul three loads to the crusher. For this he was paid 50 cents a ton.

Subsequently he made enough to have a two-horse team and a larger, stronger wagon, able to carry three tons. Shortly before graduation, however, the two horses and the wagon were stolen. He and others commented many times that if the thief hadn't interrupted his "career," Nationwide Insurance would not have happened.

By 1910 Lincoln's pockets bulged with $125 in stone-hauling proceeds, enough to enter the Massachusetts Agricultural College at Amherst, MA. Today it's the University of Massachusetts. Minot and Helen Lincoln had hoped their son would become a teacher, but he had set his mind to farming, even though he wasn't at all sure a farmer needed a college education.

His parents were unable to provide support, so Lincoln worked first in the college's cornfields and then in the barn. He earned 15 cents an hour for cleaning out the horse and cow stalls, which fit right into his interest in dairying and animal husbandry.

During his four years at MAC, Lincoln was introduced to Professor William "Pop" Hart, an affable gentleman who taught a harmless course entitled, "Agricultural Education." Lincoln only signed up for the class because it would earn him a few easy credits, but he later admitted it was "the single most significant course I ever took in college. (It was) the basis for the county agent or extension service."[3]

Hart played a key role in determining Lincoln's career, which probably was fortuitous inasmuch as the young student was foundering somewhat. All he knew was he wanted to pursue a career in agriculture. What's more important, among the dozens of lines of work he had considered, he knew he didn't want to sell insurance.

"Insurance … was for the weaklings who could do nothing else," Lincoln wrote in his book, *Vice President in Charge of Revolution.** "During two summer vacations I trimmed apple trees and did like jobs to escape the effete horrors of selling insurance."[4]

In later years Mrs. Lincoln laughed when she recalled what her husband had said in his young and impetuous days. "He told me, 'There are two things I'll never do — sell insurance and sell books.' He wound up doing both."

Lincoln must have thought "Pop" Hart had saved him from a fate worse than death when he called him into his office in his senior year.

---

* The title for Lincoln's 1960 book, written "as told to" David Karp, apparently originated from an article in the *Harvard Business Review*. At a President's Staff Conference July 11, 1955, Lincoln recommended the reading of three articles in the *Review*, one of which (unidentified) suggested "large corporations employ a vice president of the revolution" to create new ideas. At a subsequent staff conference September 19, 1955, Lincoln mused, "Perhaps we need a 'vice president in charge of the revolution' who will discuss with everyone ways to improve everything we are doing."

"Murray, I'd like you to go down to New London, Connecticut, to apply for a job."

"A job? What sort of job?" Lincoln was puzzled. He had yet to complete his senior year. (Hart and other professors arranged for Lincoln to get his degree even after he left school.)

"I don't know much about it, but it sounds like just the thing we've been talking about in class. ... They are looking for a young man who knows something about modern farming and wants to help the farmer. ... Are you interested?"

"Well, sure," Lincoln replied and headed for the job interview.[5] He beat out seven other candidates to become the first county agricultural agent in New England. He was 20 and earning $100 a month.

Although he was tall, he still looked young, "so young that my joints looked green," Lincoln himself remarked. It often made it hard for him to gain the confidence of the Connecticut Yankee farmers who resisted his best efforts to help them.

"How old are you?" Lawrence Dodge asked Lincoln one day. Dodge was a representative of the U.S. Department of Agriculture who checked on Lincoln's progress from time to time.

Lincoln told him, and Dodge's face fell in alarm.

"What's the matter, Larry?"

"Why, good grief, fellow. You aren't old enough to be an employee of the U.S. Department of Agriculture."

"Well, no one asked me my age. I didn't volunteer it."

"I'll tell you what to do," Dodge said. "You raise a mustache. You're big enough so you could have a mustache and nobody'd ever think to question your age again."

So Lincoln did, and he continued to grow one off and on throughout his life. As he said later, "I have the distinction of growing the only mustache ever decreed by the United States Department of Agriculture."[6]

But hair on the upper lip didn't help that much in

Connecticut, where the old-timers sought every opportunity to take the college lad down a peg or two. Still, he could recall having a chuckle or two on occasion.

One such came on a visit to a prominent dairy farmer in Stonington. Upon passing through the farm gate, Lincoln noticed what he thought at first were goats; then he realized they were Jersey cows, and a sorry lot they were.

"Good heavens, man. What in the world is your source of income?" Lincoln asked.

The farmer snapped back. "Source of income, young man? Hell, we don't have any up here. We live on lack of expense."

Despite the harshness of the stony land and the oft indifference to his efforts, Lincoln had some success in Connecticut. He rid a few farms of army worms, got some farmers to improve production through the use of more fertilizer, pooled the farmers' resources for the purchase of fertilizer, fencing, feed and seed so the larger lots would save farmers money, and tried, in vain, to establish a milk cooperative.

At virtually every bump in the road, Lincoln turned to his mentor, "Pop" Hart, for advice and support.

"Don't give up your ideas," Hart told him when opposition mounted to the milk cooperative. "Keep on using your head, and we'll find some way of helping you do what you ought to be doing."[7]

Hart's help came again early in 1915. He urged his protégé to consider joining the Plymouth County Trust Company, a bank in Brockton, as its agricultural representative.

"At that time bankers and industry leaders across the country were suddenly awakened to the fact that the farmer might become a sizable customer for their money and goods. The combination of enlightened benevolence and self-interest led to an interest in promoting agricultural education and hastened the development of farm organizations."[8]

For Lincoln the opportunity was "love at first sight," not for the job necessarily, but because it put him just a few miles from Easton where the apple-of-his-eye, Anne Hurst, still lived. Lincoln bought an engagement ring with his first paycheck and eight months later, on October 9, 1915, they married. They honeymooned for 10 days at Rangeley Lakes, ME, and moved in with Grandmother Lincoln.

In C.P. Holland, the president of the bank, Lincoln found another loyal supporter. "Now, young man, you just do whatever you think ought to be done around here," Holland told his newest employee. When the 23-year-old agricultural representative ran into a problem with a customer or a stockholder, Holland invariably bailed him out. Holland also offered Lincoln the wisdom of his years, serving up advice concerning a variety of matters important for a young businessman to know.

"Murray, one of the first things to do is to take care of what you've got," Holland told him one day. "You can shine your shoes even if there are holes in their soles. You can have pressed pants even if they're patched. You can have a clean shirt, even though the cuffs are frayed. And when you're before the public you want to put on the best personal appearance you can."[9]

In later years, when Lincoln was buying his suits at Brooks Brothers (he was a favorite customer of the tony New York haberdashery), he remembered Holland's fatherly advice, often expressing concern with the correctness of his appearance.

"Can you tell I've been out in the barn this morning?" he whispered to an associate at the beginning of a Nationwide Insurance board meeting, concerned that the odors picked up on his farm on Sunbury Road, Gahanna, OH, might still linger.[10]

At Plymouth County Trust Lincoln again set out to help the dairy farmers in the Brockton area by encouraging them to establish their own milk processing plant. Holland and his board agreed to finance the plan to buy out Brockton's largest milk distributor, but that wasn't going to be easy. Weston Manley was "the archvillain in the milk drama," Lincoln said.

Even Manley's own brother believed it. "Murray," he said, "you're going up against one of the meanest men in the country. I can tell you that honestly, even if he is my brother. ... Take fair warning: Watch out for him. Don't trust him an inch."[11]

Sixty thousand dollars is what Manley said he wanted for his plant, but when Lincoln offered $30,000, Manley surprised everyone by accepting the offer. What really knocked one and all off their feet, though, was the farmers' choice for plant general manager. It was Weston Manley .

"Good grief!" cried Lincoln. "It wasn't more than a few weeks ago that you told me you detested that man worse than anything in the world!"

"Yes, we did," the farmers replied, "but we figure if he was sharp enough to get all he could out of us, he'll get all he can out of others — but this time he'll be doing it for us."[12]

Lincoln's troubles did not go away. *The Brockton Enterprise* attacked him for conspiring with the farmers to raise milk prices, thus depriving infants of it. His opponent this time was Fred Field, owner of the paper, the local shoe company, and president of a competing bank. The situation for Lincoln was as black as the headlines and getting blacker.

Then he got lucky — again. Holland called him into the office.

"Murray, you're doing fine work here, and I think the milk plant is going to straighten itself out soon," Holland began. "I'd hate to lose you, but in your own interest I think you ought to go out to Cleveland and look into this proposition."

Holland handed Lincoln a letter from Myron T. Herrick, president of the Society for Savings Bank, Cleveland, former governor of Ohio and twice ambassador to France. Herrick thought the bank should have an agricultural representative, somebody to talk business with Ohio's farmers, as he had. As a young man he sold dinner bells to farmers.

Lincoln went home to Anne to tell her about the new opportunity. She recently had given birth to their daughter, Elizabeth Brett,* and he wanted to make sure she would take to the idea of moving. She did.

At the time Lincoln was taking a course to improve his business letter writing. "By golly, Anne," he said. "I'm going to see if I've learned anything in this course" and wrote a letter to Herrick expressing interest in the job.

For years Mrs. Lincoln tried in vain to break her husband of the habit of beginning a sentence with "By golly … "[13] It stuck with him throughout his life, though, as did his Massachusetts twang that created words such as "Americar," "idear" and "Cuyahogar." While in Cleveland Lincoln attended night school to improve his public speaking, but the twang was still there at the end.

Upon arrival in Ohio in 1917 Lincoln found the state to be "a fertile paradise I hadn't thought existed outside the Book of Revelation." It had no stones.[14] His start at the Society for Savings Bank was a bit rocky, however. At the outset he had neither an office nor a car, both of which had been promised, nor was he given much to do. Herrick righted the wrongs in between trips to Europe, but he would take delight in introducing Lincoln to the bank's rich and famous visitors as "my cow and pig man." That always brought a laugh.

The tall New Englander eventually won the admiration of Herrick and his associates with his innovative thinking. For example, he researched the demographics of the bank's customer base, which persuaded Herrick to advertise — for the first time. Still, Lincoln was not very happy with his lot.

---

* Elizabeth Brett Lincoln, who was called Betty, died on the Lincoln farm in Gahanna in 1931 at the age of 14. "I cannot, to this day, find words to discuss that tragedy," Lincoln wrote in *Vice President in Charge of Revolution*, p. 138.

Two weeks and two days short of Lincoln's 25th birthday, President Woodrow Wilson went before Congress and declared: "The world must be made safe for democracy. Its peace must be planted upon the tested foundations of political liberty." Four days later, on April 6, 1917, Wilson signed the joint Congressional resolution declaring war on Germany.

Because he was married and had a dependent, Lincoln was not drafted alongside 2.8 million of his fellow Americans. Nevertheless, the war had a profound impact on his future.

The Cuyahoga County agricultural agent was among those who received "Greetings" from the draft board; Lincoln filled in for him temporarily until a new agent could be appointed. That put him to working on the "Dollars from Ditches" program where he met "Uncle" George L. Cooley, a prominent Cuyahoga County farmer who became known as the "Father of the Ohio Farm Bureau."

"Uncle" George, a title of affection associates bestowed upon him, was a "doer" of the first water. Born in Cuyahoga County in 1861, he became a teacher, a farmer, an architect and engineer, a builder of barns and roads, a federal road inspector, and the organizer of the Cuyahoga County Grape Growers Cooperative, one of the first cooperatives in the nation. He also helped organize highway departments in Ohio, California and Louisiana, where he was the state's first highway director, the first so named in the United States.

By 1915, however, Cooley was back farming in Ohio and trying to deal with the county's "Dollars from Ditches" program. The goal was to clean up the ditches that drained into Lake Erie, but one of the largest went through Cooley's farm. Cleaning it meant dumping tons of dirt on his property. A settlement was reached after he and Lincoln had spent many hours together "in the trenches" and discussing a wide variety of agricultural issues.

Johnnie came marching home again in the waning months

of 1918, the Great War having been won at a cost of 112,432 American lives. (More than half died from disease, primarily pneumonia.) Lincoln returned to the bank and went about his business largely unnoticed until two years later when Cooley dropped by for a visit.

With missionary zeal Cooley had been throughout the state, helping farmers organize county farm bureaus. Now he was trying to pull them all together under a new flag, the Ohio Farm Bureau Federation.

"George Cooley, with his shaggy red hair bouncing up and down like a mop, energetically set the group in motion. ... It was plain why he became 'Father of the Ohio Farm Bureau.' No matter how large the group, Uncle George knew everyone by first name. His friends called him a walking file cabinet because he often appeared at meetings with papers bulging from every pocket."[15]

The newly organized Ohio Farm Bureau Federation needed an executive secretary, but Cooley didn't tell Lincoln that when he visited him at the bank. He only asked him to attend a meeting in Columbus February 9, 1920. Lincoln agreed to do so.

Only later did Lincoln realize that he was one of five candidates for the job. Cooley asked Lincoln to attend a second meeting in Columbus, at which time he was told the farm group wanted to hire him at $5,000 annually. The other applicants held out for $7,500.

"Do you want the job?" Cooley asked.

"Sure," Lincoln replied.

"Then take five thousand."

"I will, if they'll have me."[16]

Lincoln got the job and sent a letter of resignation to Herrick, who again was in Europe.

Herrick never replied to Lincoln, but three years later they bumped into each other in France. Lincoln asked his former boss about his lack of response.

"I know I didn't answer it," Herrick said. "I was mad at you. Why, you could have been president of that bank, but instead you chose to go with the Farm Bureau. I was disappointed in you, but I'm no longer disappointed. I see what you are trying to do."[17]

What Lincoln was trying to do was to build a farmer's organization that would extend well beyond Ohio's borders, but he needed help. In the early days his wife, Anne, often worked alongside her husband at the Southern Hotel (where they also lived initially), as did his secretary, Kathryn Gee (pronounced as the letter "G").

As a recent graduate of the Columbus Business School in the early summer of 1920, Gee sought a secretarial position with the Farmers Commercial Service Company (later the Farm Bureau Cooperative Association). The interviewer asked her to take a few letters as a test and then proceeded to dictate 20 or so. If she could have them all typed up by quitting time, he told her, she could have the job.

Although it was well past the noon hour when she began, Gee accomplished the task. Her reward was a job for most of the next 44 years as secretary to her interviewer — Murray D. Lincoln.

3

'GOOD LUCK AND HORSE SENSE'

Consumerism swept the nation in the 1920s. The war was over over there and, except for the struggling farmer, people felt good about themselves and about the future of a strong and victorious America.

Folks went on a buying binge just for the fun of it. Whether they needed them or not, they snapped up radios, movie tickets, refrigerators, washing machines, gramophones, Burma Shave, dry cleaning, bridge tables, Luckies, wrist watches, cellophane, bathtub gin, raccoon coats and Hemingway. Some, who would rue the day, bought lots of stock on Wall Street and others lots of lots in Florida.

"The clearest illustration of the new consumerism, however, was the frenzied excitement with which Americans greeted the automobile, which was in the 1920s becoming more widely available and affordable that ever before. By the end of the decade, there were more than 30 million cars on American roads — almost as many as there were families. Automobiles had, in the process, become not just a means of transportation, but the first great consumer obsession."[1]

While it was mostly city folk who were enjoying the love affair with the automobile, some farmers were experiencing the excitement, too. What they didn't get too excited about were the insurance rates. They were driving fewer miles primarily over lightly traveled rural roads, yet paying the same for insurance as city dwellers. Consequently, farmers chose to ignore insurance altogether rather than pay through the nose for it.

So, after aggressively pursuing cooperative purchasing and marketing of agricultural supplies and products for the first six years, Murray D. Lincoln, Ezra C. Anstaett and others within the Ohio Farm Bureau Federation began to work out how to provide automobile insurance — at reasonable rates — to the 85 percent of Ohio's farm population that had none at all.

It wasn't too long after Lincoln returned from his first trip to Europe* in the late fall of 1923 that he turned his attention to the insurance problem, although life insurance was his first focus. The Ohio Farm Bureau board authorized as early as April 14, 1925, an exploration into establishing a company to provide insurance, with gaining control of an existing company as "the ideal set up." There was no specific mention of automobile insurance at that time.

The idea of automobile insurance got its first full-blown airing at the Ohio Farm Bureau's 7th annual meeting in a report from Lincoln February 2, 1926:

"Folks," he began, "you may wonder why the Farm Bureau has been looking into the question of insurance. … It was with the idea of studying life insurance as applied to farmers that we

---

* Several Ohio county agents created a telegram as a joke on Murray D. Lincoln on the occasion of his first trans-Atlantic crossing, which he made with an American Farm Bureau Federation delegation. The fake dispatch to the Farm Bureau, purportedly from Lincoln aboard the U.S.S. Leviathan, read: "Mid-ocean. Feeling fine. Six meals a day. Three up and three down." From transcript of 5th annual meeting, Ohio Farm Bureau Federation, February 4, 1924, p. 99.

ran across the automobile insurance plan.

"We are convinced that more and more will the automobile become in use, that it is no longer a luxury but is now almost a necessity ..."

Lincoln told the board about "a company in Illinois" with an automobile insurance plan that "was absolutely sound and safe in principle," so safe, in fact, that the day before the Ohio Department of Insurance authorized the Farm Bureau to solicit contracts. Lincoln emphasized that "we do not propose in any way to go into competition with other mutual companies."[2]

He then handed out brochures from State Farm Mutual Automobile Insurance Company of Bloomington, IL. For nearly four years it had been selling automobile insurance through farm bureaus in Illinois.

A number of months earlier Lincoln and Anstaett had learned of State Farm and decided to find out more. What they discovered piqued their interest. In the first six months of its existence, State Farm had 1,300 policies in force, premium income of $29,222 and a surplus of $7,758.

The man behind this first blush of success was an Illinois farmer turned insurance salesman, George J. Mecherle (pronounced ma-hurl). Although he was the founder of State Farm, it was his management company, G.J. Mecherle Inc., that had the contract to sell the insurance to farmers throughout the state.

In April 1924 State Farm expanded beyond the borders of Illinois for the first time, signing up the Indiana Farm Bureau Federation of Indianapolis as its first state agent. Sixteen months later, on July 14, 1925, Mecherle came knocking on the door of the Ohio Farm Bureau and appeared before its executive committee. In a brief talk he outlined the State Farm organization and its pact with the Indiana Farm Bureau.[3]

A month later, on August 19, 1925, Mecherle was back in Columbus to appear before the full board. After Anstaett presented the staff report favoring a contract with State Farm, C.J. Halverstadt, a farmer from Leetonia, made a motion to authorize the executive committee to enter into an agreement. "Uncle" George Cooley seconded the motion, and a management contract was signed with G.J. Mecherle, Inc.[4]

Within another month, however, a problem arose. Lincoln reported to the board September 9, 1925, that it was "very doubtful" State Farm would get a license in Ohio because of the nature of the management contract with Mecherle. Perhaps this was after Lincoln bumped into Gov. Alvin Victor Donahey at the Statehouse.

"Now, you're a pretty big man," the governor told Lincoln, who stood almost 6-foot-four in his stocking feet. "You can bring all the farmers in the State of Ohio into the Statehouse, and I'm still not going to approve that company (Mecherle's)."[5]

Ohio Department of Insurance Superintendent William Safford didn't like it either, and in those days the superintendent's voice was as good as law, especially when it had the backing of the governor. He told Lincoln and Anstaett it would be better if the Ohio Farm Bureau established its own insurance company.

"The State Insurance Department apparently did not intend to license the Illinois company," Anstaett warned the Ohio Farm Bureau board October 14, 1925. "The Federation would very likely have to set up its own company."

When word got out that the Ohio farm group might get into the insurance business itself, "one of our board members ... came to Columbus to advise me against it," Lincoln said.

"Oh, Murray, don't make such a recommendation," the farmer pleaded. "What do we farmers know about running an insurance business? You'll just ruin yourself and the Farm Bureau."[6]

For many years detractors of the Nationwide Insurance Companies used the same argument: What does a bunch of farmers know about running an insurance company? By the time Nationwide had become a $40 billion enterprise, however, such questions had stopped. As for the old director, Lincoln said in later years he "got a lot of fun showing him our financial statements."

At its November 11, 1925, meeting at the Girl's Athletic Club on Fourth Street, Columbus, the Ohio Farm Bureau's executive committee authorized staff "to proceed to incorporate an automobile insurance company and the insurance service provided thereby be offered to all those eligible to membership in the Farm Bureau." The only board member who did not vote in favor of the resolution was Cooley.[7]

Right from the start the "Father of the Farm Bureau" resisted any oblique diversion from serving the farmer in the field. Consequently, he felt some of Lincoln's ideas were off the mark, such as in 1920 when the executive secretary discussed acquiring the independent telephone companies in Ohio and selling them to Ohio Bell. Cooley told Lincoln "to pay attention to feed and fertilizer and forget funny things like that."[8]

On November 20, 1925, the Ohio Farm Bureau Federation board authorized the incorporation of the Farm Bureau Mutual Automobile Insurance Company, which occurred December 17, and voted $10,000 for initial working capital. The board also gave Anstaett "the responsibility to set up the company and get it going," Anstaett said. The directive came "directly from the board; Lincoln was not present."

Anstaett suggested that somebody be named general agent of the new company. "I was nominated and chosen," he said.

Reflecting some years later on the birth of the insurance company, Lincoln said:

"If it hadn't been for Bill Safford ... and Mecherle's acquisitiveness, we probably would have become an agent for State Farm. ... Safford wouldn't license State Farm because of the Mecherle contract, although Mecherle always thought we prevented him from getting the license."[9]

For about a year after launching the insurance business in April of 1926, Mecherle's management company helped the Farm Bureau Mutual Automobile Insurance Company set up its operations under a three-year contract totaling $30,000. The services included the establishment of a "comprehensive system of records for the home office" drafts of "application blanks, policies, riders, loss blanks, reinstatement blanks, and any and all other similar forms, papers and instruments necessary in the proper conduct of the insurance business of the company."[10] It also helped solicit sales throughout Ohio, for which the Mecherle company received a percentage of every policy written.

"By the time we saw what we could do ourselves," Lincoln said, "we tried to buy Mecherle out of his contract for $2 million, but he wouldn't sell to us.* Then we tried to get the other Farm Bureaus to join with us rather than to continue with Mecherle."[11]

Lincoln went so far as to solicit the support of the American Farm Bureau Federation, but the national organization rejected him, much to his dismay. "If the AFBF had helped, we could have taken over the State Farm Insurance Company," Lincoln said 20 years later.[12]

Eventually the contract with Mecherle was settled and the

---

* Lincoln's memory of events 20 years earlier probably was a little off here. Mecherle's initial contract with the Ohio Farm Bureau Federation totaled $30,000. Beginning in the fall of 1930, however, Lincoln and his Farm Bureau associates negotiated to buy out all of Mecherle's management contracts built up over the decade and effect a buyout of State Farm. Mecherle initially sought $4 million for his company, in cash and with no deferred payments. He later came down to $1.5 million. "As soon as he (Mecherle) found out I was in back of the thing, he ducked out very quickly," Lincoln recalled in 1955. One of the go-betweens late in the negotiations was H.P. Gardiner, president of First National Mutual Fire Insurance Company, Bloomington, IL, who represented Lincoln secretly so Mecherle wouldn't know the Ohio group still had an interest.

fledgling Ohio insurance company was on its own. Anstaett sold the first policy to himself, but on a desk nearby were more than 1,000 applications for insurance ready to be processed. That was 10 times the number of applications that the state insurance department required for a license.

Not knowing quite how to price its insurance, Farm Bureau Mutual only hoped to get under the old-line insurance companies, which charged $55 annually. For six months of Farm Bureau Mutual insurance on one car, farmers paid $15 for a lifetime membership in the mutual company, which included one vote at the annual meeting; a $20 refundable deposit that went to pay expenses and losses and, at the end of six months, their share of whatever expenses and losses there were.

The company called for a premium of $9.18 on a Chevrolet or Ford in each of the first two six-month periods. Even with the initiation fee and the deposit, the annual charge was $1.64 below the old-line rate. The second year, without the initiation fee and deposit, the rate remained at $18.36 annually, well below the $55 charged by the established companies.

"Well, we just went to town after that," said Lincoln.

Somewhat surprising to Lincoln, though, was the number of policyholders who asked for their deposit back after the first six months. "We sent them their checks just as we'd promised. Then, once they'd satisfied themselves that we meant what we said, danged if they didn't send us another premium deposit so they could still be insured by us. In fact, most of them simply returned their refund check, endorsed back to the Farm Bureau Insurance Company. It was a natural suspicion." [13]

According to William Turner, author of the *Ohio Farm Bureau Story 1919-1979,* it was Anstaett who was the primary leader of the new company; Lincoln had broader responsibilities within the Ohio Farm Bureau.

"The company sprang up like a mushroom largely as a result

of Anstaett's prior spade work with county Farm Bureau boards," Turner wrote. "To support the sales efforts, Anstaett created a direct mail campaign believed to be one of the first ever used in a promotion program."[14]

The insurance company also instituted a number of other innovations, such as an illustrated sales kit, training for its sales force, a sales manual, a weekly sales bulletin and an annual sales convention, to which agents could bring their wives at the company's expense only if during the year they had sold fertilizer in addition to insurance.

The first of nine claims filed in 1926 arrived May 12, just a month after the Farm Bureau launched the company. Russell Fox, of Limaville, OH, filed it, a $25 claim for the tire, rim, tube and spotlight stolen off his car. The check was in the mail within 24 hours, the first brick in building the company's reputation for settling claims quickly. The company's policy became "Fair, Frank, Firm and Friendly."

After its first eight months, which brought it to the end of 1926, the Farm Bureau Mutual Automobile Insurance Company claimed 5,400 policies in force and posted assets of approximately $114,000, premium income of $115,000 and a surplus of $47,000. The numbers were considerably better than what State Farm reported in its first six months four years earlier.

At the start of the Depression in 1929, policies in force totaled 80,000. The assets were $1.7 million, the premium income $883,000 and the surplus $280,000. The following year, despite the crash of the nation's economy, Farm Bureau Mutual topped $2 million in assets and $1 million in premium income for the first time.

The year 1930 was noteworthy for another reason: Ezra Anstaett left the Farm Bureau Mutual fold to devote full time to the Town and Village Insurance Service Inc., which was established as a general agency in 1928 with the support of the Ohio Farm Bureau. Now an independent agency, Town and

Village is still in operation in Columbus. Six other Farm Bureau Mutual employees followed Anstaett to Town and Village: Darryl Smith, Albert Docter, Roger Snider and their secretaries.

"Anstaett, more than any one man, has been responsible for the success of Farm Bureau insurance," said Lincoln at the time. "His vision coupled with an indominatable(sic) energy, has been a constant inspiration to all of us. The rapid growth of our company is largely attributable to his efforts. ... Men of his kind wear shoes which are hard to fill."[15]

Town and Village was an interesting animal from several points of view. First, it was a knock-off of a company established by George Mecherle and State Farm in 1926 called City and Village Mutual Automobile Insurance Company.* The similarity in the names and in the mission was more than just coincidence. Its purpose was to write insurance for those who didn't qualify for coverage (because they weren't farmers) under the by-laws of Farm Bureau Mutual Automobile Insurance Company and to give to its agents a new market to sell, especially in the winter when bad weather often brought rural traffic to a standstill.

Farm Bureau Mutual was under considerable pressure at the time to broaden its policyholder base. Some policyholders had moved off the farm and wanted to continue the coverage; others wanted coverage for their children, who were moving into urban areas.

"Our directors were at first unwilling to have our insurance business go into towns and villages," said Charles W. Leftwich, who joined Farm Bureau Mutual in 1927. "They felt at that time it was not a proper course for us to take," but Lincoln and Anstaett prevailed. Farm Bureau Mutual revised its charter in 1931 to permit the writing of virtually all casualty lines of

---

*City and Village Mutual lasted only until the end of 1927 when it was folded into State Farm.

insurance.

"Farmers have found that by segregating themselves into a class they can reduce their insurance costs by one-third to one-half," a Town and Village promotional flyer explained. "People living in towns and villages can do the same."[16]

Another interesting point about Town and Village pops up in the names of its investors and officers. Anstaett was one, of course, but so was Lincoln, who became president of the company while still executive secretary of the Farm Bureau insurance company, secretary of the Ohio Farm Bureau and general manager of the Ohio Farm Bureau Corporation, under which its insurance company was formed.

Lincoln staunchly defended his position in a 1928 letter to an irate Farm Bureau Mutual policyholder. "... My conscience is absolutely clear concerning the starting of this Town and Village Insurance Company," he wrote Clarence Hunter of London, OH. "If Mr. Anstaett and myself desire to invest our money in an insurance company, I see no reason why it should be questioned."

The contractual relationship between Town and Village and Farm Bureau Mutual ended abruptly April 1, 1931, after the mutual offered to buy Town and Village. "Mr. Anstaett did not want to sell," the special committee of the board reported. "However, he named the ridiculous value of T-V as $100,000. Your committee made it very clear that such price was ridiculous and would not be considered."[17]

Although the separation was said to be "amicable," the pot boiled for some months after. In July, for instance, a dispute surfaced concerning the exclusive use of agents and sales tactics. Anstaett filed with the Ohio Department of Insurance charges against his former employer, alleging that Farm Bureau Mutual was offering to waive its membership fee to new customers if they switched from Town and Village.

For the record, Farm Bureau Mutual continued its sales effort into the towns and villages under the provisions of the revised by-laws, and three years later, in 1934, it began offering insurance to motorists in cities.

In 1928 "Uncle" George Cooley was elected president of Farm Bureau Mutual, a position that he held until 1939 when Lincoln succeeded him. Cooley was not happy with the arrangement with Town and Village and said as much in a "Dear Lincoln" letter. He informed Lincoln that a special committee had launched an investigation and, as executive secretary, Lincoln would be expected to execute the committee's recommendations for action.

Despite the dispute, it was on Cooley's watch that the company began its spread beyond the borders of Ohio, at the invitation of the farm bureaus in their respective states. West Virginia came first, followed by Maryland, Delaware, New Hampshire, Vermont and North Carolina, all in 1928. There were nearly 600 licensed agents in the seven states by the end of the year. Virginia and Pennsylvania came aboard in 1929.

Charles W. Leftwich, who retired in 1970 as a senior vice president of Nationwide Insurance Companies, was a claims adjuster in 1928. He recalled "a long-forgotten chapter" in the company's history, namely the unusual approach Farm Bureau Mutual took to service farmers in New Hampshire.

"On checking requirements for licensing in New Hampshire, we found that companies from other states could not be admitted unless they had operated for at least five years in their home state. We couldn't qualify, of course. So the discussion with New Hampshire people led to the formation of ... the Farm Bureau Mutual Automobile Insurance Company of New Hampshire." Its subsequent sale separated it from the New Hampshire Farm Bureau: Today it is the Concord General Mutual Insurance Company.

The decisions to expand beyond Ohio and to offer services to non-farmers "made a huge difference over the years in the dimension of Nationwide compared to a lot of … Farm Bureau companies that stayed largely within (their own) states and remained rural in their insurance exposure," General Chairman John E. Fisher said shortly before his retirement in 1994.

This expansion into urban areas and then into other states also was largely responsible for the continued growth of Farm Bureau Mutual during the depths of the Depression. Only once and only in one area did the company fail to post a gain over the previous year. That was between 1933 and 1934 when the surplus dropped to $827,000 from $848,000 the previous year.

"Despite all the growth, it was a lean, tight, day-to-day operation at first," recalled Bowman Doss in 1968.[18] He became a licensed agent of the Farm Bureau Mutual Automobile Insurance Company in 1933, although he first worked part time helping Town and Village Insurance sell in West Virginia.

Doss, who succeeded Lincoln as head of the Nationwide Insurance Companies in 1964, continued his story of the early years:

"I've heard more than one insurance expert say that if we had set up all the reserves we should have our first year, the whole set-up would probably have been financially impaired. Anyway, if we were nearly broke, we didn't know it and it was a case of ignorance is bliss. Somehow, we kept making headway with a parlay of good luck and horse sense."[19]

4

FORWARD WITHOUT FEAR

Charles W. Leftwich looked at the wreck and scratched his head. A Clinton County policyholder who owned the 1926 two-door Nash drove it off the road and rolled it a couple of times. "The car probably should be junked," said Leftwich, in 1927 the only field claims adjuster for the one-year-old Farm Bureau Mutual Automobile Insurance Company.

Despite Leftwich's misgivings, the Nash was repaired. Then the policyholder wouldn't accept it, "and I can't say I blamed him," said Leftwich. So cash settled the claim and Farm Bureau Mutual took possession of the car.

It was the company's first car, but like Ohio's rural roads, it wasn't too reliable. "When you started out on a trip in that automobile," he recalled, "you never knew what would happen or whether you could get back." That was not good; he was under strict orders to return to Columbus each night whenever possible to save the company a hotel bill, even though the cost of a bed was but $2.50 or $3 a night.

If employees had to travel overnight by train — and there was much rail travel out of the old Union Station in downtown

Columbus — the rule was upper berths only, not the costlier lower berths. The company reimbursed its employees, "but I certainly thought twice before spending more than a dollar for dinner," Leftwich said.

In the late 1920s and throughout the next decade, the lid was on expenses. For many years Murray D. Lincoln wrote letters and memos on both sides of the paper to save money, making him the company's first ecologist. Even the directors of the Farm Bureau felt the tight fit. They were advised to register at the Deshler-Wallick Hotel when in town for board meetings because the company had used up all its credit at the Neil House.*

There was a need to keep the cost lid on tight. The good times all but the farmer experienced in the 1920s gave way to the hard times. The collapse of the stock market October 29, 1929, was but a harbinger of the ills of a nation and prompted the headline, "Wall Street Lays an Egg."[1] By 1933 approximately 100,000 businesses had failed. The virus that had gripped the American farmer for a decade became a worldwide epidemic.

Asked if he could recall any era comparable to the Great Depression, the British economist John Maynard Keynes replied: "Yes. It was called the Dark Ages, and it lasted 400 years."[2]

"During the Depression," Lincoln recalled, "we of the Farm Bureau hung on for all we were worth. Our dues had dropped

---

* The Deshler, at Broad and High streets, became the Deshler-Wallick in 1925, the Deshler-Hilton in 1952, the Deshler-Cole in 1964, the Beasley-Deshler in 1966 and closed in 1968. As Evelyn Keseg, Farm Bureau Mutual's first woman officer, explained in a 1985 interview, the hotel didn't retain the Farm Bureau business for very long. "When we were a tiny little company, and we were having our annual meetings and the farmers were coming in, the Deshler made a bad mistake. They said they didn't want the farmers in there with their muddy shoes and their tacky clothes. (As a result) Mr. Lincoln would never allow anyone to have a meeting at the Deshler in his lifetime … (He) was vehement about that. He felt it was a terrible insult."

from $10 to $5 and then to $2 and much of the time we were collecting no dues at all. Things got very tense, although we never missed a payroll.* I think we survived because we were engaged in purchasing and service. People had to have insurance for their cars and farmers had to buy feed and seed and fertilizer, even if the prices of what they sold were very low."[3]

W.E. "Ed" West, who joined the insurance company in 1928 and rose to senior vice president and treasurer of the Nationwide Insurance Companies, remembered how close the company came to missing a payroll in the Depression.

"We had an inkling of what was coming, and Mr. Lincoln, Mr. (J.E.) Keltner and I went to the bank and withdrew sufficient cash from our accounts to meet two or three payrolls. This money was put in safety deposit boxes at the banks for an emergency, if it came.

"It did, and we actually paid all employees in cash one payday" when President Franklin D. Roosevelt closed the nation's banks.

The payroll crisis of 1933 stood out in the memories Elizabeth Kinsell had of her days as a Farm Bureau Mutual employee. In the Depression there were long lines of unemployed looking for a job — any job. Therefore, it was devastating to lose one because there was little hope of another. "Mr. West called us all into his office one by one and asked us what our family responsibilities were," she said. "The company had to let a few go, but no one was released who had anyone to support."

M.J. Morrison worked in claims in the 1930s. Claimants signed a release, which the company held on file. "All they had was our verbal promise to pay them when the banks opened," Morrison said. "They didn't expect anything else. Everybody was in the same boat."

Farmers found themselves in an overturned boat and

---

* In 1931 jobs were cut throughout the Farm Bureau organization and salaries reduced by 10 percent.

drowning in surpluses and debt. Because productivity on the American farm was high, the farmer continued to produce in the 1930s more than the consumer could afford to buy. As the Depression deepened, farm prices dropped out of sight.

"Farmers were getting less than 25 cents for a bushel of wheat, 7 cents for a bushel of corn, a dime for a bushel of oats, a nickel for a pound of cotton or wool. Sugar was bringing 3 cents a pound, hogs and beef 2 cents a pound and apples -- provided they were flawless — 40 cents for a box of 200."[4]

Despite America's malaise, the Farm Bureau Mutual Automobile Insurance Company forged ahead; not as strongly as before, but ahead. It expanded into other states and, on June 28, 1928, moved from one large room at 199 East Gay Street into the Ohio Farm Bureau's new headquarters at the Benjamin N. Huntington House, 620 East Broad Street.*

Marie Spohn began work there in 1933, typing premium notices at $14.50 a week.

"You know, when you worked in those days you had a sense of responsibility, a sense of loyalty to the company. ... If you didn't finish the work which was delegated to you, you just automatically stayed until it was finished, and they didn't pay overtime."

Being in the typing pool was a nerve-wracking experience, especially for the new hires "on the bubble." Evelyn Keseg was only 17 in 1937 when she began as a typist at $65 a month.

"The policy department in those days consisted of about 25 people typing all the insurance policies. ... The Farm Bureau would hire the top typists out of (high) schools from across the city ... and you typed in competition with people.

"You were given these policies, and you were told that you were expected to type them without errors. ... There was a list

---

* The Huntington House and the similar 19th century, Empire style Andrew D. Rodgers House at 630 East Broad Street, which Farm Bureau Mutual also acquired, were placed on the National Register of Historic Places in 1987.

of production, and you were on the list with the number of policies you'd typed and the number of errors. At the end of the month the person on the bottom of the list was just automatically fired, because that way you had great incentive to do well. Also, that way they could constantly hire better typists.

"You were typing faster and faster, and you would watch the person on your right and left. When they would take a policy out of the machine, you would think, 'Oh, my God! She's ahead of me by one!'

"You didn't leave your typewriter unless it was absolutely the only thing you could do. If you had to go to the restroom, you would go to the front of the room to Rhea Short, who was the head of the policy department, and say, 'Please, Miss Short, may I have the key to the restroom?' She would look at you with the coldest eyes I have ever encountered. ... It was not an easy thing to get the key to the restroom."

Keseg didn't get paid for working overtime, either, "but they did buy your dinner. Now, that was 75 cents for dinner, but they didn't give you that 75 cents because you might go to Jack's next door, which was a hamburger joint, and get a Coke and a hot dog, and you might have a quarter left.

"They would give the money to your supervisor, and she took the department en masse over to the Jefferson Hotel where you had a full-course dinner. This was great. Then you marched back, and you sat at your typewriter, and you typed."

The policy department's work load became even heavier after January 10, 1934. On that date the Farm Bureau Mutual Fire Insurance Company received a license to operate in Ohio.

Throughout the early years of the company the value of a fire insurance company came up for discussion many times. At one point, in 1931, it appeared as though the Ohio company would get into fire insurance through the purchase of the assets of State Farm Mutual Automobile Insurance Company in

Bloomington, IL, but nothing came of the discussions.

A notation in the December 9, 1932, board minutes of the automobile insurance company indicated something was afoot. President Cooley called upon David M. Odaffer — "Uncle" Dave — of Crawford County "to report upon the investigation that he and the President had made relative to the service being rendered by existing farm fire mutual companies."

It is unknown whether it was before or after this meeting that George H. Dunlap was making hay on a hilltop on his 87-acre farm near Cadiz in Ohio's Harrison County. Dunlap, who had been active in the Farm Bureau since the early 1920s but only recently elected to the board of the Ohio Farm Bureau Federation,* was interrupted in his labors by a farmhand who said, "Your uncle is in there," pointing to the house. "He wants you to come in."

Dunlap trudged down the hill to find "Uncle" George sitting on his front porch with "Uncle" Dave, the first president of the Farm Bureau Service Company that was established January 7, 1923. They wanted to discuss "whether or not we should form the Farm Bureau Fire Insurance Company." Little could Dunlap know that one day he would chair all the Nationwide Insurance Companies, but then and there his opinion must not have killed the fire insurance idea. The subject came up again at the March 16, 1933, annual meeting of the automobile company. The board authorized the investigation to continue.

The need for a fire insurance company arose, in part, because Pennsylvania and other states into which the automobile company was expanding were prepared to enforce laws preventing fire insurance to be wrapped into an automobile policy. Farm Bureau Mutual had to make a move in order to grow.

---

* At age 33 in 1939, George H. Dunlap was the youngest ever to be elected to the insurance company's board, but he was elected to the federation's board in 1933.

The automobile company's board adopted the name, Farm Bureau Mutual Fire Insurance Company, at its meeting December 7, 1933, and approved $10,000 as an advance to assist the new company in setting up shop.* To meet the state's requirement for a license, it obtained 100 policy applications, all from employees of the automobile insurance company, including Lincoln. This was accomplished by getting the employees to agree to have the fire portion of their Farm Bureau Mutual automobile insurance transferred to the new fire company at no additional cost.

Odaffer, who was elected the fire company's first president, wrote Lincoln in January about the company's progress. "We do not feel that we should rush into this thing too quickly; therefore, we do not want to give this fire insurance too much publicity until we are all ready to go ... To avoid many headaches caused by speed and inexperience, we are proceeding cautiously ..."5

When all appeared ready to go, Odaffer and his wife took out the first policy on April 13, 1934.

Unlike its sister automobile insurer, the fire company wrote policies for all comers, not just farmers. That helped it to get off to a faster start. By June the company wrote more than $3 million in fire coverage. Within a few more months, premiums reached to $4.5 million.6 By the end of the year, nearly 6,000 policies were in force. After 10 years in business, premium income topped $1 million. Sixty years later it is a leading fire insurer with 3.6 million policies in force and premium income of more than $800 million.

This surge of business created by a group of Ohio farmers must be put in the proper perspective. Fear gripped the nation as the Great Depression hit bottom.

"With their economy mired in its deepest depression, their

---

* An additional $90,000 was provided the following year to meet requirements in other states.

government paralyzed, and their financial system crumbling, Americans turned to (President Franklin D.) Roosevelt with desperate expectations. 'First of all,' declared the new president in his inaugural address, 'let me assert my firm belief that the only thing we have to fear is fear itself—nameless, unreasoning, unjustified terror. ... '"7

The men and women of the Ohio Farm Bureau Federation showed little fear. After establishing the fire insurance company, they turned right around and began negotiations to buy a life insurance company.

Late in 1933 the American Insurance Union offered up its bankrupt company to Farm Bureau Mutual Automobile Insurance Company, but almost two more years of negotiations went by without a resolution. In the meantime, American Insurance Union became the Life Insurance Company of America. After many months Farm Bureau Mutual acquired LICA October 8, 1935, paying but $366,782 for a virtual shell of a company it promptly renamed the Cooperative Life Insurance Company of America.

It wasn't always in difficulty, of course. John J. Lentz founded the AIU in Columbus September 21, 1894. It was a fraternal organization perhaps best known for constructing what today is the LeVeque Tower at 50 West Broad Street. For nearly 50 years the AIU Citadel was the city's tallest building at 44 stories, or 555 feet, 6 inches. The six inches were added so the tower would top the Washington Monument by a half-foot.

Groundbreaking took place in 1924, two years before Farm Bureau Mutual Automobile Insurance Company was born, and the building was completed September 21, 1927, at a cost of $7.8 million. At the time the AIU had $200 million in life insurance in force and 175,000 policyholders. Only about one-tenth of each of those figures remained at the time of the sale, along with just $16 million in policies in force in 43 states, the District of Columbia, Alaska, England, Mexico and Canada.

The fraternal organization, its members and the policyholders, and the insurance company, which filed bankruptcy in 1932, all fell victim to the Depression.

With three companies under his belt and both Anstaett and Cooley* gone from the scene, Lincoln hit full stride, and a long, quick stride it was. For those who watched his performance, he seemed headed in many different directions at once. One of them was to involve the Farm Bureau in rural electrification, as he detailed in his book, *Vice President in Charge of Revolution.*

"Now, power of any sort interested me, and when sometime in 1935, I saw that one of the first New Deal alphabet agencies was the Rural Electrification Administration, I went down to Washington to meet Mr. Morris L. Cooke, the administrator. ... I told him that we of the Farm Bureau wanted to avail ourselves of the benefit of this legislation and set up our own utility plants."[8]

This, of course, is exactly the line of thinking to which Cooley objected 15 years earlier.

"What do you know about the utility business?" Cooke asked.

"Not a thing," Lincoln admitted. "I was trained in dairying and animal husbandry."

"Well, now, we expect about 90 percent of the rural electrification to be done by the presently existing private utilities and about 10 percent by public-owned utilities and cooperatives. As you may know, it is a highly technical job, and I doubt whether you or your people are equipped to handle it."

"I'll turn those figures around on you if you'll let us try it,"

---

* "Uncle" George Cooley died in 1938. He was replaced on the insurance company's board by Dunlap. The Farm Bureau Mutual board said of Cooley at the time he retired: "In a multitude of little deeds, he exhibited a thoughtfulness unsurpassed. In the momentary crises and afflictions of many around him, he was a Samaritan, comforter and friend." Board minutes, March 30, 1931, pp. 160-161.

Lincoln said.

"Young man, you're crazy."

"Okay, but just give us the opportunity."

"Well, I suppose I must because the law states that I must. But I'll be frank: I don't have much hope for you."[9]

Lincoln rushed back to Ohio, got quick approval from the Ohio Farm Bureau Federation and, through its newly formed Farm Bureau Rural Electrification Cooperative, set up 30 rural utility cooperatives "so quickly that no other state caught up with us. ... Farmers were just itching to have electricity, and to have it from their own cooperative was a dream come true."[10] Of the first $5.5 million the REA loaned cooperatives, Ohio received $5 million.

After pumping some $100,000 of its own funds into the electrification project, the Farm Bureau slowly phased out its newest cooperative. By 1942 it was gone, but Lincoln savored the triumph for years. Still elated in 1949, he commented:

"They told us we couldn't do it. The utilities said they couldn't make any money putting power into rural areas; that it would cost $2,000 a mile to build an electric light line. By golly, we got it done for $868. Now 92 percent of our farmers are *electric farmers!*"[11]

Another battle Lincoln fought and won in the mid-1930s involved the Cooperative League of the U.S.A.,* an organization established in 1916 in which Lincoln found a safe harbor for his consumer cooperative ideas. Longtime senior company executive Dr. Robert A. Rennie, who grew up just 25 miles from Lincoln's boyhood home in Raynham, MA, said Lincoln "had a one-track mind" when it came to the cooperative movement.

The Ohio Farm Bureau Federation split, right down the middle, on whether it should accept Lincoln's recommendation

---

* Now the National Cooperative Business Association.

to join the league. "After a good deal of groaning and moaning and head-shaking and grinding of teeth,"[12] Perry L. Green, as Farm Bureau president, cast the deciding vote in favor of league membership. In 1941 Lincoln became president of the Cooperative League, a post he held until 1965.

At about the time in 1936 that King Edward VIII walked out of Buckingham Palace and into the arms of "the woman I love," Wallis Warfield Simpson, the Ohio Farm Bureau and all its affiliated enterprises took a hike to the corner of Chestnut and High streets and into the Pure Oil Building. In return, the Farm Bureau transferred to the Pure Oil Company its East Broad Street properties.*

The employees enjoyed the move. The more spacious quarters were one thing, but having shopping was even more important. Among the nearby stores were Madison's and The Union department stores, Summer & Sons cut-rate store, F.G. & A. Howell Furniture, The Boston Store, and the aroma from the bakery at Moby's department store and food market filled the neighborhood every morning.

During the next 10 years the Farm Bureau also acquired the adjoining Arcade and Schulz buildings, the Clinton building across Chestnut Street and the 245 N. High Street building, later known as the Landmark building. The latter purchase didn't come easily. The Ohio insurance department looked upon the deal with a jaundiced eye. After several months of fruitless discussions, Dunlap, then chairman of Farm Bureau Mutual, jumped in to exert a little peer pressure by making a personal visit to the department.

"I told the superintendent that we really had a space

---

* Perhaps there was a little vindictiveness associated with the Farm Bureau enterprises taking over the Pure Oil Building. In his *Vice President in Charge of Revolution,* pp. 126-127, Lincoln details how Pure Oil turned down the Farm Bureau as a gasoline customer in 1935, the year before the purchase of the building.

problem," Dunlap said. "We had done everything" to maximize the use of the office space, short of stacking people on top of one another.

Dunlap discerned a change in the mood of the regulator, who looked him in the eye and said: "Now, if you want that building to house those insurance companies, I've got no law to refuse it. If you want the building to house Murray Lincoln's cooperatives, I've got no law to approve it."

"It's to house the insurance companies," Dunlap insisted. The purchase was approved.

A block south of the 246 North High Street building was the Chittenden Hotel at Spring and High streets. Once a month virtually every employee would troop dutifully to the hotel to hear Lincoln's state-of-the-world luncheon address. Evelyn Keseg described him as being "as cold a man on a one-to-one basis as I have ever known (but) in front of a crowd, he was a spellbinder. ... He was like Elmer Gantry."

Later, in the 1940s, the monthly meeting moved to the Neil House, on High Street just south of Broad Street. "This got very interesting during the war (World War II)," said Keseg, "because we would pick up people along the way. On the way back, they would see this group of people moving up High Street and they'd think 'nylons' or 'cigarettes' ... and we would end up back here at the company with these strange people that didn't belong to us."

There's little doubt that Lincoln had the power to move people. Charles W. Fullerton also was overwhelmed by the force of Lincoln's delivery. After hearing the company's leader for the first time, the former president of Nationwide's non-insurance affiliated companies felt he "was two feet off the ground when I got back to Chestnut and High streets," he said. "He really got to me about being in service for people and if people join together they can do anything for their own benefit."

The evangelistic spirit pervaded the enterprise; nothing seemed impossible. The long hours, parsimonious pay and puritanical, Spartan atmosphere meant little to the dedicated work force. Smoking was forbidden (except in the restrooms), no dating between employees was allowed (although there were those who did, on the sly), desks had to be clean and clear at the end of each day, and the 10-minute coffee breaks at the vending machine were closely supervised. Lincoln discovered one unfortunate executive sipping coffee outside of break time and fired him on the spot.[13] Those really willing to tempt fate sneaked across the street to Doc Jackson's drug emporium and lunch counter for a real cup of coffee.

Neither rain nor sleet nor dark of night ever swayed Lincoln from his immediate focus. He was going to do his own thing, regardless, and that usually meant tossing out any speech prepared for him. His lack of attention to what his wordsmiths had so carefully crafted drove them to distraction.

Rennie was among those so frustrated during the 1950s when he wrote some of Lincoln's speeches. Lincoln would take a speech and hold it up in front of his audience and say, "I've had this speech written for me, but I'm not going to give it."

One day Rennie couldn't take it any longer. He went to Lincoln.

"Murray,* why do you have me write this speech all out? Why don't I simply outline what I think you should cover on that topic and then you can simply glance at it when you want to interject something to keep the speech relevant to the topic?"

"Oh, you don't understand, Bob. Newspapermen want copy on the particular subject the speech was assigned, and I can simply give them copies of your speech."

Lincoln became president of the Cooperative Life Insurance

---

* Rennie was among the few who called Lincoln "Murray." For most others, even those who had known Lincoln for many years, it was always "Mr. Lincoln."

Company (later the Farm Bureau Life Insurance Company*
and then, in 1955, the Nationwide Life Insurance Company)
on December 9, 1938, president of Farm Bureau Mutual
Automobile Insurance Company on April 6, 1939, and
president of Farm Bureau Mutual Fire Insurance Company on
April 4, 1946.

After so much had been accomplished by so many in the
decades of the 1920s and 1930s, often against tremendous odds,
the fact remained that the leader who emerged didn't really
have his heart in insurance.

---

* The name change in February 1939 was forced by New York State law that
said the word "cooperative" could not be used unless the cooperative had been
organized under its laws.

5

GETTING ON
WITH THE PIONEERING

Murray D. Lincoln looked out at the audience at the company's spring regional meeting in 1955. At 63, he was still an imposing figure, standing tall and straight. The Parkinson's disease that was to take his life 11 years hence had not yet manifested itself.

"I have a lot of sympathy for a lot of you folks ... who may get confused at times as to some of the moves we are making," he admitted to his audience, "but there has never been any question in my mind as to what our ultimate purpose was ... and that was to help people help themselves ... "[1]

Lincoln sensed that some of the employees did not understand the direction in which he was headed. For the past 10 years or so he had led them through the fires of controversy and a bouillabaisse of entrepreneurial endeavors that more often than not had little to do with the insurance business.

After World War II, Lincoln championed cooperative causes throughout the world with renewed, indefatigable vigor, brushing aside any suggestion that his zeal for his personal agenda might not be in the best interest of the Farm Bureau

Mutual insurance companies. To him it was all so clear: the insurance companies, the nation, the world — all would one day benefit from a global exchange of the fruits of one's labor.

"Cooperatives are the trail blazers of the new order," he would say, "an order of abundance and peace. Let's get on with our pioneering and build that world."[2]

The Depression and the war years curbed his "pioneering" only slightly. The automobile, fire and life insurance companies posted steady, but not spectacular, growth throughout the 1930s. Sales of automobile insurance were stimulated on the one hand by the arrival of financial responsibility laws in many states, making automobile insurance virtually mandatory, and depressed on the other by weak demand, particularly in the early years of the Depression.

While Vivian Leigh and Clark Gable swept Americans off their feet in *Gone with the Wind,* the Nazi juggernaut swept through Poland, throwing Europe into war again. Congress enacted the nation's first peacetime draft in August 1940, and "Be Prepared" signs popped up as President Franklin D. Roosevelt urged the United States to "be the great arsenal of democracy."

In March 1942 George J. Smith, a Farm Bureau Mutual employee in the filing department, enlisted in the U.S. Army Air Corps and became a first lieutenant. He flew 64 missions in Europe with the 451st Bombardment Squadron, based in Saling, England. He was shot down and killed August 6, 1944, while piloting his B-26 light bomber on a raid over Normandy, France. Smith was the company's first employee killed in action.

The stepped-up production of war materiel brought renewed prosperity and an end to the Depression. It also started a roller coaster ride for many in the insurance industry. In the late 1930s and early 1940s, auto insurance sales enjoyed a resurgence as more people found employment and took to the road in new cars. Loss ratios increased as a result. Then came Pearl Harbor and gasoline rationing, which curtailed driving, and loss ratios dropped. So did the rates.

The war also ended for the duration the large annual meetings of the Farm Bureau's insurance companies. So many attended the pre-war meetings they filled both ballrooms of the Neil House. During the war, however, gasoline rationing mandated that the meetings be held by mail, with only those directors residing in Columbus attending to execute routine business.

At war's end, the situation turned around again, but not necessarily for the immediate good of auto insurers. "The public went on a driving binge (and) rates could not be adjusted rapidly enough to cope with the adverse loss experience," recalled Charles W. Leftwich. The numbers for Farm Bureau Mutual Automobile Insurance showed premium income jumping more than $7 million to $21.1 million between 1945 and 1946 and losses went from $6.5 million to $10.4 million. The company's surplus dropped by almost $800,000.

A concerned Lincoln took the matter to his board. "This very production, good as it is, is creating a real problem in service," he said. "Complaints are coming from the field that our service is too slow. Policies are not getting through ... within three days of the receipt of the application. Answers to correspondence are delayed. Premium notices are slow."

The blame for many of the problems rested with the adjustments to a post-war economy. The churning of the labor force left Lincoln with "inexperienced and inefficient help" and pre-war office equipment that was unable to keep up with the increasing volume of business. He began a six-day week and a night shift to get caught up.

"Our service had completely broken down," recalled Dean W. Jeffers, a 29-year-old returning veteran.* An adjuster in Grove City, PA, before the war, he returned there in 1946 to find an "unbelievable" backlog of claims.

---

* Dean W. Jeffers served in the U.S. Marines from 1942 to 1945, saw combat in the Pacific, and rose to the rank of corporal.

"We had to clean out that backlog because the Farm Bureau Mutual Automobile Insurance Company was getting a bad reputation. The only thing that saved us was that the other insurance companies had their troubles, too.

Jeffers joined the company as a claims adjuster March 24, 1941, although for a short time previous he worked as a part time agent to supplement his income as a high school teacher in northern Ohio. The promise of $2,100 a year from the insurance company convinced him to give up teaching. During the summer of 1941 he moved around Ohio to learn the ropes — Columbus, Dayton, Canton and Perrysburg — before being assigned to Grove City, PA.

Among those who took a shine to Jeffers was Marion Foltz, superintendent of claims. He joined Farm Bureau Mutual in the 1920s after he lost his left arm in a farm accident. "He was an exceptionally strong person (and) an outstanding leader of men," Jeffers recalled. "He never really asked for any kind of an edge because of that handicap. He didn't think anything about coming up and sticking his foot on a stool or chair and saying, 'Dean, will you tie my shoestring?' He didn't let that bother him a bit."

In the spring of 1947 Foltz called Jeffers to headquarters from Pennsylvania to be a claims supervisor at $3,900 per annum. Jeffers accepted the promotion with the proviso that he be moved around the company so he could learn the insurance business. Upon reporting to work at the old Clinton Building, he wondered if he made the right move. The "desk" assigned to the newest claims supervisor was a packing crate with a blanket thrown over it. "I never forgot that," he said.

Jeffers survived the rugged start and moved on two years later to the actuarial department where product development, pricing and regulation all come together. In the role of assistant actuary, he found himself making a fire rate recommendation to Lincoln's cabinet, which at the time met at the Columbus

Country Club on the East Side of the city.

"I thought I had given all the reasons why we should go ahead and increase the rates," Jeffers said of his presentation. Then Bowman Doss, who headed up sales, "shot me out of the water so badly that I never really forgot it."* Twenty years later Jeffers was to succeed Doss as president of the Nationwide Insurance Companies.

Whether it was at this meeting that Jeffers made his first impression on Lincoln is not known, but during the lunch that followed Jeffers overheard Lincoln ask his assistant, James R. Moore, "Who is that young fellow?" To Jeffers it indicated Lincoln did not know who he was until that time.

Because of the rapid growth of the company, it became increasingly difficult for Lincoln to know the employees by name, even some of his more senior staff. Sometimes, upon leaving the 246 North High Street headquarters building, he would go out the back door to avoid seeing employees whose names he couldn't recall. "It's embarrassing," he admitted.[3]

W.E. "Fitz" Fitzpatrick, who retired in 1989 as corporate secretary and assistant to General Chairman John E. Fisher, occasionally would bump into Lincoln in the hallway. "Sometimes I think he thought my name was `There,' because he'd say, 'Hello, there.'"

On the other hand, those who knew him best were unanimous in describing the chief executive as a man who always kept his distance from all but a very few outside advisors. "Mr. Lincoln's humanitarian tendencies were usually focused on groups of people," Fisher remembered. "He was much more attracted to the opportunities for doing things that would help organized groups as opposed to being involved in one-to-one relationships. In fact, he could be sort of remote on a personal basis."

---

* At the lunch that followed, Jeffers turned to Doss and said, "You out-gunned me today, Mr. Doss, but this scrap's not over with." Doss looked at him and then started laughing. "Bowman and I got along fine," Jeffers said.

More worldly matters than insurance, such as energy, hunger, housing and the like, consumed him. To have time to deal with some of the monumental issues of the day, he hurried everywhere, trying to capture another vision. Walking down the hall of the 246 North High Street headquarters, for instance, he always was in full stride, "almost to the point of leaning forward, as though he were leaning into the wind," said Fisher.

Party politics also fascinated Lincoln, especially the politics that could benefit masses of people. By birth he was a staunch Republican, yet he was approached in 1944 to serve in Roosevelt's administration as Assistant Secretary of Agriculture under Claude R. Wickard. "You ought to come down and be one of the crowd," Roosevelt told Lincoln during a visit to the White House.

The opportunity to be involved in actions affecting millions of people intrigued Lincoln, but a team of oxen could not have pulled Anne Lincoln from their Gahanna farm. In addition, Lincoln's Republican friends urged him not to join the New Deal. So he turned down the president. It was only after the death of Roosevelt April 12, 1945, that Lincoln learned the assistant secretary's job could have been a prelude to something bigger. Roosevelt intended to replace Wickard with Lincoln and then send him out among the electorate to make speeches. If he caught on, Lincoln likely would become Roosevelt's running mate on the 1944 Democratic ticket,* a slot that

---

* In the fall of 1950 Lincoln was under intense pressure to seek the Democratic nomination for U.S. Senate and run against the Republican incumbent, Robert A. Taft. In a radio address on WRFD October 1, 1950, Lincoln declined, but switched to the Democratic Party because it "has been leading the people toward the kind of an economy that I think is going to be in the interest of the greatest number of people."

Ten years later a trial balloon went up for the 68-year-old Lincoln to join John F. Kennedy on the Democratic ticket. "Say Murray Lincoln Urged As Kennedy's Running Mate" the headline read in the Columbus *Citizen-Journal* May 10, 1960, but the balloon failed to fly any further.

Missouri Sen. Harry S. Truman filled.

"I was floored," said Lincoln upon learning of the opportunity missed. "I've sometimes said that was the nearest claim to fame I've ever had."[4]

Among the other opportunities in the early 1940s Lincoln felt he missed were an investment in an oil refinery in Iran,* the purchase of the National Refinery Company in Cleveland (acquiring oil or oil refineries always was on Lincoln's mind), and the purchase of the Ford-Ferguson tractor company.

Lincoln had heard about Harry Ferguson's revolutionary tractor design and saw in the machine a path toward alleviating world hunger and second, a benefit specifically for the Ohio farmer. Lincoln believed farmers "might as well own the company and the patents," too, if they were going to buy a Ford-Ferguson tractor for the farm, anyway.

During a European meeting of the International Cooperative Alliance immediately after war's end in 1945, Lincoln visited Ferguson in Paris. He told the inventor he wanted to buy the company to save the world from hunger.

"If this tractor would make any contribution, I'd be very happy," Ferguson said, "but do you know how much money it would take to buy this company?"

"No, sir, and I don't want to know," said the Ohio farm executive. "If you told me right now how much it was going to cost, I'd probably go home and not do it."

He didn't do it, either, but he came within a whisker of

---

* In 1946 Lincoln was approached about investing in a cooperative Iranian refinery. "It was a great (opportunity) … because it would have plunged us into international oil cooperatives on a scale that would have made our influence felt," he wrote in 1960 in *Vice President in Charge of Revolution* (p. 202). "I believe that if oil cooperatives had been established in the Middle East a number of years ago, that area would not now be drifting helplessly into the sphere of Russian influence." In a report to the Farm Bureau Insurance Companies board June 5, 1951, he said of the proposed oil cooperative: "If we could have done it, we could have changed history."

success. For months the negotiations dragged on with the president of Harry Ferguson, Inc., in Detroit, Roger M. Kyes.*
Finally, Kyes came to Columbus for a Saturday showdown.

Lincoln said he would "never forget that day because I smoked eight cigars (Lincoln rarely smoked, even cigars), and I was as sick as a horse all day Sunday."[5]

Kyes, reluctant to believe Lincoln was serious, turned the discussion to the salaries of Ford-Ferguson executives, which he wanted to preserve if the Farm Bureau did acquire the company.

"I don't know what you are getting," the Detroit businessman said, "but I'm getting $225,000 and a bonus of $110,000."

"By golly," said Lincoln, running his hand over his bald head, "I'm getting slightly less than that." He earned $18,000 at the time. The talks broke off, but Lincoln did not give up. He enlisted the help of Henry Knight, a vice president of General Motors Corporation. In one evening, from a room in the Hotel New Yorker in New York, Knight raised by telephone pledges totaling $33 million from people he knew.

The next morning Lincoln called Kyes. "I'm now ready to come up to see you with the color of money in my eyes and with the approval of the board that we can pay any salary that we can justify."[6] But it was too late. On June 30, 1947, Ford abrogated its agreement with Ferguson's U.S. company and decided instead to build its own — and practically the same — tractor.†

Lincoln was philosophical about the lost battle. "In an odd way ... the whole experience boosted my stock with the Farm

---

* Roger M. Kyes, a Cleveland economist, became vice president of General Motors Truck Corp., deputy secretary of defense under President Dwight D. Eisenhower, and then a GM vice president again. He also became a confidant of Lincoln's.
† In 1956 Lincoln toyed with the idea of gaining control of the Ford Motor Company itself by buying out the 40 percent interest held by the Ford family.

Bureau board. What was more, it enlarged their vision and their sense of the size of things we were capable of tackling."[7]

In the mid-1940s the war in Europe and the Pacific wound down and the war within the Farm Bureau heated up. Lincoln called it "a power struggle" within the Farm Bureau among those who thought he was "autocratic and arbitrary." In *Vice President in Charge of Revolution* (pp. 155-157), Lincoln said staff opposition mounted over the bureau's membership in the Cooperative League* and the hiring of two outsiders, Herbert E. Evans and Harry W. Culbreth, both of whom were to later play important roles in the Nationwide Insurance Enterprise. Also a part of the problem internally were Lincoln's forays into non-insurance ventures.

The end of the "power struggle" came in February 1945 with the resignations of four of Lincoln's top aides, including his closest advisor, Lee A. Taylor, who was assistant general manager and secretary of the insurance companies. The four told the press they did not believe the Ohio Farm Bureau should join hands with labor and pursue consumer cooperatives for the farmer. Lincoln answered: "There's no organic difference between the farmer and the laborer."[8]

Lincoln quickly took steps to shore up his ranks, afraid that the revolution might spread and other Farm Bureau employees might join it.

Among those whom Lincoln called into his office was the handsome and energetic West Virginian, Bowman Doss. (He never used his first name, Porter.) He joined the Farm Bureau Mutual Automobile Insurance Company in 1932 as a part-time agent and became a licensed agent the following year. He racked up an impressive sales and management record in West

---

* During the Lincoln era, the membership of the insurance companies in the Cooperative League received considerable scrutiny from Ohio insurance regulators. They were concerned that policyholder funds were improperly used to support non-insurance cooperative ventures.

Virginia, North Carolina, Syracuse, NY, and Ohio before moving into the home office in 1944 as assistant superintendent of agents.

"What are *you* going to do?" Lincoln asked Doss after the mass resignations.

"I'm staying, " came the reply.

"Well then, I want you to become sales manager of the entire company,"[9] succeeding L.J. Bennett, one of the four who quit.

Doss worked "day and night to stop the erosion" of employees looking to follow the defectors, then received his reward for his loyalty and for his talent as a salesman by his election as assistant secretary. A year later he became agency vice president. That was 1946.

It also was the year of what undoubtedly was until then Lincoln's most publicized speech and remarks that he, and the company, had to live with for the rest of his life. The occasion was the opening of the biennial convention of the National Cooperative Congress at the Deshler-Wallick Hotel September 9. Lincoln was its president and gave the opening address.

He spoke of "a world in revolution"; of a business economy "which looks to the future with fear and apprehension" versus the cooperatives that are "planning ahead with confidence and optimism"; of an American public "at the mercy of a profit-minded business system ... determined to exact the greatest possible toll from the consumer" and of the need for the cooperative movement to come together for the common good.

"The days of opportunity are numbered," he said. "The tides of revolution are ready to sweep into the vacuum of American unrest."[10]

In reporting on the speech, the *Columbus Dispatch* took Lincoln to task under a headline, "Cooperatives Map Plan with CIO to Run Industry and Agriculture," and said in a picture caption that Lincoln had outlined "a prospective alliance between farmers and labor, particularly the CIO, aimed to meet the coming `revolution' ... "[11] There also was the suggestion by *The Dispatch* the following day that another speaker, E.R. Bowen, had said that cooperatives had embraced communism.[12]

Neither inference by the newspaper was true. In his talk, for instance, Lincoln never mentioned the Congress of Industrial Organizations or any plan to link up with the labor organization. However, the damage was done. Lincoln and those who worked with him became virtual outcasts with the "downtown crowd" in Columbus and bore the scars from it many years afterward.*

Lincoln was never one to socialize much with the city's power brokers. Mrs. Henry Ballard, wife of the company's corporate counsel, did what she could to correct that and received a blast of cold air for her trouble.

"Now, if you and Mrs. Lincoln ever get an invitation to the Crichton Club,† be sure to accept it," she said.

"Why?" he asked.

"Well, then you'll be accepted into society in Columbus."

"Why do I want to be accepted in that kind of society?" an unimpressed Lincoln said. "I tried it in the Kiwanis Club, and I'd just go to meeting after meeting and get into such a hell of an argument with the guys around the table that I paid a dollar and a quarter for the dinner I didn't want to eat, and I got so stirred up in the argument with my fellow table members ... so I just quit."[13]

At the time of Lincoln's 1946 speech to the National Cooperative Congress, the Wolfe family of Columbus owned both *The Dispatch* and Ohio National Bank. Lincoln was among

---

* In an interview April 28, 1982, James N. Marion, associate vice president of corporate security, took issue with the title of Lincoln's book, *Vice President in Charge of Revolution,* published in 1960. "Here you are," Marion said, "newspaper editors writing editorials about him being a revolutionary and a communist, and they come out with the damn title of the book."
† The Crichton Club was a social organization formed after World War II. It met three times a year at the Columbus Museum of Art.

the local leaders who sat on the bank's auxiliary, or advisory, board.

"That lasted until that time I made the speech and said we're in a revolution," he recalled in 1956, "and the next week they abandoned the auxiliary board of directors — frankly to get rid of me, nothing else."[14]

Lincoln's message concerning the virtues of cooperatives suddenly found a much wider avenue in 1946 when the Farm Bureau Mutual Automobile Insurance Company organized Peoples Broadcasting Company* as its first affiliated, non-insurance enterprise. "We cannot overestimate the importance of the radio development as a means of communication to people," Lincoln said.[15]

The basic idea of the broadcasting company was to find sound investments for policyholder monies, but it also "was an attempt by Mr. Lincoln to reach the people through the channels of the air, rather than through the channels of a newspaper," admitted George H. Dunlap.

Lincoln found it interesting "that no really savage attack has been launched against me or any company within the Nationwide organization since we acquired our radio stations," he wrote in *Vice President in Charge of Revolution.*[16]

Peoples Broadcasting, which is today Nationwide Communications Inc., built its first station, WRFD, in Worthington, OH, and its tower facilities on 140 acres of land in Orange Township, Delaware County, just north of Columbus. RFD was an acronym for "rural free delivery," a postal term. A daytime-only AM station of 5,000 watts at 880 on the dial, it went on the air September 28, 1947, broadcasting from its studio in the Henri Boyd Inn, Worthington, OH.

Because of its low dial position, the station reached large portions of Ohio, but Dunlap saw it as a weak station that was

* The Farm Bureau had had its own weekly Sunday broadcast over WAIV since May 11, 1931, and periodic short broadcasts as early as 1927.

more trouble than it was worth.* Not so Lincoln. He had faith in the power of broadcasting. He first put Moore, at the time director of information for the Ohio Farm Bureau Federation, in charge of the new affiliate, then Herbert E. Evans when Moore† fell ill.

The cigar-smoking Evans was known around the office as one of the company's genuine "characters." Weighing in at some 300 pounds and standing more than 6 feet tall, Evans did not go unnoticed, although some had difficulty understanding his New York accent. He naturally attracted attention, including Lincoln's. He hired Evans away from the Consumer Distribution Corporation, a New York cooperative, in 1946 and installed him as personnel director just prior to the resignation of the four senior executives.

Because he was an "outsider" from New York, some viewed him with suspicion, including the board. Evans brought to the job many liberal, Eastern ideas, such as life insurance for the employees, better compensation and working conditions, particularly for women, and a retirement plan.

"What do these people need a retirement plan for?" crusty board veteran John Hodson‡ asked of Evans at a board meeting. "Farmers don't have a retirement plan. Why would *they* (the employees of the insurance companies) need a retirement plan?" Those who watched the dedication Evans had to his job remembered that he "literally put his job on the line" to get the retirement plan.

Later, as vice president in charge of Peoples Broadcasting, he

---

* In December 1974 the Ohio Farm Bureau purchased the station from Nationwide, then sold it a few years later.

† Following his retirement in 1953, Moore became president and general manager of Peoples Travel Service, established in 1950. The board of the travel agency, which is still in operation, is made up of former and current Nationwide officials.

‡ In 1941 John Hodson nominated himself to the board of the insurance companies and won election.

had an occasion to be before the board again. He delivered a glowing report on the performance of the affiliate, then sat down.

Sitting next to him was Controller Ed Keltner, who leaned over to Evans and whispered, "Herb, you shouldn't have done that. You're broke; you don't have a dime. How can you tell the board what you did?"

Evans launched his massive frame to its feet and addressed the board again.

"Look, Lincoln and you directors. I didn't mean to mislead you; I thought I was telling the truth, but Ed here tells me that I am broke." Lincoln nearly had a fit.[17]

Many years later a successor to Evans, Clark Pollock, appeared before the board to give his monthly report. Pollock painted a rosy, six-figure profit picture for Nationwide Communications, a good month's work. Nary a word of praise came from the directors.

"Are there *any* questions?" Pollock asked.

The hand of one board member went up. "Do you know," he asked, "who shot J.R.?"

The reference was to the immensely popular television show, *Dallas*, which topped the ratings in 1980 with a cliffhanger involving the shooting of J.R. Ewing, the lead character. A somewhat bemused Pollock had to admit that he didn't know.

"Well, you know, I told the wife you were going to be on today," the director explained amid the guffaws, "and she said to ask." It was the only question asked of Pollock that day.[18]

On the heels of Peoples Broadcasting came the second non-insurance affiliate, namely Peoples Development Company, formed in 1948. Like the broadcasting company, it was a vehicle for investment and also to provide affordable housing for the masses. Its first housing project, Amsden Heights, originally included 34 individually-designed homes in Bellevue, OH, at prices ranging from $8,825 to $13,475. The northern Ohio residential community featured "gracefully curving macadam drives and a large public park and playground." All the homes were built in 1949 at the request of the National Machinery Cooperative.

A variety of developments followed, such as Lincoln Village, "a model city" for 11,000 people on the West Side of Columbus, Annehurst* Village in Westerville, a Columbus suburb, Pinetree Community southwest of Atlanta, and many others.

With a company involved in housing, Lincoln took the next leap into a Newark, OH, company known as Tectum, "another example of how Nationwide Insurance invests its policyholders' dollars in their own interest" declared an advertisement for Tectum. It manufactured strong, lightweight and inexpensive ceiling tiles made from chemically treated wood. The tiles were used primarily for roofing of schools, homes and office buildings.

When he presented Tectum to the board, he admitted "This may be to some of you the craziest thing we have ever presented."[19] He saw in Tectum not only the investment (of about $500,000 initially) but also a market for farmers' wood. When production faltered and the original management did, too, the Farm Bureau Insurance Companies bought them out.

The Newark plant problems were resolved, a second plant built in Arkadelphia, AR, and Tectum International formed "to provide low-cost shelter for under-privileged people throughout the world," said Lincoln.[20] The first overseas venture was in Korea where the product, made of rice straw instead of wood, was renamed Tec-Pan. The Korean company, Tec-Pan Industrial Corporation of Seoul, never developed beyond its formation.

The National Gypsum Company of Buffalo, NY, bailed out Lincoln and the insurance companies by buying Tectum for

---

* A combining of Lincoln's wife's maiden name.

$3.1 million in cash and notes. This followed the discovery that the building product produced "effervescence"; when it became damp, it flaked, and flaked badly. "It looked like the product was not going to be anything but a loser, so we sold it," said John C. Wagner, retired senior vice president and general counsel, Nationwide Insurance Companies.

Regardless of the many diversions Lincoln cooked up, the insurance companies were on the move. To accommodate the nearly 2,000 home office employees, work began in 1948 on the razing of the Schultz and Arcade office buildings adjacent to headquarters at 246 N. High Street, erecting a new building in their place and incorporating it into a remodeling of the headquarters building. The automobile company was just shy of its first one million policies in force (it topped 1.3 million the following year), the fire company had 244,000 policies in force, and the life company's 130,000 policies in force was a record high.

As the decade of the 1940s came to a close, the Farm Bureau Insurance Companies were vibrant, expanding enterprises, spurred on by the post-war boom. President Harry S. Truman won the White House and Citation the Kentucky Derby; a little-known Richard M. Nixon relentlessly pursued Communists and former U.S. State Department official Alger Hiss, who was convicted of perjury; an assassin's bullet killed India's Ghandi; the Soviet Union exploded an atomic bomb; Israel became an independent state and opening nighters saw Mary Martin wash her hair in *South Pacific*.

In a chat with his directors, Lincoln waxed philosophical about the growth of the company and the direction he had taken it. "I am fully aware," said he, "that we could have had a much more placid experience if we were not constantly reaching out to enlarge and improve our scope of operations."[21]

They might have known, with Lincoln at the helm, the road yet ahead would be anything but "placid."

6

A TIME FOR NATIONWIDE

"**W**HEREAS,** *the President of this company has reported to this Board that the Superintendent of Insurance of the State of Ohio has directed the Board of Directors of this company to cancel and terminate the service contract entered into with Ohio Farm Bureau Corporation under date of July 1, 1945, because a number of the members of this Board are officers or members of the Board of Directors of said Ohio Farm Bureau Corporation, which dual membership, in the judgment of the Superintendent of Insurance, is an unsound insurance practice and should therefore be canceled and terminated as of the close of business on September 30, 1947 ... "[1]*

The "whereases" in the board minutes of the Farm Bureau Mutual Automobile Insurance Company continued for five cold and impersonal pages. More than a half dozen similar agreements snipped away that September day in 1947 left the leadership of the insurance companies and the Farm Bureau with gut-wrenching decisions.

It was, pure and simple, a divorce ordered by the Ohio

regulators of the insurance industry. No matter how successful the marriage had been between the Ohio Farm Bureau Federation and the Farm Bureau Mutual Insurance Companies — and it was very successful for both sides — the state regulators decreed that it end.

The rationale for their position fell into two main areas of concern: One, the arrangements involving the fees the insurance companies paid to their sponsoring organizations, and two, the interlocking directorates and managements of the insurance companies and the Farm Bureau. The regulators objected to the fact that the bureau's board members also sat on the boards of the insurance companies and therefore, in each instance, made decisions affecting themselves.

Debate on the key issues spanned several years in the early-1940s, primarily because the Ohio Department of Insurance was short of staff during World War II. Consequently, the regular examination of the Farm Bureau Mutual Insurance Companies begun in 1942 did not resume until the end of 1945.

The sponsorship program provided for the sponsoring organizations, such as the farm bureaus in Ohio, Vermont and Maryland, etc., to receive from the insurance companies payments for advertising, membership drives and other services. In return, the sponsors would sign up their members with the Farm Bureau Insurance Companies.

The state's chief examiner, Dean M. Kerr,* and his associates perceived a lack of proper accounting of the sponsorship funds: How much was transferred, and how was it spent. "We ought to have definite statements of proof of the value of such fees," President Murray D. Lincoln agreed, "and the sponsor should be able to demonstrate to any insurance department ... the services rendered.

"I feel that these fees will be continually questioned as we go

---

* Shortly after the breakup, the insurance companies hired Dean M. Kerr as government relations director.

forward ... " he told the insurance companies directors in February of 1946.[2]

Lincoln had new sponsor contracts prepared, detailing how much was paid each sponsor, and the sponsor organizations prepared invoices covering their services on behalf of the insurance companies. "We accumulated a mountain of invoices," he said. "The examiners were happier. This is what they were used to. This was what they wanted."[3]

Not exactly. They also wanted Lincoln and the other leaders to make the choice: the insurance business or the farm organization but not both.

Lincoln always suspected that "somebody underneath was up to something ... I think we just were beginning to be too effective, and they don't understand it, and what you don't understand, you fear."[4]

Throughout 1947 and into the winter of 1948 Lincoln and the board wrestled with the issue and emotions ran high. Lincoln himself wanted to duke it out with the insurance department, but the attorney for the insurance companies, Henry Ballard, held him back. Lincoln always resented that.

"I regret to this day," he wrote in 1960 in *Vice President in Charge of Revolution*, "that we did not fight. We'd done nothing wrong," and neither had any member of any board.[5] The insurance department agreed, but for the protection of the policyholders, they said, Lincoln and the others had to make the choice.*

A bitter Lincoln chose the insurance companies, resigning as executive secretary of the Ohio Farm Bureau Federation February 4, 1948, but "the separation ... was a severe emotional wrench for me," he wrote. "It took me away from the Farm Bureau after an intimate association of 28 years."[6]

Not everyone associated with the two organizations had

---

* The Department of Insurance examination didn't end formally until December 21, 1953.

regrets, however. George H. Dunlap, the powerful chairman of the Farm Bureau Mutual Automobile Insurance Company, was one who didn't.

"Right or wrong, (I) felt that perhaps the time had come" to split the organizations, he said. "Mainly the organizations in total had become very large. Mr. Lincoln's interests were in world affairs, in peace programs, and in programs beyond the boundaries of Ohio.

"It was felt that each organization could probably expand faster and meet their chartered objectives better than to keep it all under one person."

Another longtime employee of the Farm Bureau Mutual Automobile Insurance Company, Charles W. Leftwich, agreed with Dunlap.

"We regarded it as a serious setback at the time," he recalled in 1970. "Looking back, I can see, and I'm sure most others will agree, that it was a good thing for both organizations. The insurance department actually did us a great service. The separation certainly has not impeded the growth or success of either the insurance companies or the Farm Bureau. To the contrary, it has been conducive to more specialization and concentration in our respective programs."

At the time of the split, the auto, fire and life insurance companies had just posted combined 1947 premium income of $35.6 million, admitted assets of more than $51 million and 982,000 policies in force. The following year, the three companies topped 1 million policies in force for the first time.

By way of comparison, the Nationwide Insurance Enterprise in 1993 had premium income of $12.8 billion, admitted assets of $42.2 billion and 11.3 million policies in force.

On several occasions during the 1940s the Farm Bureau Mutual board and Lincoln also discussed changing the name of the insurance companies. Many were reluctant to do so, pointing to the success of the insurance operations under the bureau's banner. If it ain't broke, don't fix it was their position.

Others, such as Lincoln, saw the cracks forming as the company looked to expand into new states, and that was a real problem for the Ohioans. They had had little difficulty moving into states by invitation from "sponsors," such as other Farm Bureau organizations, but they stopped at the door of states where the resident Farm Bureau did not want them. In many of those states the farm bureaus had their own insurance operations.

Helping to drive a wedge into the cracks was the American Farm Bureau Federation, which Lincoln had quit in disgust a number of years earlier in a policy dispute. He wanted the organization to serve all the people, as the Farm Bureau insurance companies did; the AFBF wanted to serve only those farmers who were Farm Bureau members. The rift never healed.

"The inescapable truth was that the American Farm Bureau was determined to keep itself strictly a farm organization," Lincoln wrote in *Vice President in Charge of Revolution*. "It was determined to maintain that artificial and deep schism between the farmer and the city dweller."

(A little ego was involved, too. Lincoln was the only state executive secretary on the AFBF board; the remainder were presidents. "They resented me deeply as a hired hand in the parlor. They thought I had no right to be on the board."[7])

Whatever the problem, real or perceived, the AFBF was strong enough to bar the Ohio insurance group from securing licenses in about 20 Farm Bureau states. The national organization made no bones about their stance, either, lobbing in missives on the subject at every opportunity.

On one occasion in the fall of 1945, the Farm Bureau Mutual board replied to such a letter from Roger Corbett, secretary of the AFBF. "The board would not be opposed to a discussion of a change of name of the Farm Bureau Insurance Companies of Ohio," the Ohioans said, but they would be "interested to learn what would be gained by such a change."[8]

It was a bit of derring-do and a slap in the face of the AFBF, if you will. The board knew the company could not expand without a name change.

Lincoln brought up "the controversy" again in 1946 and, for the first time, suggested a new name. He expressed concern that with the growth of other cooperatives one of them would develop a national insurance program and beat him to the punch.

"Because of our experience, our objectives and our history," he said, "I think we should seriously consider changing our name to something like the 'Peoples Mutual Insurance Services' and offer this service in any state or territory of the U.S.A. It is too great an opportunity and service to miss."[9]

The name-change discussions continued into the 1950s with no resolution. Some board members much preferred the status quo. Chairman Dunlap was one. "I saw no need for a name change," he said, inasmuch as the companies were still growing within the original 13 states in which the company had a license, plus the District of Columbia. After all, the number of policies in force in 1954 was nearly 3 million, or 37 times larger than it was 20 years earlier, admitted assets topped $210 million, or 81 times what had been recorded a couple of decades before, and Farm Bureau Mutual Automobile Insurance Company was the world's fourth-largest automobile insurer — and second largest among mutual companies.

The forces behind further expansion finally carried the day in 1953 and a panel — the New Name Research & Recommendations Committee — took on the task of finding a new name. The first two choices presented to the board were Heritage and Town and Country.

Dunlap stopped Lincoln in the hall before going into the board meeting for a discussion of the new name.

"What are you going to do about the name change?" Dunlap asked.

"I don't know," said the chief executive.

"I don't like either one of them, Mr. Lincoln."

"I don't either. I think I'll appoint another committee," which Lincoln did by bringing in a flock of consultants.[10]

During the two-year process the committee discarded some 2,600 names already in use and studied the nearly 1,000 remaining possibilities. Among those that found their way into the finals were Fortuna, Defender, Foundation, Merit, Policyowners, Pathfinder and Vanguard. Lincoln's earlier choice, "Peoples Mutual," failed to survive the process.

For Leftwich, chairing the selection committee was not a happy task.

"How are you coming along?" Lincoln asked from time to time.

"Oh, we're making progress, Mr. Lincoln," Leftwich replied with a smile.

Years later he would admit the truth. "We weren't doing a thing; we were stuck."

Month after frustrating month went by, until the morning of September 24, 1954. While shaving the name that came to Leftwich seemed a natural, and he immediately tried it out on the committee, then on Lincoln.

As he entered the chief executive's office, Lincoln was looking out the window, his mind probably 100 miles away, recalled Leftwich. "Mr. Lincoln, we have a new name to suggest. Nationwide."

Nothing. No reaction at all.

"So, I put my tail between my legs and went back to my office," Leftwich said. A few minutes later, Lincoln walked in.

"You know, that name, Nationwide; it kind of grows on you."

"Do you like it, Mr. Lincoln?"

"By golly, I do."

So did the board, which approved it in November. It also approved the payment of $5,000 to a Cincinnati insurer that was considering the same name for a new life company.

Nationwide was previewed to the employees January 25, 1955, through a closed-circuit telecast in Columbus and 20 other cities and officially introduced September 1, 1955, to general acclaim. No longer would a company salesman knock on a door, announce, "I'm from the Farm Bureau," and be told, "We don't need fertilizer."

One policyholder seemed quite upset, and slightly confused, however. He canceled his policy with Farm Bureau Mutual, declaring, "I'm switching my insurance to a new outfit called Nationwide."

The new name was not the only reason the 1950s were exciting, vibrant times for the insurance companies. The employees moved into a remodeled and expanded 246 North High Street building,* described by Lincoln as "the acme of something." Dedicated in 1951, the new building gave the more than 2,000 employees the first headquarters in 25 years that they could call their own. (The much smaller Farm Bureau staff moved across Chestnut Street into the Joyce Building in 1948 after the breakup.)

Among the job candidates to interview in the new building was John E. Fisher. At 21, the young man from Portsmouth, OH, had had his share of excitement as a stock clerk in a grocery store, a shoe factory worker, a carpenter's helper, a boilermaker's apprentice for the railroad, a shoe company management trainee, a door-to-door furniture and vacuum cleaner salesman, a cost recorder in the Columbus Department of Sewage and Drains and a husband at the age of 19. He also found time to study at the University of Colorado at Boulder, Ohio University at Athens and Franklin University at Columbus.

Fisher's wife, Eloise, secured a secretarial job at the Farm

---

* The $5 million, nine-story building received honorable mention in the "Office of the Year" awards of *Office Management and Equipment* magazine, October 1951.

Bureau Insurance Companies by being a superb typist. Tiring of all her husband's part-time jobs, she suggested he apply at the company, too — for a permanent position. He was hired May 14, 1951, as an underwriting trainee, thus launching a 43-year career that ended in April 1994 with his retirement as general chairman.

It was a career that almost ended before it began. In taking the company's employment test, Fisher failed to read the directions carefully and filled in one section completely backwards. "In order to really determine what my (grade) was, they had to accommodate me by applying the directions backwards, which gave me a very high score."

Fisher clearly remembers his first day at the Farm Bureau Insurance Companies. All new employees received a ticket for a free lunch. In charge of Fisher's orientation, and ticket, was Al Herman, a slightly nervous type who, "while he was talking to me, was tearing up these little bits of paper," Fisher recalled. "I went on a little tour of the office, and when I came back to see him for my free lunch ticket, he looked down and realized that the free lunch was in little pieces at the bottom of his waste basket."

The first office for the future chief executive officer of the Nationwide Insurance Enterprise was on the street floor of the Lazarus warehouse building at Chestnut and Third Streets. The rapidly expanding insurance companies shared space there with the R. G. Barry shoe company. A problem with the heating system forced employees to open the windows in winter.

"Since the nearby railroad yard was still active, you could always tell how long someone was gone ... by the amount of coal dust on their papers," Fisher said.

Assigned to Annapolis, MD, in the spring of 1952, Fisher again ran into man-made debris on his desk. The regional office was in the old S. Kotzin Company candy warehouse at the corner of Chinquapin Round and McGuckian roads. ("Because

I later became responsible for printing for that region, I always was bugged with the fact that we were at Chinquapin and McGuckian," Fisher laughed.)

This time the windows of the warehouse were left open in summer because there was no air conditioning. Thanks to operations at a large sawmill across the street, "You could tell how long somebody had been missing from their desk by how much sawdust had accumulated on their papers," he recalled.

The year Fisher began his career with Nationwide, Gen. Douglas MacArthur was ending his after being fired by President Truman. The U.S. was trying to extricate itself from another war, although it was called the Korean "conflict." Memories of another conflict 10 years earlier, the bombing of Pearl Harbor, returned for millions of Americans through the pages of *From Here to Eternity.* Those few not reading the James Jones best-seller watched the birth of color television.

Decentralization was the watchword around the insurance companies in 1951. "We were going to sweep through the whole nation (with) 20 or 30 regional offices,"* remembered Ralph Jordan, vice president in the office of corporate relations. "We soon found out that setting up an office in a new territory with all that it implies — the costs, the trauma of moving people, of selecting people — is more difficult than when you are all excited in a meeting and saying, 'We are going to conquer the world!'"

The staging for decentralization, known as Operations Opportunity, began in Columbus in the late 1940s. Operations Vice President Howard Hutchinson had the prime responsibility for the plan, and Richard G. Chilcott, Dean W. Jeffers and Ashley T. "Mack" McCarter had managerial roles. "We were known as the three stooges," said McCarter. "All three of us came out of claims. We just worked together very closely."

As Jordan remembered, there were "a lot of slips between

---

* Only 13 were established, from New England to the Pacific Northwest.

the cup and the lip" in executing the decentralization plan. "There was a lot of agony, a lot of stress," he said.*

The New England Region came first, and it set up office on the two top floors of a furniture store in New Haven, CT. Although it had but Vermont, Connecticut and Rhode Island to service at the time, the region idea existed to get closer to the business and the customer and to improve service, which fell behind during the rapid growth of the Farm Bureau Insurance Companies in the post-war years.

In the beginning, hiring personnel willing to move from Columbus to Connecticut was difficult, but even more troublesome was holding on to them. "We recruited something like 50 girls who were going to be permanent members of our staff in New England," recalled Robert M. Culp, the first regional underwriting manager for the decentralized companies. "At the end of about 90 days, we had something like seven or eight of the 50 left. They went back home — back to Columbus."

That experience taught Culp and his associates to do a lot more of the hiring in the local area, bring the new hires to Columbus for training and then return "home." The other was never trust a truck driver. On the way over to the region, one moving van overturned on the Pennsylvania Turnpike and scrambled the region's furniture and one set of record cards — thousands of them all over the highway. Each was gathered up and refiled, a lengthy and laborious task.

A second moving van driver met up with a friendly young lady at a truck stop along the way and that truck disappeared. The Pennsylvania State Police looked for the van for five days before finding it parked up a country lane under some trees. "Never did find the truck driver," Culp said.

There was considerable disagreement then and now whether

---

* "Every one of the moves has gone off like clockwork," Lincoln told the Third Annual Institute of Modern Management, Chicago, February 9, 1954.

decentralization of the Farm Bureau Insurance Companies was an idea whose time had come. Some believe the plan was overly ambitious; others believe it did wonders for the companies.

McCarter, in charge of the Carolinas region in 1951, firmly supports the latter position. "When we put decentralization into effect, people had to step up to their jobs and do them," he said. As a result, "the development of people ... was really phenomenal. That's really when growth took off."

Fisher agreed. "I don't think these opportunities would have arisen that allowed many younger employees to try their wings. ... I must say I got an earlier opportunity at supervision and management because I joined the companies right at the beginning of decentralization."

Decentralization also set the stage for a profit-center management philosophy, "a vital asset to Nationwide," Fisher maintained. "We have been able to achieve an entrepreneurial attitude by setting incentives and objectives on a localized basis with operations almost like individual insurance companies."

The advances in telecommunications and the computer make expansion of the regional concept much less likely today, said Fisher, who saw to it during his term as chief executive officer to consolidate some of the old regional offices for greater efficiency and economy. He believed the companies may have been "decentralized to the extreme."

McCarter, who retired in 1980 as senior vice president, office of the president, also benefited from his regional experience, receiving a promotion to the home office in 1956 to head up field operations. That put him in closer touch with Lincoln, one of the few executives in the company taller than the 6-foot-3-inch McCarter.*

After just six months in his new job at headquarters,

---

* In the 1950s and 1960s, Richard C. Brough, operations controls, was considered the tallest at 6 feet 6 inches.

McCarter was surprised by Lincoln. He strode into McCarter's office, plunked himself down in a chair and stretched out to his full length. "He looked like he stretched from one end of the room to the other," said the field operations chief.

"I want to ask you some questions," Lincoln began.

"All right."

"Number one: What do you do? And number two: Do you think you are worth what we are paying you to do that?"

After recovering from the unexpected frontal assault, McCarter spent the next 15 minutes detailing his responsibilities and answering more questions from Lincoln. McCarter finally realized that Lincoln's questions probed for answers reflecting the corporate, cooperative philosophy. "He had the feeling that if the philosophy was right and understood, the finances would take care of themselves. ... I don't think he cared about what I was being paid."

It wasn't too long after that discussion that Lincoln startled McCarter again with another visit.

"I've got to go to New York. I'd like you to go with me."

Although swamped with work, McCarter could not refuse, but he had no idea why Lincoln wanted him to tag along.

Once aboard the company plane — by the mid-'50s the companies had acquired two — the two men engaged in conversation, interrupted only by Lincoln's habit of taking 10-minute catnaps mid-sentence. Upon awakening, the conversation would pick up right where he left off. As the Convair 240 approached New York, Lincoln asked:

"Did you know this plane has a shower in it?"

"No."

"It does, by golly. Have you ever taken a shower at 10,000 feet?"

"No."

"I have. On the way back if you want to take a shower, take one."

"Are you trying to tell me something, Mr. Lincoln? Do I

need a shower?"

"No, I just thought sometime you would want to tell somebody you took a shower at 10,000 feet."

McCarter took his shower* on the return trip and told the story repeatedly for many years thereafter.

Dr. Robert A. Rennie recalled the chief executive was "pleased as punch" that the companies had an airplane. It was another way for Lincoln to demonstrate to others the rewards of a cooperative enterprise, although funds from the insurance companies financed the aircraft.

Rennie, an economist who taught at Johns Hopkins University and consulted the likes of the Federal Reserve and the American Telephone & Telegraph Company, also joined the Farm Bureau Insurance Companies in 1951. Lincoln told Rennie his job would be "to find out what the needs of consumers are for financial services."[11]

The two men came to respect each other enormously, although Rennie never did buy into Lincoln's cooperative philosophy.

"While I saw the cooperative movement as a good way to counter the power of monopolies or monopolistic competition, I thought that it had very serious limitations," he said. "Lincoln put his emphasis on the need to get consumer cooperatives into the picture, along with farm cooperatives. However, consumer cooperatives have monopoly elements, too. In economic terms, we call it 'monopsony,' which means that the buyer exerts power over the producer.[†]

Lincoln saw consumer cooperatives as a way to save the world,

---

* Apparently taking a shower in the company plane was high excitement, but an executive from the Swiss-based Movenpick supermarket chain declined the experience when it was offered by Edward F. Wagner, head of Nationwide Development Company.

[†] Webster's *New World Dictionary* defines "monopsony" as "a situation in which there is only one buyer for a particular commodity or service."

with the result the cooperatives would gain the upper hand over the producer, Rennie explained. "I've never seen a time in history when a group of people got together in their own selfish interest and had sufficient market power that they didn't really infringe on the rights and welfare of the people on the other end of the economic spectrum.

"Lincoln and I debated this endlessly. This is probably one of the reasons he didn't take me to his bosom more fervently," Rennie said.

The cooperative movement seemingly consumed Lincoln, many thought to the detriment of the insurance companies. In August of 1954 he told the board:

"I asked Mr. Doss, our executive vice president, to take over the general direction of our insurance activities ... in order that I could direct my major attention to our subsidiaries. With the coming of the improvement in these areas, I next asked him to begin to step into that picture so I could devote more time to these outside relationships ... "[12]

Thus Lincoln took another step away from running the companies, preferring to turn the day-to-day operations over to his senior officer. It was the last key assignment Doss received from Lincoln. Four months later their relationship changed dramatically.

7

THE RATTLING OF PINS

In the 1950s America's white-collar workers outnumbered blue-collar workers for the first time. Bureaucratic corporations, fat as bacon, swallowed up thousands of office drones, as William H. Whyte Jr. described in his 1956 best-seller, *The Organization Man*. The burgeoning middle class, euphoric in a peacetime economy, flocked to the tree-lined suburbs. Consumerism surpassing that of the 1920s returned, demanding everything a suburban homeowner could want — from queen-sized mattresses, power mowers and garbage disposers to "hi-fis," dishwashers and finned automobiles. Charge accounts and new-found "plastic" boosted consumer credit 800 percent between 1945 and 1957.[1]

"In the cold war struggle," Murray D. Lincoln said with remarkable vision, "victory eventually will go to the side which devises a system to get the most goods to the most people." As president and chief executive officer of the Farm Bureau Insurance Companies, Lincoln set his course with that cooperative philosophy in mind.

In addition to the insurance companies, he had his broadcast facilities, a manufacturing enterprise that provided construction materials for the homes his real estate development company was building, the shell of a mutual fund, a finance company — Approved Finance, Inc., acquired in 1951 to provide low-cost financing primarily for policyholders buying automobiles — and the Alliance Manufacturing Company of Alliance, OH.

A maker of the "Lift-A-Dor" garage door opener,* television antenna rotors and other electronic devices, Alliance was bought for $6.26 million in August 1954 chiefly to use its favorable earnings ($2 million in the first eight months) to offset losses at the Nationwide-associated ceiling tile manufacturer, Tectum. When Peoples Development Company sold Alliance two years later, it realized a tidy $5.8 million profit.

At the time of the sale, Farm Bureau Mutual director Perry L. Green told Lincoln: "Murray, this transaction may be legal, but it isn't right to make money this fast."[2]

Lincoln also reveled in the prestige of being president of the Cooperative League of the U.S.A. and of CARE,† which he co-founded in 1945. He flew around the country and the world,‡ performing the duties of his many offices and searching for new enterprises to conquer in the name of the insurance companies or the cooperative movement, or both.

According to a memorandum written in early 1954 by Paul

---

* The garage door opener became better known later under a new marketing name, "Genie."
† The Cooperative for American Remittances to Europe, CARE in its original form, became well known for its relief packages to people in nations decimated by World War II. In 1953 CARE became the Cooperative for American Relief Everywhere.
‡ In the late 1940s and early 1950s the Ohio Department of Insurance examined Lincoln's overseas trips carefully. After one extensive journey to Europe they criticized expenses charged the Farm Bureau Mutual Automobile Insurance Company, "having no branches in Europe."

Boardman,* project director of Peoples Development Company, Lincoln and his associates were out beating the bushes for investment opportunities. In the prior two years alone, Boardman noted that the insurance companies looked at "steel processing, recovering pig iron from slag piles, lift trucks, fruit packing company, house trailer company, roller bearing manufacturing, concrete pipe manufacturing, upholstering pads for auto industry and the pottery business, etc."[3]

It was his involvement in these and other outside activities that caused Lincoln to turn over to Bowman Doss the day-to-day insurance business. Lincoln promoted him to executive vice president in January 1951 with the comment: "You, I think, are the best-liked, most popular man in the company."[4]

Doss, then a month shy of his 43rd birthday, was very pleased. In the six short years since moving to the home office as assistant superintendent of agents, he had achieved the loftiest of positions next to Lincoln, a perch on which no other ever had sat. By the fall of 1954, Doss clearly had the inside track to succeed the chief executive, then 62. In Doss' words, "Everything looked rosy."

Lincoln cared little for the affairs of running a multi-million-dollar enterprise but enjoyed immensely the power it gave him. Perhaps that is why he virtually ignored the question of succession, a question to which more than a few in management and on the board sought answers. Factions formed throughout the organization, to the detriment of the company.

Several years later Lincoln told Dr. Robert A. Rennie: "If I should ever appoint a successor ... he would be dead because everybody would be converging on him." He probably was

---

* Paul Boardman, described by Lincoln as "a cold, analytical banker type," joined Peoples Development Company in 1952, was named vice president and general manager of Nationwide Corporation in 1956, and retired in 1964.

right, so perhaps it was out of compassion that he never draped anyone with the coveted mantle.

Nevertheless, at the urging of Roger M. Kyes, his friend from the Ferguson tractor days, Lincoln agreed to hire in 1949 a management consulting firm from New York, Slade, Rogers & Vieh.* A revised organizational structure, which included Doss' promotion, the decentralization plan and a new executive salary program were products of the consultants' work.

Still, Lincoln was not entirely happy with the recommendations and actions, so in January 1954 he hired another New York management consulting firm, McKinsey & Company, which before and since performed many services for the enterprise. Its original charge in 1954 called for an audit of executive salaries, including incentive compensation, to make the Farm Bureau Insurance Companies more competitive. As the firm got into the project, however, the emphasis turned to the structure of the organization with a view to national expansion.

Three prime considerations motivated McKinsey's management study: (1) the rapid growth of the organization; (2) a similar growth pattern for the subsidiaries, and (3) the need to have in place strong management and maximum operating efficiencies before the territorial extension of the insurance companies.

"There is a limit ... to how far an executive can stretch his capacity to plan, administer, and control the operations of a 200 million dollar organization," McKinsey said in its report to the board of directors December 1, 1954. "Fortunately, Farm Bureau's chief executive (Lincoln) has already recognized the importance of concentrating his attention on long-range planning and the review and appraisal of end results.

"He realizes he cannot perform these major executive

---

* The firm later became Rogers, Slade & Hill, then Rogers & Slade.

functions effectively if he retains his present responsibility for operating decisions in the insurance, finance, housing, building materials, radio and electronic companies."[5]

The board approved the plan December 1. Two days later a meeting to unveil the strategy to all senior executives and managers was held at the Chittenden Hotel in Columbus. The day became known as "Black Friday."

With the top staff all seated, Lincoln rose to speak. "I'd like to talk to you this morning about organization," he began. He briefly detailed the growth of the insurance companies, the increased competition, the need to strengthen the structure and the promise of an improved compensation package.

"I am fully aware that some of the organization changes may appear to be major," he continued. "It is my conviction, however, that this is the time to take such steps."

He revealed the organizational chart prepared by McKinsey & Company, confirming that Doss would serve as executive vice president. "This means he will have full authority and operating responsibility for the insurance companies and the subsidiaries," Lincoln said.

"Before I turn the meeting over to Bowman, I want to reiterate that this is my plan of organization," the chief executive said emphatically. "I am heartily in favor of it."

Doss, who had worked closely on the plan with McKinsey's John Tomb, presented the few remaining changes but provided even fewer details. He introduced Howard Hutchinson, vice president of insurance operations and the new number three in the organization, and Robert W. Heffner, vice president of personnel, who also worked on the plan with Doss. That was it.

The assembled were stunned; "in shock," according to one executive in attendance. There were so few names on the chart. The executives "didn't know what was going on," said Ralph Jordan, then an administrative manager and later a vice president in government relations. "They didn't see where they were; they hadn't been given a clear slot."

Harry W. Culbreth, vice president for public relations, was among those who clearly saw where he was headed, and he didn't like it one whit. By being slotted as the research assistant to Lincoln, he felt demoted and, what's more important, pushed aside for a shot at the one job he coveted more than any other: Lincoln's.

While Doss was saying "every one of us has a right to feel very optimistic about the future," those left out of the loop plotted to overthrow the plan. Instead of seeing "the door of opportunity swinging wide," as Doss did, they saw it slamming in their face. Before the weekend was over, Culbreth and other key executives met to plan their rebellion.

Lincoln handed the ball to Doss, who promised "to give the promotion of our philosophy the greatest whirl it ever had." Immediately the executive vice president began to feel the heat generated by the proposal. In the December 17 issue of *The Dividend*, the employee newspaper of the insurance companies, Doss tried to put out the fires.

"I know it would be even better if I could announce today the people who will fill all the jobs in the proposed organization," he wrote. "I cannot! I cannot because, at this moment, there are several key positions yet to be considered. … We will share all information about this plan soon after the first of the year."[6]

Before the end of the year, however, the rebellion was in full swing. Culbreth, Charles W. Leftwich, P. Lee Thornbury, general counsel, J. Edward Keltner, vice president and controller, W. E. "Ed" West, vice president and treasurer, Herbert E. Evans, vice president, Peoples Broadcasting, and others all wrote memos to Doss or Lincoln, some enclosing their own organizational charts. Those with perceived power wanted to hold on to it; those without power wanted to gain it.

Evans summed up what was happening. In a memorandum to Lincoln, he wrote: "We have developed organization bulwarks all over the place, manned by fighting adherents ready to defend their programs and budgets almost to the point where the major company interests are secondary. These bulwarks are defended at all costs."[7]

Culbreth certainly was ready to defend his territory against Hutchinson and Doss, each clearly positioned ahead of Culbreth in the new chain-of-command. Rennie was sitting in Culbreth's office when Culbreth grabbed the McKinsey chart and headed for Lincoln's office. He confronted the boss.

"Do you know, Mr. Lincoln, that under this reorganization plan Bowman is the only person reporting to you?" It was true. Every one of the reporting lines went through Doss, the only executive reporting to Lincoln. Culbreth intimated that Doss was trying to take over the company.

Lincoln, rubbing the top of his head, examined the chart, then tore it up. "We are not going to do this," he said, apparently fed up with having to deal with so many disgruntled factions within the organization. Never again would Lincoln allow the preparation of an organizational chart, believing that his executives used them as a crutch to avoid making decisions they ought to make.

At the moment of Culbreth's confrontation with Lincoln, Doss was in his office in conference with Hutchinson and Dr. William Brown, a consulting psychologist the insurance companies had hired in connection with the reorganization. An agitated Lincoln stormed in, interrupted the meeting and announced, "I'm going to call the whole thing off."[8] He did, too.

On April 7, 1955, the board formally rescinded its acceptance of the reorganization plan and virtually all management changes reverted to the way it was before December — with one notable exception: Doss.

"To make a long story short," he said some years later, "the board reconsidered, which reminded me that the board can taketh away whatever it giveth. They reduced my position from executive vice president to first vice president with a big salary reduction.* I was placed in left field with no particular responsibility or accountability — just to drift. Well, I drifted and drifted."

For the next nine years Doss was an executive without portfolio, "driving an empty desk," as one board member put it. Lincoln told his executives Doss would "concentrate on certain difficult problems that would be assigned from time to time," but there were few assignments of significance. Lincoln had little contact with his first vice president, preferring that Doss be dispatched to meetings outside the office as a "floater." The chief executive even went so far as to tell the executive staff in January of 1956 not to involve Doss in operational details or decisions "and quit sending him memos."[9]

"I had to do that to Bowman," Lincoln said many years later. "I was looking to him for leadership and all I ever got was, 'Well, Mr. Lincoln, if you will just tell me what you want me to do, I'll do it.'"[10] Lincoln hated that.

Several times Doss considered leaving Nationwide, "but I believed so thoroughly in the company. Now, I knew I hadn't been treated right and that hurt ... (but) it didn't seem like it was right to leave. ... I figured that if they wanted to, they could fire me, but I'll be damned if I was going to leave."

At the time of "Black Friday," all the regions reported to Dean W. Jeffers, director of operations under Howard Hutchinson. The regional managers were "worked up" over the Doss situation, Jeffers recalled, so he invited Lincoln to

---

* At the time of his promotion to executive vice president in 1951, Doss received a salary increase to $35,000 annually. His salary doubled to $70,000 for the first three months of 1955 before the reorganization plan was abandoned; then he fell back to $50,000 annually.

address the managers at a meeting in Pittsburgh to calm their concerns.

As he often did, Lincoln rambled in his talk, never mentioning Doss' name. Consequently, "the regional managers shut him out, just like that," said Jeffers. Sensing a problem, Lincoln stopped and turned to Jeffers:

"Jeff, what's wrong with these people?"

"Mr. Lincoln, they want to know what happened to Bowman Doss."

Lincoln just glared. Jeffers called an immediate coffee break and tried to explain to his boss that putting Doss on the shelf hadn't been well accepted in the regions. The managers expected, and deserved, an explanation, Jeffers said.

"Young man," a furious Lincoln snapped, "don't you ever tell the president what to do!"[11]

Jeffers knew he came close to being fired that day, but he continued to rise through the management ranks. In 1956 Lincoln popped into Jeffers' office. After several minutes of rubbing his bald head and making small talk, he got to his point.

"Jeff, I want you to take over the sales department," he said. The job carried the title of vice president.

"Sure," Jeffers replied. "I haven't been in sales in quite a while."

"I know. Now, Dean, there's a question as to whether or not sales should be a part of decentralization or whether sales should set out separate and apart from everything else and report directly to the president. ... I want you to tell me where you think sales should be."

Although some disagreed with his decision, Jeffers said sales should report through the line operation. He would continue to report to Hutchinson, even though the two men "knocked sparks off each other," Jeffers acknowledged. He also knew he was stepping into a position during a time of "great uproar."

The mid-1950s were not only a period of corporate divisiveness, the casualty company as well as the automobile insurance industry in general had fallen into one of its periodic down cycles. In the five years ending 1953, auto premium income for Farm Bureau Mutual was up 172 percent,* well beyond the 60 percent industry gain. The company's costs associated with the increasing number of policies[†] and claims and an expanding administration due in part to the rapid growth and decentralization of the companies adversely affected the surplus.

To maintain a conservative 2-to-1 premium-to-surplus ratio, every $2 in premiums requires $1 in surplus. If an insurance company's volume of business is rapidly expanding, it often is difficult to expand the surplus at the same pace and ratios get out of hand. In 1953 Farm Bureau Mutual's premium-to-surplus ratio was an overheated 3.9 to 1.

Lincoln heard through the office grapevine that if "this blankety-blank president of ours hadn't kicked us into so many of these subsidiaries, everything would be all right ... "[12] A senior salesman approached him with a similar line of complaint:

"Well, now look, Mr. Lincoln. What do you want us to do? Do you want us to put these companies back on their feet, or work on your philosophy? What do you want us to do?"[13]

What the chief executive wanted was to help people help themselves through a wide variety of enterprises which need not have anything to do with insurance. He maintained that profits from the subsidiaries saw the insurance companies through the difficult mid-1950s. With each new subsidiary came an expanded potential customer base, he believed.

Speaking at a management meeting some 20 years later,

---

* In 1949 premium income for Farm Bureau Mutual was $42,125,000; in 1953 it was $114,429,000.

[†] In 1949 the expense per policy was $15; in 1956 it was approximately $20.

General Chairman George H. Dunlap praised Lincoln for his "vision and inspiration" in establishing subsidiaries and affiliates for the benefit of the policyholders. "It required not only foresight but a great deal of courage as well" to move into such diverse fields, he said. "The early years were not easy ones for these operations. Indeed, their very survival, in many instances, was a result of the assistance and the wholehearted cooperation of the Nationwide Companies."[14]

In the early 1950s, however, the wisdom of Lincoln's approach was questioned as the insurance business drifted lower. The Farm Bureau Life Insurance Company, for example, plodded along with small sales volume, "primarily insuring people under age 40," noted the internal managerial newsletter, *Issues.* "Lincoln was aware that life insurance was, in effect, for people who died too young or too old, and that prompted him and others to ponder the needs of the 'in betweens.'"[15]

The Korean War had ignited inflation "to a then shocking 7 to 9 percent at a time when people were used to 1- and 2- percent increases," the newsletter continued. "Nationwide Life products - primarily annuities - were paying less-than-inspiring returns of about 3 percent. The in-betweens were dangling in the wind."

Rennie, then vice president of research and reporting to Culbreth, believed as Lincoln did: A fixed-return financial instrument was not all that it was cracked up to be in inflationary times. The two men agreed that even the "in-betweens" deserved a hedge against retirement monies being eaten away by inflation. Lincoln cited his own experience of having bought a life insurance policy as a young man only to discover that "thanks to inflation, (it) is just about covering my electricity bill."[16]

Rennie, who taught at Johns Hopkins University, recalled the College Retirement Equities Fund, established by the Teachers' Insurance Association. It was an equity annuity, but as Rennie told Lincoln, it probably couldn't be sold by the Farm Bureau Insurance Companies' exclusive agency force because the agents were not licensed to sell securities.

He went to Culbreth. "Let's train our agents in selling mutual funds." Neither Culbreth nor Lincoln understood mutual funds, Rennie said, but he got a green light. Unfortunately, he kept seeing a red light when he tried to get the company attorneys interested in drafting the necessary documents. He went back to Culbreth and Lincoln.

"Why don't we buy the management company of an existing mutual fund? Then we'll have one with a record."

"By golly, let's do it," the chief executive told Culbreth, who didn't believe in the proposal but knew how strongly Rennie felt about its inherent merit.

Rennie canvassed mutual funds with assets less than $50 million and kept asking: "Do you want to sell? Do you want to sell out?" Finally, he got a "yes" from Ralph L. Bouma in Detroit and changed forever the Columbus-based organization and the insurance industry itself.

His discovery was Mutual Income Foundation, Inc. (MIFI), the investment manager and underwriter for a small, common stock mutual fund founded by Bouma May 5, 1933. In 1951 its assets totaled about $2.5 million. Approved Finance, created in 1951 as a wholly-owned subsidiary of Farm Bureau Mutual, bought MIFI for a mere $25,000 and gave it a $10,000 capital infusion.

MIFI marketed its own fund, Mutual Investment Fund, until 1957 when Heritage Securities, Inc., was established as a Nationwide associate company and became the distributor of the fund. Heritage subsequently was renamed Nationwide Financial Services, Inc.

Today Nationwide Financial Services is the highly successful distributor of equity-based products, including the shares of six Nationwide mutual funds. In 1993 Nationwide Financial

Services had nearly $3.5 billion in assets under management. For its first three years under Approved Finance, however, MIFI lay virtually dormant. The marketing people at the Farm Bureau Insurance Companies wanted no part of it, recalled Rennie. What's more, he was being called the "Benedict Arnold" of the insurance industry. He remembered the belligerent tone of many callers:

"Didn't I recognize that fixed income, the guaranteed dollars, was the foundation of the life insurance business, and had been for a century? And here I was talking about variable dollars. I would destroy the life insurance" business, the callers said.

Jeffers found himself wrapped up in the fray as well. At the time he was New England zone manager, which included Connecticut. Despite the indifference to the undertaking at Columbus headquarters, Jeffers agreed to experiment with selling mutual funds in Connecticut. "It wouldn't be anywhere today if he hadn't done that," said Rennie.

At a New York press conference June 30, 1954, Lincoln announced a new mutual fund, life insurance and retirement income "package." The plan "brings to persons of modest income the professional services of estate planning normally available only to the wealthy," Lincoln told the financial press.[17]

It was a milestone, if somewhat hesitant, launch, marking the first time mutual funds and insurance would be sold together. The first year also saw 828 Farm Bureau insurance agents trained and licensed to sell securities, and it started a firestorm in both the insurance and securities industries. Some companies, such as Massachusetts Mutual Life Insurance Company and Northwestern Mutual Life Insurance Company, issued orders banning their agents from selling both funds and insurance, although more than a few continued to do so surreptitiously.

By 1959 the opponents were in full cry, but it certainly wasn't because Nationwide's Heritage Securities, Inc., was doing so well. Its assets totaled but $4.6 million. Nevertheless, Nationwide and its executives were under attack.

Edward "Ted" Stowell, Ohio's superintendent of insurance, opposed "dual licensing" of agents as well and even went so far as to issue a rule banning such activity. However, the plan drew so much national attention that Stowell scheduled public hearings in Columbus June 23-25, 1959. Representatives of the securities and insurance industries came from throughout the country to participate and to listen. They overflowed the first hearing room, then a second. Finally the hearing moved to a third room large enough to accommodate the masses.

Lincoln parked himself on a benchseat next to his administrative assistant, J. Richard "Dick" Bull. Sliding onto the bench immediately behind them was Alex Hutchison, vice president of sales for Metropolitan Life, which vigorously opposed "dual licensing." Hutchison hoped to listen in on Lincoln's conversation but heard nothing for several hours. Finally, Lincoln leaned over to Bull; Hutchison leaned forward to eavesdrop. He heard Lincoln say:

"Dick, you better put another nickel in the meter. We are going to be here awhile."[18]

They were, too. For three days the debate raged. In his testimony, Lincoln asked the question, "Who ... is better qualified to sell mutual fund shares than the trained life underwriter who is acquainted with the prospect's family status, his financial circumstances, his obligations, his hopes and desires?" He said it was "in the public interest that the prospect be offered a choice of products and that the offer be made by someone who is qualified to help him make that choice ... "

Noting that Nationwide was the first to sanction and encourage the sale of mutual funds, Lincoln concluded by saying, "from the standpoint of our policyholders, it may be the wisest thing we ever did."[19]

Rennie, who became known within the company as the

"Father of Mutual Funds," discussed the vagaries of the dollar, the economy and inflation, which demanded a balanced approach. "I want to state categorically that from an economic point of view, the sale of mutual funds is a greater offset to inflation than is the sale of life insurance," he said.[20]

Milton Ellis, a Metropolitan Life vice president, led the industry's opposition. According to a report in *The New York Times,* he testified "the Met" believed that "the interests of the public will best be served if the sale of life insurance and the sale of securities are kept separate and distinct. ... It seems to us that any life insurance company which authorizes its agents to sell securities is in a very real sense advertising that it no longer has confidence in its own products of guaranteed dollar contracts."[21]

Six weeks after the hearing, Stowell determined that he did not have the authority to enforce his own ruling banning dual licensing. Nationwide had won a resounding victory.

Even after the ruling, however, the animosity toward Nationwide continued in some quarters of the industry. For instance, Jeffers felt the heat while appearing on a panel at the annual meeting of the National Association of Life Underwriters in Denver in 1961. Also on the panel were the sales vice presidents of several companies, including Northwestern Mutual, Prudential Life, National Life and Accident and the moderator, Burkett W. Huey, managing director of the Life Insurance Agency Management Association.* Jeffers realized he was "the mustang among purebreds."

As Huey began his introduction of Jeffers, the audience became noisy and unruly and several hundred walked out of the packed auditorium. Jeffers rose to speak, but fellow panel member Robert Templin, of Northwestern Mutual, pulled him back. "Let Huey calm them down first," Templin advised. "I'll

---

* Since renamed the Life Insurance Marketing and Research Association.

quiet them down," Jeffers said, and proceeded to give his presentation.

"When we had the question and answer period ... the questions were to come up on written cards," the ex-Marine recalled. "The first one was just yelled up, some question that had to do with mutual funds. I turned around to (Huey) and told him, 'That question is so absurd that I wouldn't dignify the questioner with an answer.' Well, you could have heard a pin drop in the whole doggone place."

The noise made by the many, many pins Lincoln and his associates dropped throughout the decade of the 1950s rattled his own companies and several industries. Mutual funds represented just one step in the march to fulfill Lincoln's cooperative dream, to fashion one's own destiny. These were the acquisition years and his staff pursued a wide variety of undertakings, including other insurance companies. He believed it "cheaper to expand by acquiring more companies rather than assuming the cost of extending our own companies, involving as it would the establishment and training of a new sales force."[22]

National Casualty Company of Detroit was among his first insurance company targets. At the time the Farm Bureau Insurance Companies eyed several other insurance businesses, such as Midland Mutual Life Insurance Company of Columbus, but Lincoln insisted the acquisition be a casualty company. What is more important, 47-year-old National Casualty gave him that giant step west he yearned for so much: It had licenses to do business in all 48 states, Hawaii and the District of Columbia, and to write in those states all lines of insurance except life.*

---

*Within the Farm Bureau there was strong support for establishing National Casualty as headquarters for western expansion. In doing so, the advocates reasoned, there no longer would be a need to change the name of the Farm Bureau Insurance Companies (see Chapter 6). The decision to continue Columbus as headquarters for all operations necessitated the name change.

The Farm Bureau Mutual's investment advisers believed at the outset in 1950 that the Curtis family in Detroit owned the majority of stock in National Casualty. They had the biggest block, believed to be about 20 percent, but the remainder was scattered. Farm Bureau Mutual hired Paul F. Jones, a former Illinois insurance commissioner, to round up not less than 55 percent of National Casualty and gain control without loss of agents or business in force. This accomplished, Lincoln successfully wrested control from the Curtis interests and installed Jones as president.*

When Jones died in November 1953, Lincoln was eager to take his place as president, but the board didn't nominate him at first. It tried to elect fellow board member Dunlap instead, and a frustrated Lincoln wanted to know from his Nationwide chairman why the board preferred Dunlap and not Lincoln. Dunlap found himself in a tight spot. He had to think fast to assuage the perplexed Lincoln.

"Now, Mr. Lincoln, you're the head of a large mutual company. You're a national figure. You're an international figure. If the directors elected you president, all the papers would pick it up that a mutual company president is elected president of a stock company. If they elected me, I'm so unknown the newspapers would pay no attention to it."

"Well, golly. It's nice we can laugh about it," said Lincoln, feeling a mite better.

Dunlap drove home his tale. "We could have elected you president, but it would have been a divided vote, and I thought that would not be good. Now, if you just let the matter alone and come to the next meeting, you'll be elected president unanimously." After Dunlap worked his persuasive magic with the board, it elected Lincoln, as Dunlap promised.

---

* Less than a year later Lincoln reported to the board of the Farm Bureau Insurance Companies that it had a chance to sell National Casualty "and make a million dollars." No buyer was mentioned.

National Casualty was "a rather humorous disappointment," to John E. Fisher's way of thinking because Nationwide used the Detroit-based insurance company as a vehicle to pioneer merit rating of automobile insurance. From the earliest days of the Farm Bureau Mutual Automobile Insurance Company, the car model, the age and residence of the customer, etc., determined the premium. At the urging of customers, however, the "merit" variable, granting a reduced premium to customers with good driving records, came to market through National Casualty.

"Lo and behold, our agents viewed the availability of merit rating through National Casualty as access to a nonstandard insurance company," Fisher recalled. "They tended to put their good drivers in the Nationwide insurance portfolio and the bad risks in the National Casualty company, which became a high-risk business unintentionally."

Nationwide General Insurance Company, created in 1957, took on the responsibility for merit rating automobile insurance until other Nationwide companies could be properly converted; then Nationwide General dropped merit rating and became a payroll deduction and direct response auto insurance company — and a leader in its field.

National Casualty continued as a health and property/casualty insurance provider, thanks to its introduction, first in Ohio and then primarily in the southeast, of NA$P – No Accident Savings Program. "It was the principal vehicle on which National Casualty's property and casualty division justified its existence" in the early 1960s, said Eugene F. Hull, retired vice president, Nationwide Property & Casualty Insurance Company. According to the *National Underwriter,* an industry periodical, "a risk has to be almost unbelievably bad" to be denied insurance under NA$P.[23]

However, during 1963 and 1964 National Casualty posted underwriting losses of $1 million and $1.4 million, respectively.

As a result, it stopped writing automobile and fire insurance.

Retired board chairman of Nationwide Mutual, Frank B. Sollars, blamed National Casualty's unprofitable years on its entry into the sophisticated, complex, international reinsurance business. "Small companies like National Casualty don't get messing around in the reinsurance business," he said. "Let's face it: You have to match brains with the sharpest people in the world. ... How could a little bitty company hire people to do that.?"

Fisher remembers well National Casualty's ill-conceived entry into the international reinsurance market, and it "has been haunting us ever since." In the early 1960s the company engaged "a fast-talking Englishman," Ronnie Driver, described by Fisher as "sort of an English aristocrat and a great raconteur."

Driver and his partner, Henry Weavers, lived the good life. On his visits to Detroit and National Casualty, for example, Driver always secured the best suite at a downtown hotel and regaled company officials during his stay. While in London, Driver motored about in a chauffeured Rolls Royce and booked the Elizabeth Taylor/Richard Burton suite at one of the British capital's top hotels.

By the same token, Nationwide and National Casualty officers, such as Hutchinson and Peter G. Korn, who succeeded Lincoln as president of the Detroit insurer, would trip back and forth to London, ostensibly to check on the reinsurance business — only they really didn't grasp what it was they were to check. It later became obvious they had virtually no control over the high-risk kind of business Driver and Weavers were doing.

National Casualty "trusted him far too long," said Robert M. Culp. As a result the company carried on its back for many years large, long-term liability risks — medical malpractice, asbestos and the like — that went far beyond its expertise.

"Of course, they lost millions and millions of dollars over

that deal," Sollars said. "You know, to my disappointment ... they're still bleeding from that."

At the end of 1993, some 30 years after Driver, Fisher estimated Nationwide Reinsurance still held more than $65 million in reserves to cover National Casualty's liabilities. "We are just going to have to outlive it," he said.

The book on National Casualty all but came to a close in 1994 — except to continue working through its losses —when its individual health insurance products were signed away in a modified co-insurance and reinsurance treaty with Washington National Insurance Company of Lincolnshire, IL. National Casualty's St. Louis operational headquarters was shuttered, leaving but a shell through which Nationwide's Scottsdale Insurance Company and Nationwide Group Life and Health could write other lines of insurance.

8

OVER-THE-COUNTER
AND THROUGH THE WOODS

N obody ever would say Murray D. Lincoln lacked extraordinary vision. However, his problem in the 1950s was the lack of capital to invest in the expansion of the insurance companies as well as in the many outside ventures he believed could "help people help themselves."

As the chief executive of a mutual institution owned by the policyholders, the only capital he could put to work was the surplus funds, or profits, and even then only under regulatory scrutiny. At $41.6 million in 1954, the surplus was incapable of supporting the multi-faceted and rapid national and international expansion on the scale Lincoln sought for the insurance enterprise.

"We can never accomplish what I vision is worth trying by the use of insurance funds alone. They are too restricted," he told the Farm Bureau Insurance Companies board at a milestone directors' meeting in the summer of 1954.[1] He then turned over the podium to General Counsel P. Lee Thornbury, who outlined the plan crafted for a publicly held company to raise the capital for investment.

The board had heard Lincoln speak of his vision before. For instance, six years earlier he spoke to them about the importance of investments, forcefully pointing out that insurance companies were becoming major players in underwriting American business. "Big companies are going direct to life insurance companies who take over a whole (stock) issue," often to the detriment of the individual who lands one step further away from control of his or her investment, he said. "The significance of all this is that the average individual is … not coming into the stock market, largely because of fear; therefore, he has turned to the insurance company to do his investing."

Lincoln also made a strong case for Farm Bureau Insurance Companies investments in "sound cooperative enterprises" as well as gaining control of an investment trust company that could then "make the investments in all these different enterprises. That would be particularly important if we could get a company already on the Big Board (New York Stock Exchange), because the examiners raised a question on our cooperative investments not being quoted on the Big Board."[2]

Although Lincoln always spoke of the insurance companies as cooperatives in the broadest sense, the industry regulators did not. In the main they refused to allow the insurance companies to invest in cooperatives.

In the post-war era, government regulators pecked at those who strayed beyond such traditional investment bounds. In 1952, for example, the New York Insurance Department insisted that Farm Bureau Mutual could not own a majority of the outstanding common stock of a finance company, which it did when it created Approved Finance, Inc., a year earlier. Under regulatory pressure, the insurance company reduced its interest in Approved Finance to 49 percent through an offering of additional shares to the public.

Ohio followed in 1955 with further restrictions. An amendment to the state's insurance laws prohibited casualty or fire companies from acquiring more than 25 percent of the outstanding securities of any noninsurance company. Consequently, the mutual casualty company sold one-half of its 49 percent interest in Approved Finance to Farm Bureau Mutual Fire Insurance Company.

Confronted as he was in 1954 with the certain enactment of this law, Lincoln looked for the key to unlock these shackles as well as to attract substantial outside capital for investment in large operations, "large enough to be competitive."[3]

The answer lay in the activation of an eight-year-old corporate shell, Service Insurance Agency, Inc. On September 29, 1955, it became Nationwide Corporation, a non-insurance, downstream holding company owned by Nationwide Mutual and Nationwide Mutual Fire. The soon to be publicly held corporation would engage in the business of holding, seeking and acquiring controlling or substantial interests in other companies, primarily those in the insurance field.

It also was the first new company created bearing the name, Nationwide.

"As I see it," Lincoln told the employees, "Nationwide Corporation is one of the most effective means of extending our insurance organization westward — in other words, of making it nationwide in fact as well as in name."[4]

Two of Lincoln's close, outside financial advisers, Raymond Smith of A.M. Best & Company and J. C. Bradford, whose Nashville, TN, securities firm still bears his name today, pushed for the public corporation, but it did not go down easily with the board. Some members, including Chairman George H. Dunlap, feared a diminution of the insurance companies, a loss of control and unbridled growth through acquisitions, which he opposed.

"If I understand it, there will be no limit to your ability to expand the services, except our ability to sell stock to pay for companies?" the chairman asked the president.

"That's right," replied a confident Lincoln. With the ability to raise capital through a public company, the sky was the limit for him. Later, he went on to explain that "we are not accumulating this piece of machinery and power to make money for a few stockholders but to put the power back into the hands of the people ... "[5]

On March 30, 1956, Nationwide Corporation filed a registration statement with the Securities and Exchange Commission covering the public offering of 800,000 Class "A" common shares. There also were 2,015,500 Class "B" shares, converted from shares held by the two mutual companies.* The auto company retained 91.27 percent of these "B" shares, which were not offered to the public, and the fire company owned the remaining 8.73 percent. Each class elected six directors to the board, the "outside" directors representing the "A" shareholders and "inside" directors drawn from Nationwide's family representing the "B" shareholders. Dunlap and Lincoln became the first chairman and president, respectively.

To make the stock more attractive to wary investors, Nationwide Corporation bought Nationwide Life, which in 1956 passed $1 billion in insurance in force. It thus became the sweetener in the package. Also in the initial mix was National Casualty Company of Detroit, in which the corporation increased Nationwide's holdings from the original 55 percent to 92.9 percent.

On April 27, 1956, trading in Nationwide Corporation Class "A" stock opened at $19. Lehman Brothers, lead underwriters of the issue with J.C. Bradford & Company, presented Nationwide with a check for $13.9 million, the proceeds from

---

* George H. Dunlap opposed the two classes of stock, fearing a deadlock with no opportunity for progress. "I was on vacation (when) they called a special meeting, and it went through as recommended. I tried my best to make it work," he said in a 1982 interview.

the offering. Allowing for the two-for-one stock split in 1962, the issue traded over-the-counter at bid prices between $5 in September 1974 and $41.50 in March 1983.

The corporation quickly put its new-found capital to work. In 1956 and early 1957 it acquired a one-third interest in Chicago-based North American Accident Insurance Company, a 70-year-old accident and health insurer; a 50.71 percent interest in Michigan Life Insurance Company, at 29 the oldest old-line legal reserve company in Michigan, and a 51.13 percent stock interest in Northwestern National Life Insurance Company of Minnesota,* a mutual and stock company based in Minneapolis.

On the basis of a November 1956 analysis of Northwestern National by Nationwide's chief actuary, Charles W. Leftwich, Lincoln saw in the Minnesota-based company "one of the cleanest specialized insurance companies that there is in the northwest." Its size impressed Lincoln: $300 million in assets, some 500,000 policyholders and $1.6 billion of insurance in force. However, the acquisition did not go smoothly, largely because, as Lincoln explained it to the board, it involved "one very tricky and very bothersome thing, and that is that the policyholders have a vote … "[6]

The policyholders had a vote because the mutual company was linked by charter to the stock company. Acquiring Northwestern National stock would not necessarily mean gaining control unless the company's participating policyholders also agreed to it, and they didn't. Led by President John S. Pillsbury Jr., a third generation descendant of the flour company family, Northwestern National thwarted Lincoln's best efforts to gain total control.

John C. Wagner, an attorney who retired in 1982 as senior

---

* Northwestern National Life Insurance Company of Minnesota was organized in 1885 as the Northwestern Aid Association. It adopted its present name in 1901.

vice president and general counsel, recalled a conversation with Lincoln concerning Northwestern National. "Mr. Lincoln, if you are ever going to have a showdown with this company, you are going to have a real problem because policyholders are hard to solicit." In the opinion of counsel, the policyholders controlled the company.

Lincoln chose to ignore the warning. "Murray always had the idea that reasonable minds and calm discussions would solve any problem," said Wagner. "If he just had a chance to sit down with the tough guy (in this instance, Pillsbury) and tell his story, he would win out. Well, it didn't happen."

There is no question Northwestern National became Lincoln's toughest battle, and it disturbed him. "Boy, this is the first time I wake up in the night in a cold sweat," he admitted. "And, God, if we make a mistake here, I'll start for South America! ... (but) you don't pick up a $300 million firm and not sweat it."[7]

It was not that Lincoln didn't try to win over Pillsbury. Before acquiring any Northwestern National stock, Lincoln set up a meeting in Minneapolis with Pillsbury "on the theory that we'd like to work with management." A luncheon was scheduled November 19, 1956, at the Minneapolis Club, but Pillsbury didn't show. He called Lincoln at his hotel later that day, at which time Lincoln again pressed for a meeting, informing Pillsbury of Nationwide's interest in an investment in Northwestern National. "He wouldn't see me," said Lincoln.

Four days later Nationwide appointed the Bradford securities firm as agents to acquire Northwestern National stock. The executive committee of Nationwide Corporation, at its November 27 meeting, authorized the purchase of shares at up to $110 each.

Upon learning three weeks later that Nationwide was buying blocks of his company's stock, a "displeased" Pillsbury tracked Lincoln down at the Biltmore Hotel in New York. He believed

Lincoln had told him earlier on the telephone that Nationwide would not buy any shares until it had the cooperation of Northwestern National's management. That's what Lincoln preferred, but after the rebuff, he pursued the purchase plan.

The first meeting with Pillsbury came January 7, 1957, just a few hours after Lincoln knew Nationwide had in hand better than 40 percent of Northwestern National's shares, with more on the way. He led a delegation to the target company's Minneapolis office to register in Nationwide's name the 80,085 shares acquired and to pay a courtesy call on Pillsbury. "I wished him a happy New Year and told him that we probably would have some reason to talk together in the future," Nationwide's president said.

"I understand you're registering quite a bit of stock up here today," Pillsbury said perfunctorily.

"Yep."

"Well, have you bought — you don't need to answer — but have you bought the Texas stock?" asked Pillsbury, referring to Dallas Union Securities Company that also had acquired a large, and key, block of Northwestern National's stock. At that point Lincoln already knew the Texas stock was his, too.

"Well, we have the assumption we are going to get it."

On that note and still with his hat and coat in hand, Lincoln prepared to leave, but Pillsbury, warming up considerably, twice pressed the Nationwide delegation to stay longer. "Finally, I started to go out a third time," Lincoln recalled, "and he said, 'Now, wait a minute. I'd like to have you meet our top men.'" In trooped the executive vice president, general counsel, controller and one or two other senior officers.

"I thought that was the first evidence that maybe he was getting ready to be friendly," said Lincoln. Following the hour-long meeting he would say of Pillsbury: "By golly, if he's an insurance man, I'm a minister."[8]

In a letter dated January 25, 1957, three days before

Northwestern National's annual meeting, Lincoln notified Cyril C. Sheehan, Minnesota's insurance commissioner, that "a clear majority" of the Minneapolis company's stock (or proxies) was in Nationwide's hands.* Furthermore, he assured the commissioner Nationwide had no intention of moving the headquarters of Northwestern National and that the jobs of its agents and employees were secure.

However, because a quorum of shareholder votes was not represented at the annual meeting, Nationwide raised a point of order, suggesting that under its Articles of Incorporation, Northwestern National should adjourn the meeting to a later date. Pillsbury overruled the point, stating that the quorum provision was invalid. Furthermore, he said, sufficient member votes, which included the mutual policyholders, were represented at the meeting.† After filling five vacancies on the board, the meeting adjourned.

Nationwide immediately sought relief in the federal and state courts, and for more than a year the lawyers went at it. An out-of-court settlement announced April 17, 1958, avoided a proxy battle and all but closed the book on Nationwide's only unfriendly takeover attempt. Three Nationwiders acquired seats on the Northwestern National board: Lincoln, John W. Galbreath, a developer from Columbus who was a director of Nationwide Corporation, and "Judge" Paul D. Grady of Kenly, NC, who was chairman of Nationwide Mutual Fire Insurance Company. Lincoln also was elected to the executive committee.

A disappointed Lincoln wrote the final chapter in the 1961

---

* A block of 400 shares from Hylmar E. Karbach of New Braunfels, TX, and tendered to Nationwide January 22, 1957, at $106.99 per share, put Nationwide in a majority ownership position. The acquisition of stock continued in 1957 with Nationwide finally securing 113,728 shares, or 51.13 percent.
† Each participating policyholder of Northwestern National had voting rights on the basis of one vote for each $1,000 of participating insurance, up to a maximum of 100 votes.

annual report of Nationwide Corporation. "Northwestern National … sound and substantial, seemed to us to offer a great opportunity for strengthening what I like to call the 'machinery' through which we operate. So, in 1957 we purchased 51 percent of the outstanding common shares, paying around $106 per share.* Many people told us this was too much to pay for a stock that had been selling at $70-$80, but it's my opinion that what you pay for a property isn't as important as what you intend to do with it."9

J.C. Bradford & Company, through its affiliated Aragon Corporation, bought Nationwide's Northwestern National shares early in 1962 for $17.4 million. Nationwide realized an after-tax profit of $3.95 million and Bradford described its purchase as "an unusual deal with a tremendous profit potential." A year later Northwestern National stock split 8 to 1.

The battle for Northwestern National and Lincoln's strategic agenda for Nationwide's expansion caught the attention of the national and industry press. The *National Underwriter*, for instance, described Lincoln as having "turned gunslinger with an acquisitive bent."10 *The Wall Street Journal*, in a lengthy and generally positive 1957 article, noted:

"While running this intricate corporate machine and its hard-driving expansion program, Mr. Lincoln continues to preach his gospel of producer-consumer cooperation. … Not long ago, while he was in the midst of rounding up Michigan Life and Northwestern National Life stock, he said in a signed article in Nationwide's house organ: 'I worry about the growing concentration of business in this country. Mergers and consolidations are centering control in the hands of fewer and fewer people.'11

"Meanwhile, he flies about the country in a company-owned

---

* The cost of the stock was $106.61, or $12.1 million.

DC-3, hunting out new companies to be added to the Nationwide chain, planning stock issues, conferring with investment bankers. ... In all this change of pace Mr. Lincoln sees no inconsistency — regardless both of cynics who suspect him of empire-building ambitions and of conservatives who charge he's undermining the American Way of Life with his co-op propaganda."[12]

Earlier Jack M. Kaplan, another of Lincoln's close advisers, also saw an inconsistency and forcefully said so. Kaplan had been president of The Welch Grape Juice Company, Inc., during the years leading up to its sale in 1956 to the National Grape Co-Operative Association, Inc. Lincoln had a hand in getting that co-op deal done.

In a scathing "Dear Murray" letter, Kaplan took issue with Nationwide's multiple acquisitions, including "the dream" Lincoln had of capturing control of Sun Life Assurance Company of Canada.* (He didn't.) He told Lincoln he and his associates knew very little about valuating insurance companies, market conditions, financing and how to negotiate acquisitions.

"Both you and your team, Murray, are naive and inexperienced in this area," Kaplan wrote. "It is frightening to think of your group negotiating transactions involving millions, aided only by brokers interested in big commissions at your expense." (Kaplan pointedly put Lincoln adviser Roger M. Kyes in the latter group.)

In Kaplan's opinion, Lincoln no longer could operate as he did "20 years ago, when you were small. ... The man who makes the decisions doesn't fritter his time and energy in collecting the facts. ... What you are doing in flying around

---

* According to his investment officer, Dr. Robert A. Rennie, Lincoln's interest in acquiring controlling interest in Sun Life spurred that institution's conversion to a mutual company. Nationwide Insurance Companies realized a net gain of almost $1 million on the Sun Life investment after backing away from a takeover and selling its stock.

the country in your own plane, conducting 'preliminary investigations,' is fundamentally unsound."

Kaplan wrote that he had "the growing feeling that, like all other mortals, you are in danger of being converted from saint to sinner. ... What are you really after in trying to grow so big so quickly? Is it greater efficiency? Or does Murray Lincoln, just like the rest of us, merely lust for power and glory? Who will you be building this empire for? Who is going to handle it after you are gone? Can you name a man in your present organization big enough to do it and big enough to carry on your dream of saving the world?"[13]

These were questions that many at Nationwide asked, especially after Lincoln backed away from the reorganization plan that ostensibly put Doss in line for the presidency. Those not in the line of succession wanted to know who was. After all, at the time of Kaplan's biting missive, Lincoln was within two months of his 64th birthday.

Another consultant in whom Lincoln put a great deal of faith was Ernest Dichter, founder of the Institute for Motivational Research in New York. In a report to Lincoln and the board in the mid-1950s, Dichter also addressed the all-consuming succession issue.

"In the early days, sales and human relations in your companies had a oneness," he wrote in his report. "Later a split developed between sales and human relations (the reference being to Howard Hutchinson and Harry W. Culbreth, respectively), and fundamentals were forgotten ... and the philosophy became a sideline.

"Now, something's got to happen to restore this sense of unity, of the oneness of your sales and human relations and your philosophy," Dichter continued. "To Hutchinson, Culbreth is an egghead, and to Culbreth, Hutchinson is just a salesman."

"I get such a kick out of that," Lincoln told the board while reading to them the consultant's evaluation.[14] Obviously he cared little that the infighting between the two men who hoped to succeed him was splitting the company into camps.

It was clear, however, that he knew what was going on. Some six months later, in a talk to the executive committee, Lincoln recalled that a year earlier his senior executives were engaged in "a death struggle." He said he told them that "if they didn't get straightened out by the time of the next annual meeting that he would ask for their resignations. They now have come to an understanding, so that's no longer a problem."[15] Everyone sitting around the table knew that was not true.

Whatever infighting or jockeying for position went on, it made very little difference to Lincoln. His concentration in the 1950s went far beyond the walls of headquarters in Columbus. During the decade it was as if everyone at Nationwide worked within the eye of a tornado. All around them Lincoln was stirring things up, what with decentralization, the introduction of mutual funds, the creation of a public company in Nationwide Corporation and the subsequent acquisition binge.

Lincoln's rapidly shifting agenda reflected the world around him. Man climbed the highest peak for the first time, only to be topped by the first satellites. Polio vaccine and the H-bomb became a reality; the first could save man and the other could destroy him. Fame and a $64,000 fortune came and went for TV quiz show contestants who were given the answers in advance. The prince of Monaco fell head over heels for a Hollywood princess. A future president saved his political career by mentioning his dog, Checkers. In Alabama a young black preacher with a dream led a bus boycott. "Yankee Go Home!" was the cry in Fidel Castro's Cuba and American Leaguers hurled similar epithets at Casey Stengel's winning teams. Broadway was more blunt: *Damn Yankees,* it said. A television show spurred sales of Davy Crockett raccoon hats, which finally brought some sanity to a nation spinning in vertebrae-wrenching hula hoops.

While attorneys were spinning webs in court over who should control Northwestern National, Nationwide acquired majority interest in Michigan Life Insurance Company; one-third ownership of North American Accident Company, Chicago; 89 percent of Northern Life Insurance Company, Seattle; the shell of an Arizona company in Pacific Life Insurance Company for future western development, and the bank Lincoln always wanted. A bank, he said, "is the only thing that can manufacture money legally."[16]

Lincoln was an enigma when it came to monetary matters. He rarely discussed his personal financial affairs, but in his ramblings to the board one day he bragged how he had invested $200 in February and made a $20,000 profit by November. In the next breath he mentioned that he had sold three colts off his farm for $19,000, adding:

"George (Dunlap) once said I'm officially one for not making money, but individually he thinks I am."

"That's not what I said," Dunlap snapped.

"What did you say?"

"I said that in connection with certain charges from certain industrial people that Mr. Lincoln was a communist, that he was no communist because he liked to make money too well himself."[17]

He didn't mind making it for the good of mankind, "but Mr. Lincoln did not like for anybody to talk about making a profit," recalled one of his successors, Dean W. Jeffers. "It was almost as if it was a bad word" because the objectives of the mutual companies, his cooperative, were to provide a service to the policyholders or members. "If all we're going to do is build bigger insurance companies, make more money, then count me out," Lincoln said.

Jeffers mentioned the unmentionable one day in giving a pep talk to a sales management group at the Neil House in the mid-1950s. The industry was in a down cycle and so was Nationwide. "If we are going to grow, you have to keep proper financial ratios between your premiums and your surplus," he told the assembled. The next day, Lincoln called him into his office.

"I understand you had a meeting with some of our management people at the Neil House yesterday," the president began, having been tipped off as to the discussion.

"Yes, sir, I did."

"And you talked about the need for this company to make a profit."

"No, sir," said a concerned Jeffers, who went on to explain what he had said. However, Lincoln felt that Jeffers had really discussed the principles of making a profit.

"You shouldn't have done that," Lincoln said, launching into a stern sermon on cooperative values. When finished, he dismissed from his office a visibly shaken young executive.[18]

Jeffers walked down the hall and straight into the office of his friend, Ashley T. "Mack" McCarter, who was getting ready to fly to Chicago.

"I'm going with you," Jeffers announced.

"Hell, I don't want you to go with me to Chicago," countered McCarter.

"I'm going. I've got to get out of here. I almost got fired a few minutes ago."[19] Jeffers accompanied McCarter to Chicago.

Some years later, in private conversation with Jeffers, Lincoln recalled the incident and admitted, "Jeff, I almost fired you that day."

Louis E. Dolan came to know how Lincoln *really* felt about making a profit, and therein begins another Nationwide Corporation tale.

Attorney Dolan was not yet 35 when he joined Nationwide's tax department in 1954. While working in the company's library in the evening, Dolan often was visited by Lincoln, who would wander in and sit down for a chat. On occasion, Dolan said, the president would ask for advice on personal matters. At the time Dolan also was handling Chairman Dunlap's personal taxes. Lincoln and Dolan became close, and when Dolan left in 1957 to join The Ohio Company, a regional investment banking firm in Columbus, he handled some of Nationwide's business, including work on the sale of Tectum Corporation.

Early one spring day in 1962, Lincoln telephoned. "Can you meet me for lunch at 10:30 at the Athletic Club (of Columbus)?" he asked Dolan. They agreed on 11:30 a.m.

Through the lunch hour and well past it Lincoln spoke of his dreams for Nationwide and the cooperative movement, "not the least of which was buying A&P (The Great Atlantic & Pacific Tea Company, Inc.) and making a co-op out of it," Dolan said. Finally, as the clock approached 4 p.m., Lincoln got to the point of the meeting.

"I'm here because I'm offering you to be my successor *across the board*," meaning, Dolan said, the insurance companies, Nationwide Corporation, the affiliates — everything.

"Mr. Lincoln, I'm honored beyond words," a breathless Dolan replied. "I'm simply flabbergasted at the thought (but) the reason I must decline is that I'm not cooperatively-minded. I'm profit motivated."

To Dolan's amazement, Lincoln leaned over and, even though the dining room was empty of others save one server, he whispered, "So am I, but it's too late for me to admit it. I realize what keeps the old gray mare going is profit."

Catching up to the rapid pace of the conversation, Dolan said, "There's one company that I would dearly love to succeed you in, Mr. Lincoln, and that's Nationwide Corporation. ... I would love that opportunity."

Lincoln banged his hand on the table and said, "By golly, you got it! When can you start?"[20] Dolan joined Nationwide Corporation in June 1962 as a vice president, was elected vice president and general manager in January 1964, succeeding retired Paul Boardman, and the following April was named executive vice president.

Nationwide's chief executive was enough of a pragmatist to know the insurance companies and the corporation had to make money to achieve his far-flung goals. Acquiring a bank was one of them. Lincoln suggested to the board that the investment department look into the stock of some bank holding companies, such as BancOhio Corporation, Northwestern Bank Corporation, and the First National Corporation, "because I think we ought to get some stock in some of these banking institutions around the country."[21]

Lincoln believed unnamed forces in the community were "scared to death" that Nationwide would acquire a bank. "They are afraid we will do something that will change the conventional, orthodox way of doing business," he told the executive committee.

"Jokingly I said to the president of the Ohio National Bank (later BancOhio National Bank and then National City Bank, Columbus) some time ago when he asked us if we still owned the little Grove City bank* — and by gosh, I just so regret that when our group across the road there (the Ohio Farm Bureau Federation) had it that they let it go ... but we got another one cooking anyway."

Continuing his story, Lincoln said he told the banker, "Well, we don't want to sell any banks; we want to buy Ohio National, and he thought that was a great joke, my having the temerity (to) suggest to him that we buy (the bank). So I went down to him the other day, and I said, 'Now look, mister. I think you thought I was joking the other day. ... I'm not joking. If this

---

* In the 1940s the Ohio Farm Bureau Federation acquired an interest in the First National Bank of Grove City, OH. Lincoln said the farm bureau then "ran into a hornet's nest" when a federal examiner questioned the propriety of such ownership. The stock was sold in 1954.

thing (Ohio National) is going to be put on the market, at least we'd like to know about it.'"[22]

What Nationwide had "cooking" was the purchase of a much smaller financial institution at 8-10 East Broad Street, Columbus, which Lincoln had eyed for at least 10 years. Upon the death of Brunson's founder, William Rindsfoos, the Brunson Savings and Loan Company and the Brunson Bank and Trust Company were put up for sale by the trustees of the Rindsfoos estate.

Organized in 1917, the thrift showed assets of $3.4 million in 1958, while the assets of the bank, founded in 1922, totaled $9.3 million. Both were acquired by Approved Finance for $1,250,500 and the stock transferred to Nationwide Corporation.

Brunson always was seen as "an important first step in our getting hold of other, bigger things," Lincoln said,[23] but Jeffers remembered it "didn't sit well" with the downtown Columbus leadership. Also, it didn't sit well with Ohio Superintendent of Insurance Arthur I. Vorys, who claimed in a suit filed against Nationwide Corporation, Approved Finance, the insurance companies and Lincoln that they had violated the state's rule against insurance companies owning more than 25 percent of another corporation.

A few days after the Brunson purchase May 15, 1958, Kyes of General Motors warned his friend of the dangers lurking in the acquisition. According to Lincoln, Kyes said it was unwise to buy a bank in a capital city, "in the very shadow of the state regulatory bodies. GM learned long ago to buy its banks out in the sticks, where nobody cares much about you." Furthermore, he predicted Vorys' action. "He sees it as an instance in which a little guy (the insurance superintendent) is fighting a big, bad institution (Nationwide)," Lincoln said Kyes advised. "Anything the superintendent can do to bring us to heel will increase his stature."[24]

Vorys left public office before the courts finally ruled in Nationwide's favor. In the words of chief counsel, P. Lee Thornbury, it was "a smashing victory." However, he also saw it as but a harbinger of more litigation over the issue of the common directors of the insurance companies and the non-insurance companies in which the major investments were held by the insurance companies. The issue of common control would continue to be a thorn in Nationwide's side if not resolved, Thornbury believed.[25]

In the winter of 1963 Lincoln approved the sale of Brunson. Dolan priced the property and peddled it by letter to prospects. One of those who responded was John G. McCoy, president and chief executive officer of City National Bank and Trust Company of Columbus, later Bank One, Columbus. He and Dolan met to discuss the sale.

"You know, we are really interested in that Brunson Bank, but not at your price," McCoy said.

Dolan responded that the price was firm.

"Well, you're whistling Dixie if you think you are going to get that for it. We've had somebody look at the bank, and they told us what it's worth, and that's what we are willing to pay for it."

Dolan again stuck to his price.

"Well," McCoy said, "you'll never get that; you'll never get it."[26]

When Brunson sold in the spring of 1964, "we got exactly what we asked for," Dolan said. The buyers were a group of Columbus businessmen, who changed Brunson's name to Citizens Savings & Loan Company. The price was $2.9 million, giving Nationwide an after-tax gain of $998,887. Dolan explained to the press that the sale freed up the corporation to seek bigger game in banking. "We want to have controlling interest in a much larger bank," he admitted.[27] Subsequently Nationwide made overtures to several larger financial institutions, including the $500 million Bank of Commonwealth, Detroit, but none was pursued very vigorously.

Although it was out of the banking business, Nationwide was very much in business as the 1960s unfolded. At the turn of the decade, Nationwide Life topped $2 billion in insurance in force, just five years after surpassing the $1 billion mark. It would pass the $3 billion, $4 billion and $5 billion milestones before another 10 years went by. In 1960 the auto, fire and life companies combined had more than 3.5 million policies in force and assets of more than $507 million.

Yet ahead in the decade of the 1960s were perhaps Nationwide's most tumultuous years.

9

INSURANCE AND
OTHER THAN INSURANCE

A
t times it was difficult for the casual observer to discern exactly what business Nationwide was in. This was particularly true in the decade of the 1960s, when the company produced almost as much news about its non-insurance activities as its insurance businesses.

There were significant insurance developments, to be sure. For example, automobile insurance sales turned overseas for the first time with the founding of Neckura in West Germany,* and while one Nationwide Corporation stock offering died aborning, another made it to Wall Street.

In addition, the move west that began in the 1950s continued with considerable vigor. Northern Life Insurance Company in Seattle joined the Nationwide Corporation family January 8, 1963, followed 20 months later by San Francisco-based West Coast Life Insurance Company. The price for 89 percent of Northern, which wrote primarily individual and group life and health policies in 20 midwestern and western states, was $29.8

---

* See Chapter 10.

million. Nationwide spent $32.1 million acquiring West Coast, which realized about 75 percent of its premiums from California. In 1965, a year after its purchase, West Coast surpassed $1 billion in life insurance.

To finance the purchase of Northern Life, a $28.9 million stock offering of 1.75 million new shares in Nationwide Corporation was scheduled for December 12, 1963. Kuhn, Loeb & Company, Inc., and J.C. Bradford & Company led the underwriters. As the day approached for the issue, however, Nationwide Corporation's over-the-counter stock slipped from more than $16 per share bid price to about $13 per share.

"I was furious that our stock had sunk so much," said Louis E. Dolan, vice president and general manager of the corporation. Murray D. Lincoln, on the other hand, took a more cavalier approach. "Well, our stock is where it deserves to be. That's what people are willing to pay for it."

At a series of board executive sessions in December 1963, Dolan recommended that the offering be called off. After all, he reasoned, a $3 difference on the 1.75 million shares to be offered would mean a "loss" to Nationwide of $5.25 million. On the eve of the issue, the executive committee voted to postpone, then withdraw, the company's registration statement filed with the Securities and Exchange Commission.

The SEC told Dolan "that there never had been a company pull out of an offering the night before it was to become effective." Counsel John C. Wagner remembered that Nationwide was "criticized severely by some of the Wall Street people" for calling it off.

The cancellation of the issue "will not alter our plans for development, nor even slow them," a disappointed Lincoln wrote in the corporation's 1963 annual report. "We shall continue to search intensively for investment opportunities of all kinds ... (including) companies in industries other than insurance."[1]

"Other than insurance" is what interested Lincoln most, partially as a means of offsetting the vagaries of the insurance industry but also to pursue his cooperative interests. Incredibly ambitious plans for a variety of cooperative enterprises took shape in the decade of the 1960s.

One that *almost* bore fruit began with a small news item in 1949. It quoted John A. Hartford, chairman of The Great Atlantic & Pacific Tea Company, Inc., as saying that if the government was successful in its anti-trust action against the world's largest grocery chain, he would "convert the whole works into the biggest consumer cooperative you ever saw."[2]

The day after the item appeared, Lincoln fired off a brief letter to Hartford in New York. "If you do this," said Lincoln in reference to Hartford's comment, "I believe you have a historical opportunity for a possible solution to your immediate problem ... I am in New York frequently and would like to confer with you on this matter ... "[3]

Hartford replied two weeks later. He said he had been misquoted. "I did not say that I was planning to turn our company into a consumer cooperative, nor do I have any such intentions," he wrote. "Perhaps, however, at some future date when things have quieted down, I will be able to avail myself of your kind offer to discuss this situation."[4] Before they could meet, Hartford died in 1951.

Throughout the 1950s Lincoln kept his eye on A&P. By the end of the decade he had a battery of attorneys and advisers working on ways to wrest from Hartford's heirs and foundation control of the $5 billion, 4,500-store grocery chain and turn it all into a giant cooperative for farmers and consumers alike. In the end A&P was just too big for Nationwide to swallow.

Until the day of his retirement, Lincoln spoke of his grand design, even though the interest of others had waned. "I was surprised to find that some of our own people apparently don't see a relationship between Nationwide and the A&P," he observed. "Perhaps I've overemphasized the importance of buying it, converting it into a cooperative and making A&P the largest consumer-owned enterprise in the world. ... I had taken it for granted that our people would see a huge new market for insurance of all types with the 20 million regular customers of A&P. ... A start, at least, could be made with group insurance for the 125,000 employees of the A&P."[5]

On that final word in January 1964, a 15-year-old dream died.*

Another dream of his was to gain control of Investors Diversified Services, Inc., a Minneapolis investment company whose assets from five mutual funds topped $3 billion in the early 1960s. Lincoln saw the potential of using all the IDS salesmen to sell Nationwide Insurance and all the Nationwide Insurance agents selling IDS mutual funds. "It would have been a tremendous combination," in Wagner's opinion.

In the summer of 1960, Lincoln wrote to Allen P. Kirby, chairman and president of Alleghany Corporation, which controlled IDS through ownership of 48 percent of its voting stock. Alleghany also owned controlling interest in the New York Central Railroad. "Would you be willing to discuss the selling of this (IDS) stock to the companies I represent?" asked Lincoln in a June 30 letter.[6] The overture met with a cool reception. "Nationwide Bid Spurned," reported the Columbus *Citizen-Journal* in its January 21, 1961, edition.

By then the Alleghany/IDS picture appeared murky. Texas oilmen Clinton W. Murchison and his brother, John, who had

---

* After Nationwide backed away from A&P, the Ohio Farm Bureau Federation tried unsuccessfully to enlist the support of other state and national farm organizations to purchase, with Nationwide's help, a sizeable block of A&P stock. "It was to get some power in the hands of farmers," explained C. William Swank, executive vice president of the bureau. "We wanted shelf space ... and we said if we can't get the Campbell Soup company and the Heinz company to talk to us out on the farm, if we own the shelf space, they'll have to talk to us."

successfully fought for control of IDS in the 1950s only to lose it to Kirby in a stockholder suit in 1960, launched a proxy fight for control of Alleghany early in 1961. To retaliate, Kirby enlisted the aid of Lincoln and Nationwide to acquire more Alleghany stock for the purpose of, as Lincoln said, "letting Mr. Kirby get control."

Kirby knew, of course, of Lincoln's interest in IDS, and he played to those desires. IDS and Nationwide even went so far as entering into a "memorandum of understanding" April 11, 1961, to explore the advantages of the 3,400 IDS salesmen and Nationwide's 6,000 agents selling the investment and insurance services of both organizations.

To gain more information about the IDS sales operation, Lincoln sent one of his top operatives, Vice President of Sales DeanW. Jeffers, on an "undercover" mission to an IDS training seminar in Minneapolis. "The president of IDS, Grady Clark, knew about our little undercover operation, but nobody else did. My fellow trainees knew only that I was from Columbus," Jeffers recalled. On the final day all the trainees met the top sales executives of IDS at a small reception. "As I started through the receiving line, I hear this voice: 'Dean Jeffers! What are you doing here?!' I had been spotted by Wes Fesler, former head football coach at Ohio State University (in Columbus), who had become a regional sales director at IDS. My cover was blown."

By mid-August, though, the joint effort plan was dead. Clark wrote Lincoln that "such a combined effort would not be feasible."[7]

Nationwide Corporation began buying Alleghany stock in small amounts a week before the April announcement of the possible joint sales effort, but it wasn't until the fall that it became heavily involved. By having the corporation itself "aggressively" join in the purchase of shares, substantial charges to the surpluses of the casualty and fire companies could be avoided. On October 4 the board authorized the automobile, fire and life companies to make additional purchases of up to 1.5 million shares of Alleghany, to be voted with Kirby's holdings.

"I felt comfortable to absorb it if we went that way and quite comfortable to get along without it," said the chairman of the investment committee, George H. Dunlap.

(From time to time, Dunlap had difficulty supporting Lincoln's grandiose plans, especially when it came to spending money. "Mr. Lincoln, I don't think I can explain this to the investment committee," he would say. "You better come and do it." Lincoln would respond, "Jawge, if this doesn't have your support, there isn't any point in my talking to them.")

By the end of December 1962 the Nationwide Insurance Companies had some 700,000 Alleghany shares, represented by common and preferred stock and warrants for common stock. In the same month the board authorized a loan to Kirby of up to $5 million (it was never used) and entered into a formal agreement with him that at any Alleghany stockholder meeting through December 31, 1967, the combined holdings would be voted "for a slate of directors to include persons nominated by Nationwide and persons nominated by Kirby."

It wasn't long before the bickering began over the number of shares Nationwide should acquire and the number of seats on Alleghany's board.* Kirby didn't want Nationwide to have more than he of either. He suggested three seats, Lincoln insisted on six, or nearly half the expanded 13-member board. Another dispute arose over the allocation of officers. Kirby had in mind installing his own people while throwing Nationwide a bone,

---

* Nationwide looked at acquiring for $16.5 million at least 1.5 million shares of Alleghany from Bertin C. Gamble, president and chairman of Minneapolis-based retailer, Gamble-Skogmo, Inc. Gamble also held options on up to 2 million more shares. Kirby later acquired from Gamble more than 1 million of his Alleghany shares.

namely the position of secretary, "if one were required."

On April 18, 1963, Nationwide's board authorized Lincoln to negotiate the stock holdings on the basis that the company be permitted to nominate Alleghany's chairman or president and the secretary or the treasurer. Following a meeting April 9, 1963, at New York's Recess Club between Lincoln, Kirby and senior officers of both sides, Kirby at first appeared satisfied with Nationwide's proposal but later rejected it. The negotiations ended May 15, 1963.

"I'd be less than truthful if I didn't say that I was disappointed when the possibility of our getting majority control (of Alleghany) disappeared," Lincoln reported to the Nationwide Corporation board.[8] His reference concerned a grand scheme to issue more corporation stock to buy out Kirby's Alleghany interests, use Alleghany to acquire control of Montgomery Ward, "and give Sears Roebuck some real competition."

On December 4, 1963, Kirby emerged victorious in the proxy fight with 56 percent of the voting stock of Alleghany. Lincoln became a director of Alleghany, the New York Central Railroad and IDS as well as a member of the latter's executive committee.

Three years later, in 1966, Alleghany offered to exchange its shares for those of New York Central. Overnight Nationwide became one of the major shareholders of the railroad, receiving 177,787 shares of the railroad for 883,700 shares of Alleghany. The insurance companies immediately turned around and sold nearly half of the railroad stock. An internal memorandum in 1970 stated that the "positive effect" from the sale of New York Central (then Penn Central) stock was nearly $2.5 million over the total cost of $10 million.

Until the 1960s, Nationwide rarely captured much national attention. Lincoln often railed against the inadequacies of the company's advertising. However, on February 14, 1962, it entered the world of network television as sponsor of the new weekly ABC-TV show, *News and Comment,* hosted by Howard

K. Smith. It was a high-profile undertaking, inasmuch as this was the first show for the award-winning Smith after leaving CBS-TV four months earlier.

"In my opinion," Lincoln said in a memorandum to the sales staff, "our sponsorship of a newsman of Howard K. Smith's caliber will do much to establish Nationwide nationally as one of the most *responsible* insurance organizations in the country ... " In addition, he said, people will learn what the company stands for, "what it can do to meet human needs," as well as perform a "unique public service."

Lincoln admired Smith for his "independence of mind and his rational, forthright approach to the news ... his knowledge, his integrity, and his courage — virtues that Nationwide as an institution would also like to be known for." He admitted that not everyone will agree with Smith's commentary, but "we shall make no attempt to 'censor' Mr. Smith ... let the chips fall where they may."[9]

The chips fell favorably for Nationwide for 39 weeks, even though Smith's commentary often stirred many souls. On the 40th show, November 11, 1962, the roof fell in.

Smith's subject was *The Political Obituary of Richard M. Nixon,* based on the former vice president's unsuccessful gubernatorial bid in California less than a week earlier. Among those the Sunday show interviewed about Nixon's political career was Alger Hiss, the State Department official pursued by Nixon when he was a member and an investigator for the House Un-American Activities Committee in the late 1940s. Hiss later went to jail for perjury.

In a brief, advance story on the television show, the earliest, out-of-town edition of *The New York Times* headed its story, "Hiss Versus Nixon." Omitted were the names of the other participants, such as Congressman Gerald Ford, thus leaving the impression Hiss was to have the entire 30-minute show to attack Nixon. (Hiss was on the air for 2 minutes, 31 seconds.)

In later editions the headline changed, but the earlier one stirred up California where, Smith said, the far right "Birchites ... went off like rockets." Before the ink dried on the script Saturday night, telegrams and telephone calls of protest flooded ABC-TV. Initially, all the calls came from California, then spread east to other cities, indicating to Smith an organized reaction to a show that had not even aired.[10]

Some television outlets canceled the program before seeing it or the script, including Great American Broadcasting's WTVN-TV (Channel 6)* in Nationwide's home city of Columbus. Millions did see the show, however, and the letters, telegrams and telephone calls flooded not only television stations but Nationwide as well. The company received 3,500 letters, 85 percent of them unfavorable, but only 43 customers canceled their insurance. Many assailed Lincoln personally, including the American Legion.

Lincoln said the decision by some stations not to air the show "strikes me as coming close to censorship," which he vigorously opposed. About Smith, he said, "We have never tried to tell him what he should talk about or whom he should have on his show. To do so would be a violation of our contract."[11]

Actually, the morning of the show Nationwide's Jeffers, vice president of sales, and Harry W. Culbreth, senior vice president, human relations, telephoned Smith and his boss, James C. Haggerty, news vice president for the American Broadcasting Company. They discussed the protests, but Nationwide made it clear the responsibility for the show rested with the network.

Nationwide's sponsorship ended June 30, 1963, when ratings fell well below the guarantee in the company's contract. "Some of our detractors will interpret our action as capitulation in the face of criticism," acknowledged Calvin Kytle, vice president-public relations, in a memorandum to Lincoln, the directors

---

* WTVN-TV, which aired the show six days later, is now WSYX-TV.

and senior management. "Some of our supporters will see it as a denial of our publicly expressed principles. Neither would be correct. ... It is important that our action be clearly understood for what it is — a practical, dollars-and-cents advertising decision, and nothing more."[12]

The November 11 show had an interesting impact on the affiliation talks Lincoln began in 1960 with T. E. Leavey, co-chairman of the board of the Farmers Insurance Group. The Los Angeles-based company would make a wonderful partner for Nationwide, Lincoln believed, "eliminate the expansion expenses now being incurred by both organizations" and create "an organization big enough to successfully compete ... at the lowest possible cost."[13]

After watching the Howard K. Smith show in Los Angeles, Leavey became quite upset and decided to call Lincoln to complain about Nationwide's sponsorship of the program. The telephone rang in Lincoln's Gahanna, OH, farmhouse, getting him out of bed.

"Hello," a sleepy Lincoln answered. It was after midnight in Ohio but three hours earlier on the West Coast.

"Murray. This is Tom Leavey. I just watched your Howard K. Smith show, and I just don't understand why you would want to be associated with ... "

Click.

Lincoln hung up on him and went back to bed. They never spoke again.

Nationwide and Farmers did, though. For many years Dr. Robert A. Rennie, senior vice president, investments, dreamed that Nationwide one day would acquire Farmers and, as a result, overtake Nationwide's chief rival, State Farm Mutual Automobile Insurance Company. He approached John E. Fisher with a plan just a few months after Fisher became general chairman and chief executive officer October 1, 1981.

Rennie had been acquiring Farmers stock for Nationwide,

but investment talk soon turned to a discussion of acquiring the California company. Fisher believed if that could be accomplished before Farmers expanded east and before Nationwide spent any more money on its Western expansion, "why, we could really balance out Nationwide. So we began to try to conceive of a means of approaching Farmers without having the deal die for us right at its outset."

It wasn't too long before Farmers Insurance Group President Richard Lindsley got wind of Nationwide's stock purchases (eventually more than 3.3 million shares), and several times he asked if "we had, you might say, adversarial intentions," said Fisher. The response always was no; Fisher had no appetite for a hostile takeover attempt.

Rennie proposed that the two insurance carriers first might have a jointly owned service company, thus positioning Nationwide for a later merger of some kind. Fisher presented the first half of the concept to Lindsley who, in turn, put it before Farmers Chairman John Sullivan. He suggested a meeting in Los Angeles at a private club where the rules were so strict, "you weren't supposed to crackle your newspaper," Fisher recalled.

"Look," the elderly Sullivan began, "if you guys want to make us an offer, let's not beat around the bush. Tell me. Make me an offer. If it's good for my shareholders, we'll consider it. But let's not play games!"

Sullivan had assessed Fisher and Nationwide perfectly.

Rennie worked up a package of Nationwide assets, which included cash and stock, "as much as we could conceivably afford," Fisher said. Rennie wrapped everything into the stock's potential, "including the radio stations, all of Nationwide Corporation — you might say almost anything that we could find that we could classify as part of the package." The aim was to have Nationwide emerge the senior member of the deal.

Fisher and Rennie took their package to Sullivan and Lindsley, meeting in secret at the Brown Hotel in Denver. Neither side wanted to stir up their agency forces or the shareholders unless the talk became serious. It didn't.

"Mr. Sullivan just sort of laughed at us," Fisher remembered. "He said, 'I don't think that mixed bag is something that I could really convince my shareholders as being a good deal.' So, he said no thanks."

Nationwide hardly came away a loser. Over the years it disposed of its Farmers stock, realizing a profit of more than $72 million.

"Lincoln delighted in floating trial balloons ... just to keep the board thinking," said Robert M. Culp. As vice president of business operations, he chased one of those early 1960s balloons with Rennie, namely the Ryder System, Inc., Miami, which primarily leased trucks. The initial idea was to have Nationwide insure Ryder's truck fleet, but to Culp it clearly would be a losing proposition. The two men then turned their attention to providing insurance on passenger car leases after Jim Ryder, the system's founder, initiated a prototype leasing program with a few auto dealers in Maryland, Delaware and the District of Columbia.

Ryder's leasing service would be launched in Nationwide's operating territory, and its agents would insure each vehicle as well as receive a fee on all leases negotiated by them.

"We think we can prove, to individuals as well as fleet operators, that they can lease more cheaply than they can buy," Lincoln said at the time. "In fact, we asked a sampling of our three million car-insurance policyholders whether a lease package (covering fuel, all maintenance and insurance) would appeal to them. ... Two out of three ... told us it would."[14]

Once again Lincoln was ahead of his time, by 20 years or so in this instance. A long-term pact with Ryder never materialized because, in part, private passenger car leasing was not accepted by large numbers of customers in the early 1960s.

Another balloon that burst involved Greyhound Corporation. Under a joint venture plan negotiated in 1963 and 1964, Nationwide Corporation would activate its Pacific Life Insurance Company, acquired in 1958, and sell 60 percent of it to Greyhound. The public carrier also would receive options to buy the remaining 40 percent of Pacific from Nationwide over a 10-year period.

Lincoln was "disappointed" that Greyhound insisted on those terms; the original plan provided for a long-term relationship. Even so, the sale of Nationwide travel accident policies by Greyhound ticket agents, in much the same manner air travel insurance was sold at airports, "should be very profitable," he said.[15] The two parties abandoned the venture, however, after Greyhound demanded an even larger piece of the pie.

Nationwide Corporation was successful with its second public offering of 2.5 million Class "A" shares, which provided $34.5 million in proceeds. They were used to pay off debt incurred in the acquisition of Northern Life and to acquire West Coast Life. This was in July 1964, three months after the biggest shakeup in Nationwide's 38 years.

10

THE GLOBAL PERSPECTIVE

Although the roots of Nationwide are deep in the rolling farm country of Ohio, branches of its operations extended throughout the nation and across the seas by the 1960s.

Murray D. Lincoln's interests, of course, were global, and he pushed the enterprise and its officers and directors to follow his lead. "A stone dropped in the Indian Ocean causes a ripple that washes our doorsteps," he would say. "The struggles of people in faraway places to end their misery affect our own plans and our own welfare as directly as if those faraway people were right here in our own state."[1]

Europe saw Lincoln the first time in 1923 as a member of an American Farm Bureau delegation, but after World War II the frequency of his trans-Atlantic excursions increased considerably, as did those of his associates. Most of Lincoln's formal duties overseas involved cooperative endeavors, however, such as the International Cooperative Alliance. He never was one for insurance industry trade memberships. Those responsibilities he assigned to others.

His successors — Bowman Doss, Dean W. Jeffers, John E. Fisher, D. Richard McFerson — all served the insurance industry in the United States and overseas in senior capacities. Fisher, who served as chairman of the International Cooperative Insurance Federation* and as a director of the International Insurance Society, once described Lincoln's farsighted vision as "rather sweeping."

For a short time Lincoln served as a director of the Rochdale Insurance Company, incorporated in New York but with ties to one of England's largest insurance companies, the Cooperative Insurance Society of Manchester. It was, in fact, a request for reinsurance from CIS to Nationwide that launched the Ohio company into the international insurance business. As for Rochdale, Lincoln resigned as a board member in 1955 rather than submit to a New York State Department of Insurance inquiry, which he viewed as an affront to a man of his stature. It was, he said, an "inquisition ... reserved for a convicted criminal."

Peoples Development Company (later Nationwide Development Company) and other elements of the insurance companies explored all manner of overseas projects in which Lincoln had, or wanted to have, an interest. Among the proposals: a $1 million hotel at the airport in Zurich, Switzerland; a fertilizer plant in India; supermarkets in West Germany; mutual funds in Europe; oil and life insurance in the Philippines and Tectum International in Korea, to name but a few.

Lincoln's last international venture before his retirement at age 72 involved a proposal to build an oil refinery in the Dominican Republic. In a letter to Donald Reid Cabral, president of the provisional government, Lincoln wrote: "We are particularly interested in this project because we believe it

---

* Since renamed the International Cooperative and Mutual Insurance Federation.

can open the way to a cooperative enterprise which can be of primary benefit to your people, while being of great interest to our cooperative movement in the United States."[2]

So many international projects Lincoln proposed, such as this refinery, were foul balls rather than home runs, yet he expected the Nationwide staff to run each one out. There were exceptions, among them the Puerto Rico operations and Neckura, both born in the Lincoln era. Then, too, were Nationwide's worldwide reinsurance activities, and its role in the founding of Allnations, Inc., an international insurance development firm based in Columbus but an affiliate of the International Cooperative and Mutual Insurance Federation.

In the spring of 1955 Lincoln received a letter from Rafael Pol, then president of the Cooperative League of Puerto Rico, asking if the then-still Farm Bureau Insurance Companies had an interest in doing business in the commonwealth. Lincoln did, of course, but because of the inability of cooperative and insurance interests to come together, little came of the inquiry until November 1959 when planning for Nationwide's Puerto Rico operations began anew and in earnest.

Initially Nationwide believed the island commonwealth could be the jumping off point for expansion into Latin America. Senior Vice President Howard Hutchinson took the lead. "He said we would have on one hand the advantage of a community where Spanish was spoken and an additional advantage where currency transactions would be in U.S. dollars," recalled W. E. "Fitz" Fitzpatrick, who retired as corporate secretary and assistant to the general chairman in the fall of 1989.

Fitzpatrick began his 29-year career with Nationwide as manager of national accounts, but because he previously had worked for insurance companies in Bogotá, Colombia, and was fluent in Spanish, he soon found himself increasingly involved in the international arena.

After several months of talks, Hutchinson led a small

Nationwide delegation to San Juan in April 1960 to meet with the senior representatives of the local cooperatives, including Pol and Ernesto del Rosario, comptroller for the Los Caños Sugar Cooperative and general agent of Employers Mutuals of Wausau and CUNA Mutual Insurance Company. After failing in numerous attempts to form a business alliance with the Cooperative Life Insurance Company of Puerto Rico and its many fractured interests, Nationwide Mutual and Nationwide Life independently secured licenses in the fall of 1961 to write business in Puerto Rico. Nationwide Mutual Fire obtained its license two years later.

Nationwide also acquired from Employers Mutuals of Wausau its personal lines portfolio on the island and hired del Rosario, first as general agent and later as branch office manager.

The plan to use Puerto Rico as a training center and jumping off point to the Caribbean, Central and South America never developed, however, although some efforts at acquisitions were made. For instance, Fitzpatrick looked at La Nacional, a well run but small insurance company in Guayaquil, Ecuador, that Dr. Robert A. Rennie had turned up, and then explored other opportunities in Peru and Colombia. Others, such as Eugene F. Hull, then manager of international insurance programs, looked at cooperative ventures in Argentina and Chile as well.

"It was my recommendation that we not get involved directly in an insurance operation ... in South America," Fitzpatrick said after weighing all the options. "Nationwide just wasn't ready to move into an entirely different environment ... a different kind of culture."

Fitzpatrick's thoughts became fact: Nationwide never went beyond Puerto Rico with a Latin American insurance operation. Yet, at the time insurance sales in the commonwealth began in 1962, the international movement was still very much alive.

In a memorandum to Bowman Doss April 23, 1962 (with a copy to Lincoln), Rennie proposed the creation of a new corporate enterprise, Nationwide International, Inc., in which all the insurance companies' overseas functions could be concentrated.

"The functions of Nationwide International would begin with insurance activities," Rennie wrote. "This is where our strength lies. Insurance organizations are also one of the basic needs of newly developing countries because they must begin to mobilize people's savings before they can achieve economic growth. Foreign aid will not do the job.

"I would foresee Nationwide International acquiring a strong financial interest in local insurance companies throughout the world ... (and) serving in partnership with the International Finance Corporation and other international agencies in providing equity and loan capital for oil development activities, food marketing and processing functions, and distribution activities abroad."

Rennie pointed out that many American companies operating overseas sought investment outlets for many millions of dollars in earnings. "These companies do not want either control or management responsibilities in enterprises using these funds," he continued. "They merely want effective use of their money in partnership with responsible management."

In conclusion, Rennie noted that "we have a magnificent opportunity here to do many of the things we have been talking about for several years."

Contemplation of the internationalization of Nationwide came as Soviet cosmonaut Yuri Gagarin contemplated the world from space, the U.S. contemplated aerial photographs of Soviet missiles in Cuba and Rembrandt's *Aristotle Contemplating the Bust of Homer* sold for a record $2.3 million. As the East Germans erected a monstrous wall in Berlin, yet another was breached at the University of Mississippi with the aid of some 13,500 federal troops.

As 1962 came to a close, the Nationwide Insurance

Companies had grown to 13,000 employees and agents who generated combined assets of $556.6 million. The $328.7 million in premiums earned came from 3.8 million policies in force.

This growing mass gave Lincoln the strength to push his global vision. In July of 1962, as Rennie prepared to depart for an investment symposium in Cambridge, England, he received one of his few direct assignments from Lincoln. "Bob," he said simply, "I want to operate in Europe."

Rennie was a studious man, and among the subjects that captured his interest over the years were Nationwide's prime competitors, namely Allstate and State Farm. Allstate was of particular interest, however, because it owed much of its rapid growth to its partnership with retailing giant, Sears, Roebuck & Company. He would recall many times with obvious dismay how Allstate had far outdistanced Nationwide, despite "having been organized in 1931, five years after we had been, and they were three times what we were at that point (1962). So, I figured there must be some synergism between department store sales and insurance."

At the Cambridge symposium Rennie deliberately engaged in conversation anyone and everyone who might enable him to fulfill Lincoln's wish. Among those he collared was Peter H. Cross, an international business broker based in New York, who revealed to Rennie that a West German retailer named Neckermann wanted an insurance partner. Rennie "leaped at the opportunity," telephoned Lincoln, and within 48 hours was in Frankfurt for the first discussions with Josef* and Peter Neckermann, father and son, respectively.

Before World War II the elder Neckermann owned two

---

* Josef Neckermann was an equestrian known throughout the world of show jumping. He won many international competitions, including individual Olympic medals at the 1960 games in Rome, the 1968 games in Mexico City and the 1972 games in Munich.

department stores in his hometown of Wurzburg and a small mail order business in Berlin, lost everything after the war, and started up again in 1949 with another mail order house and then a retail outlet in 1951. In the following decade the Neckermann organization grew to 20 large department stores, 15 smaller ones, more than 120 retail appliance outlets, a large mail order operation and a travel agency that became one of the world's largest.*

In the early 1960s Josef Neckermann needed additional sources of capital for expansion and conducted numerous discussions with Sears executives, including Chairman and Chief Executive Officer Charles H. Kellstadt. The Sears capital agreement never happened, but Kellstadt planted the seed of an insurance partnership with Allstate. When Peter Neckermann joined his father in business in 1962, his task was to find the insurance partner. Allstate was the first and only choice. Even after Nationwide entered the picture, the Neckermanns had reservations. After all, the Ohio company had neither the international experience nor the technical experience to market insurance within a large retail organization.†

Nevertheless, Rennie brought with him to Frankfurt a chemistry that cast a spell on the Neckermanns. "I liked him from the very first moment," said Peter Neckermann. "He was a very special person, and I think the best representative Nationwide could ever have."

---

* The entire Neckermann operation was sold in 1977 to a large competitor, Karstadt. Peter Neckermann placed much of the blame on his father's inability to buy city land immediately after World War II as cheaply as had some of his competitors. Consequently, the company always had to live with higher operating costs and that constantly drained the company's capital, Peter Neckermann said.

† Nationwide had a brief, unsuccessful stab at a retailing joint venture with Heck's discount stores in the Baltimore area.

The conversations between Peter Neckermann and Allstate continued until his first visit with the Nationwide board January 7, 1963. "I achieved two things at this time," he said. "I first convinced myself that these are special people, really special, because of their honesty, their straightforwardness. ... Their whole idea about business was so different from the ones which the Sears people showed. The difference really came out loud and clear."

Peter Neckermann also achieved his goal of finding a partner, convincing Nationwide to pursue an agreement. When he returned to West Germany, he also convinced his father and his board to go forward with Nationwide. "I felt ... the human relationship is more important than specific knowledge," he told the directors.

Tough negotiations followed, with Nationwide first considering acquiring a German insurance company. The dearth of healthy, inexpensive and available insurers and the regulatory environment in Germany made this route unpalatable, so a new company was formed. Nationwide insisted on 51 percent of the joint venture because it understood the insurance business. The Neckermanns relented on the condition the leadership of the new enterprise, originally called Neckuna, be German "to make sure this company is seen in Germany as German and not an alien company," said Peter Neckermann.

Walter H. Stelling, Nationwide's director of European projects, became the first chairman. Peter Neckermann was named vice chairman, then chairman in September 1966.

Automobile insurance became the initial focus (fire and life were added later) because Germany had compulsory insurance and car sales were booming as the nation entered its remarkable post-war recovery. Therefore, a large number of policyholders could be developed in a short period.

Not all welcomed the agreement. Some competitors in Germany made every effort to block regulatory approval of

Neckuna. Also, some members of the powerful Insurance Committee of the International Cooperative Alliance, particularly the Swedes, objected to the joint venture because it placed a non-cooperative, the Neckermann organization, in competition with cooperatives. "So they (the Swedes) went all out to defeat our plan," said Doss. They circulated to the Insurance Committee throughout the 70-nation membership a scathing paper[3] condemning Nationwide.

The issue came to a head at a meeting of the Insurance Committee in Vienna. Doss, a member of the executive committee, braced himself for the anticipated attack. "We all listened to the Swedes' condemnation, and it was severe," but although Doss had the opportunity to reply and was prepared to do so, "something told me, on the spur of the moment … to ignore it. … I didn't respond."

Doss wasn't sure he had made the right decision until the group took a break. "The word going about during the coffee break was that the Americans outfoxed the Swedes," he said. "That was about the last we ever heard of this problem. Today, everybody gets along fine."

What Lincoln had initiated two years earlier did not happen during his term as president of the Nationwide Insurance Companies. On July 15, 1964, three months after he retired, his successor, Doss, signed the joint venture agreement between Nationwide Mutual Fire Insurance Company and Neckermann Versang KGaA.

The name, Neckuna — in German, _Neckermann und Nationwide_ — didn't last long. A German company with a similar name brought suit, which was settled out of court. Nationwide and the Neckermanns received DM100,000 (est. $50,000) in return for giving up the name Neckuna. "That was the first profit we had … and the only profit we had for years," Peter Neckermann said. Neckura was the alternate name choice.

Neckura, which sold its first policy March 15, 1965, is unique to the ways of German automobile insurance. The premium is discounted at the outset and increased at the time of renewal if an accident occurred in that period. Traditional German insurance companies employ a simple merit-rating system: a discount in the premium is earned only after an accident-free year. At the outset Neckura is very competitive for new drivers, but becomes less so for drivers who pile up accidents.

"This whole approach in Germany was supposed to be a self-purging type of mechanism," explained Enus Burigana, who served as Neckura's chairman from 1989 to 1992. "It would behoove the accident-prone drivers to go to another company and not stay with Neckura" because the rate no longer would be competitive. "The loss-free driver, however, would benefit in insuring with Neckura because his discount was much greater."

Many of those Neckura signed up initially were foreign workers who flocked to the high paying jobs in West Germany in the 1960s. In 1970 the country's economy went into a tailspin, taking the German insurance industry, and Neckura, with it. The company, which became saddled with high risk customers largely because the foreign workers didn't know how to drive well, found itself in very difficult straits. Peter Neckermann remembers:

"Many foreign workers lost their jobs and returned home ... without paying their premiums. ... Neckura suffered tremendously. Now, we have to admit a management mistake which Ernest H. Klepetar (the company's president) and I did not realize soon enough. So, we had a great deal of loss ... almost all of our capital."*

In the spring of 1971 Neckura desperately needed an infusion

---

* The loss was estimated by Peter Neckermann to be DM4 million (more than $1.1 million).

of capital to save the company. After one negotiating session between Peter Neckermann and then Nationwide General Chairman Dean W. Jeffers in the basement of his Columbus home, the two men agreed that in return for about DM20 million (est. $5.5 million) in capital, Nationwide would acquire 60.65 percent interest in Neckura.

Although now refinanced, the future of the Neckermann companies concerned Peter Neckermann. To continue the expansion, he sought, and gained, a merger with Karstadt, a much larger German retailing organization. The insurance business he offered independently to Nationwide, going to Jeffers in 1975.

"I give you the opportunity, if you want, to buy the whole Neckura business," Peter Neckermann told the general chairman, "and, if after this merger, you want to come back and be part of that, it's your prerogative. But, I want to avoid that you wake up one morning and you are in bed with Germans who look like Allstate and who are not looking like Neckermanns."[4]

Jeffers got the message and in December 1975 the Nationwide board approved the acquisition of 100 percent of the shares in Neckura and declined to give Peter Neckermann the repurchase agreement he sought. Almost two years later he left Germany and joined Nationwide in Columbus, first as director for international and economic analysis under Rennie and then adding the title of vice president in the investment department.

Nationwide formed a new agreement with Karstadt to continue selling insurance across store counters, but increased its efforts to create an independent sales force. Klepetar retired and was succeeded as president first by William Parlin and then, in 1979, by Patrick S. Roberts, who spent a total of 17 years in Germany with Neckura before returning to Columbus in 1984 to become vice president of sponsor/endorser relations.

At year-end 1993, Neckura's written premiums on auto, fire and life policies totaled DM337.5 million (est. $222.8 million).

As long as it remains economically viable, Neckura has a life within the Nationwide Insurance Enterprise, President and Chief Executive Officer D. Richard McFerson said late in 1993. "Our marketplace is really America. Nationwide is not going to be devoting any significant time or resource to expand beyond America, at least not in my tenure," which is expected to continue until the turn of the century. Therefore, Neckura is "in a holding pattern," he said.

One international Nationwide activity begun alongside Neckura and the Puerto Rico venture and extending well beyond the borders of America is reinsurance. It is a vital, complex and little-understood element of the insurance industry in which Nationwide is a major writer, particularly in the area of property reinsurance.

Reinsurance is the method by which insurance companies, in effect, hedge their bets. Companies reinsure to avoid exposure to too much loss on a single event or when they write more business than they can reasonably handle.

Nationwide maintains reinsurance treaties in nearly 40 countries worldwide although the majority of the activity is in the U.S. and Europe. Companies often work through intermediaries, brokers such as Guy Carpenter & Company of New York, which receives a reinsurance proposal and then "shops" it around to the major reinsurers, such as Nationwide, General Reinsurance, Prudential Reinsurance and others. The Nationwide underwriter "prices," or rates, the risk, thus dictating how easy or difficult it will be for the intermediary to market the proposal.

Don Johnson, then vice president of underwriting, is credited with getting Nationwide into reinsurance, beginning in 1962, although it had dabbled in it for some years before that. Johnson sat on the board of the International Cooperative Reinsurance

Bureau, an arm of the International Cooperative Insurance Federation.* Robert M. Culp, regional underwriting manager in Connecticut, and Patrick L. Doyle, who began at Farm Bureau Mutual in 1951 as a claims adjuster, were among the first Johnson brought in to staff the new reinsurance department. They were joined shortly thereafter by Burigana, who helped set up the accounting and controls operations.

"We were really not at the forefront of this thing," Burigana recalled. "As a matter of fact, it was difficult for us because we were a mutual company with a reinsurance department within Nationwide Mutual. Most reinsurance is done with stock companies. ... This was a real hurdle for Nationwide to cross."

The early days were "a little wild and woolly," he said, "but your word was your bond. You could totally rely on a person's word."

Well, almost totally. In the early days of Nationwide's reinsurance experience, the Cooperative Insurance Society of Manchester reinsured 5 percent of Nationwide Mutual Fire's premiums, the 5 percent representing almost $1 million in 1958. As a member of the International Cooperative Alliance, the British society had an obligation to share those funds with the ICA, "but it kept them to itself," said Culp. "Well, when the other members found out" what was going on "under the table, all hell broke loose" at the ICA.

Lincoln quickly heard about the uproar, called Johnson and Culp into his office and demanded to know what all the skyrockets were about. After the two executives explained, the president told them, "You better get your passports real quick and get over there (London) and see if you can put this fire out."[5]

They did, although it caused considerable anguish among the ICA members, Culp said, as well as some house cleaning.

---

* When Johnson went on the federation's board, Burigana took his place on the bureau's board and later served as board chairman of the bureau.

As a direct result, Johnson filled a vacancy on the reinsurance bureau's board.

Culp, who retired at the end of 1983 as vice president of the property and casualty insurance subsidiaries, had to make a second hurried trip to London a few years later to put out another fire created by Maurice Rutty. He was a former Lloyd's of London underwriter who opened up his own underwriting business in offices right outside the Lloyd's building, hence the term "fringe market." Except for a bad apple now and then, the fringe operators are highly regarded and legitimate business people who market for a commission the leavings — usually 10 percent or so — of a reinsurance package from which Lloyd's already has taken the lion's share.

Nationwide contracted with Rutty to serve as an underwriter for the Ohio insurer in the London market. "Unfortunately," Culp said, "he had a get-rich-quick scheme, which was to write as much of any or all business he could find, regardless of quality or price." After the first audit, Nationwide discovered what he was doing and fired him, but the damage was done. The business he wrote in Nationwide's name "you just can't dump overboard," said Culp. "You own it until it expires.

"It was a several million dollar mistake, absolutely. It was a flat-out mistake."

In the main, though, Nationwide has held its head high in the rough-and-tumble, high-finance world of reinsurance. It is a respected international player, and the activity provides Nationwide with the opportunity to diversify its risk on a global basis.

Another international venture in the early 1960s that is little known outside Nationwide's inner circle was the plan to create a domestic, jointly-owned holding company with the Singer Company, the sewing machine people. The purpose of the holding company, to be called the Singer-Nationwide Corporation, was to acquire and develop insurance (and reinsurance) companies in Latin America, Europe and other areas of the world where feasible.

The concept was another attempt to emulate the highly successful Sears-Allstate retailing operations. Singer products were sold in 181 countries through more than 5,000 company-operated retail stores that employed 45,000 in addition to 20,000 independent sales agents. Lincoln viewed each one of those people and the outlets as an opportunity to sell insurance.

However, his dream was not to be realized. Immediately prior to the filing of the new corporation's registration statement with the Securities and Exchange Commission in November 1963, Singer's president, Donald P. Kircher, decided he really didn't want to be in the insurance business.

Perhaps it was just as well. Although in his heart Lincoln still had a greater sense of purpose and a clearer vision of direction than the average man, his body rebelled against continuing the pace required of running such a multi-faceted organization as Nationwide. The time to stop and reflect on a life well spent approached more rapidly than he knew.

11

THE MATTER OF SUCCESSION

Where is the next generation of leadership coming from?" Murray D. Lincoln asked the directors of the Nationwide Insurance Companies at the end of 1963. "What are we doing to find, develop and train that next generation of leadership? I don't expect to stay around here forever … "[1]

For the first time in 37 years, the seemingly indefatigable 71-year-old leader indicated a willingness to step aside for a new generation of helmsmen. It was time, and well past time, in the opinion of many who worked closely with Lincoln, but it took a special arm-twisting visit from a board delegation to convince him of that. For nearly two years, one could not help but notice the decline in his health: His vigorous gait slowed, his strapping physique slouched and his spell-binding rhetoric was halting and slurred.

The state of his health, rather than his age, was the greater concern. "This became a great embarrassment for everyone," according to Dr. Robert A. Rennie. "Plus, Mr. Lincoln didn't want to give up. He hadn't accomplished all that he wanted to accomplish." Yet, he finally agreed it was time to get the best leadership available "to carry Nationwide forward to its great new objectives." He suggested that the board create a search committee.

Two weeks later confusion as to his true intent remained, however. In a confidential memorandum to Lincoln, Calvin Kytle, vice president of public relations, tried to clarify the matter. He wrote:

"Although there may be no necessity to actually name your successor immediately, it is most important — and becoming more so every day — for our people to be assured that some orderly process is at work through which a satisfactory successor is going to be named.

"When we talked, you implied that such a process was at work, referring to the special board committee which had been set up at your urging. I suggest, on the contrary, that this committee is confused both as to your intent and its assignment."[2]

Kytle, who long supported Harry W. Culbreth's interest in becoming Lincoln's successor, suggested the president write the chairmen of the four insurance companies, stating his intentions, establishing the criteria for a successor, and asking that a successor be appointed and announced quickly "so that you will have as much time as possible to break him in before he takes office."

There is no indication that Lincoln took Kytle's advice, nor even the hint from the directors who earlier provided for the day he would step down. In 1960, when Lincoln was 68, the boards of the Nationwide Insurance Companies and Nationwide Corporation signed agreements to retain Lincoln as a consultant for five years after his retirement at a combined annual salary of $60,000.

However, his December 1963 message to the board concerning a successor stirred up the "wannabees" at headquarters. Lincoln said more about whom he did not want to see as president than about those he did. For example, about George H. Dunlap — who made no secret of his desire for a line position — he said, "If Jawge ever succeeds me, I swear I'll turn over in my grave."[3]

Dunlap recalled walking with Lincoln one day and "listening more than talking" to the president as he rambled on about successors. When stopped by a red light at Broad and High streets, Dunlap managed a question.

"Mr. Lincoln, are you trying to suggest or tell me that you would like me to get the board in condition to accept Mr. Culbreth as your successor?"

"No, sir! Let him get there himself, and what he's doing will keep him from it!" The reference was to Culbreth's open campaigning for the job.

Senior Vice President Bowman Doss firmly believed Lincoln wanted Culbreth to be president of the insurance companies and Louis E. Dolan to be president of Nationwide Corporation. As for Doss himself, becoming "chief executive officer of Nationwide ... never entered my mind," he said, and even if it had, he knew he would not have Lincoln's support.[4] Parenthetically, Doss never acquired the title of chief executive.

Future General Chairman and Chief Executive Officer John E. Fisher, administration manager of the Virginia regional office at the time of Lincoln's retirement, recalled that the board tired of the interoffice skirmishes. Not only did Culbreth believe he should have a shot at Lincoln's job, so did Senior Vice President of Insurance Operations Howard Hutchinson. A former washing machine salesman, he came up through the ranks primarily on the side of agency operations and often was allied with Doss, behind whom he stood organizationally in the line of succession. He was considered a capable executive, but he could not bear the thought of Culbreth at the helm and therefore battled him for it.

As a result of the many internal skirmishes, the board turned to Doss, a man who, Fisher said, "kept his hands clean during those days of contention." Some viewed Doss as a compromise candidate and, at the very least, a temporary respite from the devisiveness stirred up by Culbreth and Hutchinson.

Chairman Dunlap, who long had been friendly with Hutchinson, said of Doss's candidacy, "it did take some doing to encourage them that this was the best thing to do — not to make any issue on the matter of the presidency at this time. Somebody said in the (March 4, 1964) board meeting, 'If Mr. Lincoln will recommend him (Doss), then I'll vote for him.'"

Director Max M. Scarff, who chaired the search committee and who supported Doss, went down one flight to Lincoln's 7th floor office and brought him back up to the board meeting. "He feebly made such a statement," Dunlap said. "Not too strong, but he made it all right." Doss received the unanimous nomination for president and general manager of the insurance companies.

At the conclusion of the board meeting, Lincoln returned to the executive floor, walked haltingly into Doss's office, and sat down, almost in an exhausted heap. "The board says it's time for me to retire," Lincoln said, "and I told George (Dunlap) that I hoped he would treat you better than he had treated me."[5]

At the annual meeting of the companies April 2, the board elected Doss* president and named Lincoln president emeritus. "I hope my actions in this new role will speak louder than my words," the 56-year-old former school teacher from Waiteville, WV, told the board. In addition to the four insurance

---

* On his way home from the annual meeting, Doss was pulled over by a policeman for speeding along East Broad Street, Columbus. Doss tried to explain: "I'm sorry, officer, but I've just been elected president of the Nationwide Insurance Companies. I've had everything else on my mind but what I was doing." The policeman offered his congratulations and let Doss go without a ticket.

companies, Doss became president of 11 other Nationwide organizations* at the same time.

Lincoln had prepared a statement for the meeting but because of poor health, he could not deliver it. In it he said he felt it appropriate to say a few words inasmuch as "this kind of thing doesn't happen around here very often." Doss was only the fourth president in 38 years, following: Lee B. Palmer, 1925-1928; George L. Cooley, 1928-1939, and Lincoln, 1939-1964.

"Well, what years these ... have been! Excitement, crises, disappointments, opportunities missed and opportunities grabbed, fights of one kind or another, defeats, victories — I've enjoyed every bit of it. ... I can't begin to tell you the satisfaction I've had in watching and helping this institution grow in size, in influence, in scope, and to me most important, in purpose.

"... As much as we've done, really we've just begun. ... We've got to keep moving. ... We've got to do more to spread ownership and responsibility to individuals. ... It's concern for people that can lift Nationwide to ever greater heights of achievement and influence."

Lincoln's comments then turned to his successor. "Bowman Doss is a good man," the statement continued. "He's a good executive. ... He's become a genuine international cooperative leader, but most important of all, to me anyway, Bowman has a twinkle in his eye and that lets the humanity shine through."

Finally, he addressed the issue of his health, which he had not done previously.

"I'm fully aware that for some time rumors have been flying around on the grapevine, not just here in the building but

---

* Nationwide Development, Nationwide Mortgage, Nationwide Premium Accounts, American Enterprises, Heritage Securities, Approved Finance, Approved Consumer Discount, Approved Discount, General Credit, Nationwide Transport, and the Nationwide Foundation.

throughout the community, about what's wrong with me. ... I'm frank to tell you that until a month or so ago I didn't know for sure myself what was the matter, but now I know.

"What I have is Parkinson's disease. This is a progressive disease which affects muscles in the arms and legs and other parts of the body. This is why I've been shuffling instead of striding along. This is why my voice doesn't hold out very long at a time. This is why I may not look as if I'm responding to you when you talk to me.

"One thing that Parkinson's does not ordinarily do — and I find this extremely comforting — is to affect the mind. The doctor tells me I'm no crazier than I was 30 or 40 years ago. ... But I have one more piece of good news, which I've saved to the last. It's possible for surgery to arrest the progress of Parkinson's disease," a procedure which he announced he would undergo at St. Barnabas Hospital in New York in two weeks. When he returned to Columbus, Lincoln concluded, "I still feel I'll be able to fill the job of vice president in charge of revolution!"[6]

Doss had his own revolution in mind. After he had sat on the sidelines as a noncombatant for nearly a decade, few expected the gentlemanly West Virginian to emerge victorious. "Faith and determination will win," he would say.

On March 4, the day Lincoln told Doss he would be elected president at the April 2 annual meeting, Doss fired those who had made his life so difficult. His prime targets were Culbreth, senior vice president of human relations, and two of Culbreth's underlings, Kytle and Forest R. Lombaer, vice president of personnel. Their resignations were accepted at the annual meeting, at which time the board eliminated six other vice presidential positions, including the one previously held by Doss.

The headline in the morning Columbus newspaper read, "Major Shakeup at Nationwide – Drop Eight Veeps, Three

Quit Company."* The election of Doss received mention in the fifth paragraph.[7] The *Wall Street Journal* didn't report the news until three days later, adding little to the story.

Despite the considerable number who offered their congratulations as well as consoling words, the thought of retirement devastated Lincoln. After the April 2 board meeting, he went home to his suburban horse and cattle farm, "Linhurst," and to his wife, Anne, also afflicted with Parkinson's disease. There Dolan found the president emeritus, sitting alone on the porch swing in the twilight, pad and pencil in hand.

Tears welled in his eyes as he struggled to speak of the events of the day. Because of his affliction and emotional state, the words did not come easily. When he could not utter the words, he wrote them on his pad.

"I will never again set foot in that building," Lincoln said, so deep was his hurt. He said Doss wanted him to collect his things and within 24 hours get out of the office he had, in effect, occupied since 1926. "I was asked not to return," Lincoln added, although he subsequently did as a director, but he had no office.[8]

Lincoln also reiterated his 1962 promise to designate Dolan as his successor as president of Nationwide Corporation. Its annual meeting was a week later, April 10, and it created yet another power struggle for Lincoln's job at the corporation.

Dunlap, Doss and Dolan were all considered in the running. Dunlap was board chairman but for many years coveted a senior staff position and a Nationwide paycheck as well as an office. He got the latter in 1962 after going to his friend, Dolan, with the request: "Get me an office." Dolan forgot about it until Dunlap returned a few weeks later.

---

* Louis V. Fabro, manager of media relations, personally carried the announcement to the newspaper with instructions to ask the editor "to make sure he didn't say there had been a shakeup at Nationwide." After seeing the headline the next day, Fabro said he "didn't know whether to go to work that day or stay home."

"When I ask you to do something," the chairman said in a very low, emotionless voice, "you don't have to do it, but if you are not going to do it, I wish you'd tell me."

"What are you talking about?" Dolan asked.

"I asked you to talk to Elmer Rule (corporate secretary) about getting me an office."

An embarrassed Dolan told Dunlap to sit tight while he visited with Rule. "Well," said Rule, "I know George is pretty powerful around here, and I guess I'd better find him one." He did, next to Ashley T. "Mack" McCarter's office, and Dunlap "just beamed," said Dolan.

With Lincoln's retirement, Dunlap spied his opportunity to secure a line position as president. Doss, who went on the corporation board upon his election as president of the insurance companies, said "several of the board members tried their best to get me to agree to be president of the corporation," in particular Scarff of New Carlisle, OH, and the North Carolinian Paul D. Grady. Although they campaigned hard to get Doss the votes, he professed to be not interested. "I didn't think it fit with what I wanted to do," he said.

Lincoln, meanwhile, wrote his letter to the board on behalf of Dolan, as promised. He did so in pencil on the back of a letter addressed to him from National Casualty Company. His secretary, Kathryn Gee, typed it up on corporation letterhead, dated it April 9, the day before the corporation's board meeting, and delivered it to Dunlap. It read:

"As perhaps my last official act as a member of this board and president of this corporation, I would like to nominate and recommend Louis Dolan as my successor as president.

"Since he has been in our employ I think he has amply demonstrated that he is eminently qualified for this position. He has youth, is aggressive, is a lawyer and, as several outsiders have remarked to me, he is an excellent negotiator in corporate matters.

"He has had extensive experience in the field of corporate

finance, and has won the respect of the people with whom we have contact. Therefore, I hope you will see fit to so elect him. (signed) Murray D. Lincoln, President."

There is no record that Dunlap ever presented Lincoln's recommendation to the board: Dolan believed Dunlap did not, so as not to mar the path to his own election.

After Dunlap's re-election as chairman and his appointment as acting president, the April 9 meeting recessed until April 28. "George advised me that the board had decided to proceed with a national search for a new president," Dolan said, "and that I definitely would be included among the prospects." The minutes of the meeting do not reflect such a decision.

By the time the meeting reconvened April 28, much arm-twisting had taken place. Doss' name surfaced, then was withdrawn. Harry E. Isham, retired vice president and treasurer of United States Steel Corporation and a director of Nationwide Corporation, approached Dunlap.

"Why don't you take the job?" he asked.

"There's no point in considering it," the chairman replied, believing he did not have sufficient votes. Yet, "the discussion kept on, and I was nominated anyhow and elected without any negative votes. I'm not saying that all members present voted for me ... but I was elected without negative votes."

Dunlap became the corporation's president "for the ensuing year or until his successor is duly elected and qualified." The board gave Dunlap an annual salary of $40,000, and elected Dolan executive vice president and general manager at $50,000 a year.[9] Despite his $10,000 raise and new title, Dolan was "devastated. ... I'm sure it showed through." It also was clear to him that the search was over and that "I was going to have to continue, in effect, doing the work" of the president's office.

Lincoln did not attend either meeting. He flew to New York and checked into St. Barnabas Hospital. Four days after his 72nd birthday, he underwent radical brain surgery April 22.

Dr. Irving S. Cooper, director of the hospital's department of neurosurgery, headed the international team of physicians from Argentina, Japan and the Netherlands. They performed a new surgical technique called cryosurgery, using an extremely cold probe to kill diseased tissue in the brain. Two weeks later the hospital discharged Lincoln, who then treated 23 of his doctors and nurses to a trip to Washington, DC, in appreciation for the care he had received.

With the return of Lincoln to Columbus, where he convalesced on his farm, bouts with apprehension struck Doss. " I knew that I was following a great man … the board and the people all knew that." Later that year, when Lincoln began to regularly attend board meetings again, Doss felt that his predecessor always was looking over his shoulder.

Chris Renzella, a member of the building maintenance staff, pushed Lincoln to the boardroom in a wheelchair. It was, as Rennie described the scene, "pretty tragic" because the president emeritus could neither talk nor control his physical functions. He would sit off to one side, with staff, and pass notes from time to time. When he needed a drink, McCarter or one of the other senior staffers would support the cup to Lincoln's lips.

Doss embraced the Nationwide philosophy and, to a large degree, Lincoln's personal cooperative philosophy, too. At a regional sales meeting at Cedar Point, OH, in the summer of 1964, Doss was introduced by regional sales superintendent Chester C. "Chet" Gay as "a guy we've known and loved for years, and now he's in charge." With Doss as president, "we can forget all this cooperative stuff," Gay said, winning a warm round of applause from his audience.

Doss responded. "Now, my friend, Chet, has just said that this now is the beginning of an era when we are going to forget all that cooperative stuff. I want you to know that you could not be more wrong, and that this institution is totally dedicated to the philosophy of Murray Lincoln and others who have gone before us and built this company ... and, by God, we're going to continue to operate under that kind of direction."[10] J. Richard "Dick" Bull, administrative assistant to Doss, said the group "was a little stunned."

Lincoln would praise Doss for his work in the national and international cooperative movement,* but Doss had to concentrate on the insurance operations after he became president. He and others knew the severity of Nationwide's casualty underwriting problems that began in 1962, but Rennie said "Lincoln couldn't have cared less. He wanted somebody to carry on his effort to advance the world cooperative revolution and spend 90 percent of his time on it, as he did. Bowman didn't do that."

There were times, Doss said, that Lincoln "could have treated me a little better," even after he became president. Lincoln continued to dictate letters and memos to management and to directors, often undermining Doss' position. Doss recalled one such missive in particular.

"He sent one letter addressed to the board saying that the board made a mistake in selecting me as president. He sent that to me and asked *me* to distribute it to the board. ... Well, I did it (but) it was not nice at all. He could have done much better than that."

All through 1964 and 1965 the thoughts of Murray Lincoln flowed out in written form, just as if he never left the president's office. In the summer of 1965, for example, his rambling message to the board of the Nationwide Insurance Companies began:

"So far as I can remember, I have never before missed two consecutive board meetings in the 40 years I have been

---

* Doss served as a director and chairman of the Cooperative League of the U.S.A., a member of the executive and central committees of the International Cooperative Alliance and as chairman of the executive unit of the Insurance Committee of the Alliance.

associated with the institution. It is very aggravating to put up with these physical handicaps, but I'm trying to remember and be grateful for the fact I have lived 73 years without a major illness. Therefore, I would again admonish you all to take care of your health and keep your insurance paid up."[11]

Despite his infirmities, Lincoln still flitted about the country, often accompanied by Renzella to push the wheelchair. As 1965 dwindled down, though, Lincoln's ability to attend meetings, travel and write lengthy missives dwindled, also. Curiously, in one of his last messages to the directors of the insurance companies October 18, 1965, he reported that his doctor said "I was 100 percent improved from when I left the hospital." He was to have a cataract operation that month . . . to "clear up the eye situation; then I can concentrate on improving my speech."

It never improved, nor did his general health. It steadily deteriorated, requiring him and Mrs. Lincoln to have full-time nursing care at their Gahanna home. He left his farmhouse for the last time November 3, 1966, entering Grant Hospital, Columbus, for treatment of pneumonia. He died November 7 at the age of 74.

At Nationwide's headquarters flags flew at half-staff. The home, regional and district offices closed November 11, the day of the funeral at First Community Church on Cambridge Boulevard. The church's former minister, Dr. Otis Maxfield, conducted the service, and Doss, Dunlap and Scarff were pallbearers alongside Richard G. Chilcott, vice president, public relations; P. Lee Thornbury, retired senior vice president and general counsel, and Herbert E. Evans, retired president and general manager of Peoples Broadcasting Corporation.

Lincoln lies buried at Blendon Central Cemetery in the Columbus suburb of Blendon Township.* A single headstone

---

* At the time of Lincoln's death, the cemetery was in the community of Central College. The community no longer exists, having been annexed in 1988 by the city of Westerville, OH.

marks his grave and the graves of his daughter, Betty, and his wife, Anne, who died in 1970.

On the occasion of the 100th anniversary of Lincoln's birth in 1892, Fisher, who retired in 1994 as general chairman of the Nationwide Insurance Enterprise, described Lincoln as "a unique visionary, and he used that power in service to his fellow man."

12

TWO CHANGES OF THE GUARD

Bowman Doss inherited much more than a title when he stepped into Murray D. Lincoln's shoes as president and general manager of the four Nationwide Insurance Companies in 1964. The enterprise that began 38 years earlier with three employees and a $10,000 loan now counted more than 7,200 employees (2,500 in Columbus), 6,700 agents, 4 million policies in force and admitted assets of nearly $600 million.

Doss also took on some major problems, not the least of which were 1963's operating losses, the largest ever for property and casualty operations. While the life company produced substantial gains, both Nationwide Mutual and Nationwide Mutual Fire struggled mightily.* Lincoln, in an article for the employee magazine, *Nationwide World,* in the spring of 1964, referred to getting "our companies into the black, and (building) a sound financial operation as the basis for our broad social purposes" as "unfinished business" for the enterprise.

---

* In 1963 Nationwide Mutual's operating loss was $19.9 million. The operating loss at Nationwide Mutual Fire was $1 million. Nationwide Life recorded an after-tax profit of $3 million.

An internal memorandum summarized the "unfinished business" at hand. It noted that "a trend of worsening claims experience developed in 1962 and operating gain dropped to a very modest $400 thousand in that year from $5.5 million and $7.1 million in 1960 and 1961, respectively." Premium income in 1963 was up 13 percent over the previous year, but the summary report stated that "unfortunately, not all of this growth was of good quality." Good quality means low risk, and therefore less likelihood of claims.

The rapid expansion of Nationwide into 17 new states and Puerto Rico during the previous five years created new dilemmas. At the end of 1962, no new state was in the black; "each of these areas is a major problem," a staff report said. In 1963 all further expansion was put on hold until the situation improved.[1]

The entire industry, which reported significant increases in automobile accident claims and fire losses in 1963, had its difficulties, too, but "Nationwide appeared to be hit particularly hard," according to the memorandum prepared by the company's director of budgets, Ted Collum.

Besides incurring adverse claims experience, the company received a new directive from the Ohio Department of Insurance that seriously affected Nationwide Mutual's surplus. The directive required the company "to adopt a much more conservative method of valuing" its investments in affiliated companies. Consequently, Nationwide Mutual's surplus fell more than a third, to $59.2 million, lowest it had been since 1958.

There was much finger pointing to blame others for Nationwide's troubles, and Doss was the lead-off hitter. In a confidential memorandum to the board, all vice presidents and the regional managers, Doss ripped into what he perceived to be the rapid, but ill-timed and ill-conceived, expansion; increased claims costs; insufficient attention to functional standards, such as an adequately trained agency force; an outdated rating plan; a lack of customer awareness, and on and on for 19 pages.[2] Many of these complaints originated in the field, where managers and agents alike were unhappy and confused by these and other issues, such as the processing delays, mixed sales signals and a perceived lack of support from headquarters.

Doss concluded, however, that "probably the greatest underlying cause of the problems now confronting our companies is the failure of top people to give direction and to provide the leadership that is expected of them."

Clearly here was a denunciation aimed at Lincoln, the man who put Doss on the shelf for nearly 10 years. The rebuke came just six months after the 71-year-old leader retired. Doss appeared determined to prove Lincoln had been wrong about him. He set sail on his own course, tossing overboard much old baggage in the process.

"The companies have just come through an extended period of interoffice tensions," Doss continued in his memorandum. "This was a transitional period of several years in which top management watched and waited with great uncertainty, and even apprehension, for a great and much admired leader to step down and a successor to be chosen.

"It was a period that permitted — perhaps even caused — a struggle to fill a leadership vacuum, a struggle that bred jealously, scapegoatism, and unhealthy rivalry and led to a weakening of the whole corporate structure.

"It was a period that led to unresolved conflicts, postponed and unmade decisions, hazy objectives, poor communications, ineffective motivation, unrealistic growth, ragged teamwork, hesitancy, confusion, incompetence, and a steady, general deterioration in morale ... in efficiency ... and in productivity."

Doss proposed new, vigorous leadership to right the wrongs, heal the wounds and cure the ills. "But let's not make the mistake of just trying to repair the old model," he said. "We must go to work on a new model. Let's turn this thing around and build a New Nationwide."

The directors accepted his report with "a unanimous expression of satisfaction," Doss told staff. Despite the stormy business conditions, as previously noted, he said "the climate has seldom been so favorable for us to achieve united solutions to our problems."[3]

Among his first tasks, Doss believed, was to improve morale, "to rally the personnel. I took over the DC3 that Mr. Lincoln had used and I flew from region to region," giving speeches and shaking hands.[7] In the field, Doss was in friendly territory, much more so than at the home office. Having come up through sales, he understood the role of the agent and, although somewhat autocratic, was a good motivator in that arena.

Old-timers in the agency force often tell the story of the speech Doss made to the Leaders' Conference in November 1953, and Doss himself repeated it on a number of occasions. He was executive vice president at the time of the New Orleans meeting, held to honor the top producing agents, who were entertained at the company's expense.

Frustrated by the company's poor performance at the time, specifically the bad loss ratios, Doss launched an attack on 11 agents present (whom he did not name), each of whom had cumulative loss ratios of more than 65 percent. The loss ratio of one agent from the New York City area was a whopping 81 percent over a three-year period.* That meant it cost the company 81 cents in claims and claims expenses for every dollar of insurance he sold.

"Now it looks to me like it all adds up to the fact that we are

---

* The loss ratio is usually determined by dividing the losses, or claims, by the earned premium. (Each day a policy is in force represents a day of earned premium.) For example, $400 of incurred losses, divided by $1,000 of earned premium equals a loss ratio of 40 percent, which is a very acceptable figure.

paying these agents big money to lose the company big money," Doss told the group. "Oh, you didn't think I would ever get around to doing this, but let me say that one might kindly raise the question, 'Why is the company paying out more money to bring such individuals to a meeting like this?' Now, that's pretty rough medicine, isn't it?"

Doss said the company wanted a loss ratio "that is not too high or too low; it is not right in either extreme. ... This is going to require the attention of everyone. I don't think you ought to put your backs up too much and think that all fingers are being pointed at you. Get your house in order, and we'll take care of others."

"Taking care of others" included canceling 54 agents in the first nine months of 1953 and placing 132 more on probation. Others, he said, "have not cooperated. Some of us have sat up night and day to try to get them to cooperate, and I am down here to tell you that it's going to be corrected!"[4]

Earl F. Peitz, retired senior vice president, recalled, "It was the first time anybody ever jerked the agency force up like that and said you've got a responsibility for more than just production; you've got a responsibility for profit, too."

In the audience that day was Paul R. Ashbrook, twice Agent of the Year and a perennial member of the President's Club (the successor to the Leaders' Conference) as one of Nationwide's top agents for 38 years. He recalled "the tremendous ovation" Doss received after his talk, but said it also illustrated the constant pull-push between the home office and the agency force. The company would want more sales, "and the agents would say, 'What? Get *more* business?' And we'd go and do that, but then they'd say, 'Well, now we've got too much business because we're losing money.' So, we have to start throwing people (customers) out," Ashbrook said.

Bob Pierce, of Annandale, VA, agreed. He joined Nationwide as an agent in 1966. "What always struck me is that it seemed like we were always vacillating, jumping from one point to the other. ... Nobody knew what was going on."

There was one person at least who always seemed to know what was going on and used it to his advantage, namely George H. Dunlap. The farmer from Cadiz, OH, wielded considerable power as board chairman of the Nationwide Mutual Insurance Company and as president of Nationwide Corporation, a position he had gained by outmaneuvering his competition, including Doss. The only real "threat" to Dunlap's power at the corporation was his aggressive executive vice president, Louis E. Dolan.

Dunlap, an astute executive with a prodigious memory for details, knew little about the running of a public company, in Dolan's opinion. "George was just over his head in many of these corporation matters, finance matters, because he just never had any occasion to be exposed to them." In the corporation's 1964 annual report, both men signed the message to shareholders and appeared together in a photograph. In the report the following year, Dunlap stood alone: Dolan was gone.

Several issues of contention contributed to Dolan's forced resignation September 20, 1965, all concerning the struggle for control of the corporation. Many believed, for instance, that a *Forbes* article less than five months after the election of Dunlap as president led to Dolan's downfall. It referred to Dolan as "successor-apparent" to Lincoln and as the only one of more than 40 Nationwide vice presidents "remotely equipped" to serve as president of the corporation. Then it quoted an unnamed Nationwider as saying, "When Lou Dolan is elected president during the next year or so, it'll be only a formality. He's already doing the job."

Forbes also referenced Dolan's "longer-range plans" and "his insurance companies," concluding that "considering what he has done in four short months, Nationwide should be quite a combination when Dolan gets through with it."[5]

Such was the concern for the tone of the article that Nationwide's public relations department issued a memorandum to all vice presidents, noting: "As in most articles of this kind, the writer and his editors are free to make their own interpretations about personalities."[6]

However, a year went by before Dunlap terminated Dolan's employment. It came on the heels of a luncheon talk Dolan gave to representatives of the San Francisco investment community June 16, 1965. In his speech he mentioned the "professional study"[7] underway to consider a merger of West Coast Life Insurance Company, a San Francisco institution acquired in 1964, and Northern Life Insurance Company of Seattle, acquired a year earlier. This is what Dolan hoped would happen. "There was a great overlap of territory and considerable opportunity for cost reduction," he maintained.

Dunlap felt Dolan stepped beyond the bounds of his authority. At a private luncheon in Columbus, Dunlap reamed out his executive vice president. "He came down awfully hard on me," Dolan recalled painfully. "Whew. He just got on his stiff lip and said, 'I don't want that happening again.' To the best of my knowledge, that was the only thing that ever came between us."

Three months later, and at Dunlap's urging, the Nationwide Corporation board voted September 17 to terminate Dolan, effective three days later.

Dunlap's innate ability to maneuver boards was a skill Doss never acquired. "It seemed that almost from the beginning of Doss' presidency his board relations were strained," recalled John E. Fisher, whose view of the top was from his position as director of policyholder relations in the home office. "He wanted to assert himself in Nationwide Corporation, where it appeared to me there already was some stress between the inside directors and outside directors. My observation was that Mr. Doss ... was losing ground with the board members."

There appears to be little doubt that Doss got off on the wrong foot with Dunlap and some directors by announcing to the board at his first meeting as head of the insurance companies, "Now that I'm elected president, I'm going to run the companies."* As Fisher said, Doss was not always the most diplomatic executive.

This was the first indication that Doss either cared little for the board-management relationship or really didn't understand it. Frank B. Sollars, a former president of the Ohio Farm Bureau, joined the Nationwide Insurance Companies boards in 1968 and immediately ran into difficulty with the president. As a new board member, Sollars also had difficulty understanding many of the more technical reports — and suspected some of his fellow directors did, too.

"John, why don't we do an indoctrination or a training program for board members, especially the new ones?" Sollars asked Fisher. "This is a pretty important position to have and a lot of responsibility." At the time, the boards of the Nationwide Insurance Companies governed a billion-dollar business.

"That's a great idea," Fisher replied, "but I'm going to have to take it to Chilcott because he's my boss, and Chilcott will have to go to Bowman." Richard G. Chilcott was vice president of public relations to whom Fisher reported.

Chilcott did not receive an enthusiastic response from Doss, "but we decided to go ahead, whether Bowman thought it was a good idea or not," Sollars recalled. Not long after he was summoned to Doss' office.

"I understand what you are doing, and you should have cleared this with me first," Doss told Sollars.

The hair on Sollars' nape stood up. The rugged Washington Court House farmer had heard enough.

---

* Retired Vice President Roberrt M. Culp, who attended the meeting, called the challenging remark "a fatal error. ... I can remember saying to myself, the end has already begun."

"Now, Mr. Doss, you work for me; I don't work for you. I'll be glad to bring this up in a board meeting if you want, but this is going to really embarrass you if we do. We are going to go ahead with this." And he walked out.

It is true over the years some directors struggled with understanding the complexities of a multi-billion-dollar enterprise; they are the first to admit it.* It also is true that some outsiders look upon the Nationwide boards with derision because most of the directors are farmers, not pinstriped corporate moguls.

Fisher "pondered over the years why a farm-based board could be so successful in this business." He concluded selling insurance and farming were not that different. For example, farmers face the problem of overcapacity and underpricing just as in the insurance industry. "One reason we have a price war is overcapacity and that leads to underpricing. Farmers have overcapacity in their farm commodities, (and) they are almost always underpriced."

Both the insurance industry and farmers know how to cope with countless natural disasters — floods, droughts, tornadoes, blizzards. "They tend to know you can live through things like that and survive." Also, farmers "are great at coping with regulations" that govern how, when and what crops to plant as well as the price to be paid for them. "So, they really come out of a fairly heavily regulated business," as does insurance.

Perhaps most important, though, is that farmers have a strong work ethic and "the capacity to live on lack of expense," Fisher said. As a result, "they have helped keep the company expense conscious."

---

* For about 20 years beginning in the early 1970s, the responsibility for bringing new board members up to speed fell to Patrick L. Doyle, vice president, office of the president. "It's a very complex company," he said. "It takes a board member three years to start to understand what it's all about. I've been here since 1951, and I don't know what it's all about!" He retired in 1994.

These were things Fisher came to appreciate in the years after he returned to the home office in 1966. It was Chilcott who reached out to the Virginia regional office for Fisher to head up policyholder and sponsor relations, primarily because of a report Fisher wrote critical of Nationwide's public relations efforts. "In effect, I said we don't have a public relations program," Fisher recalled writing.

Once back at the home office, he wondered whether a job really existed for him inasmuch as Chilcott persuaded Doss to downsize what was known as the Advisory Committee of Policyholders. Lincoln encouraged the establishment of the committee in 1952, inviting elected regional committee members to meet in Columbus once a year to voice their concerns regarding products and services. "We gave this plan a good hard try for 14 years, but it didn't quite click," Doss said.[8] The committee disbanded in 1966, a victim of the cutbacks forced by the underwriting losses.

About the time the Advisory Committee was on its last legs, Fisher also learned that the contracts of two sponsors had been terminated, thus giving him even less responsibility. He became quite concerned about his future at Nationwide. "Taking the job in public relations looked like a dead end," he said.

Fisher often would tell how his wife, Eloise, thought his whole career developed through a series of "dead-end jobs," the first of which was as office services manager in the Annapolis, MD, regional office. Another came upon his initial return to Columbus in 1956 to work on field office matters. He taught work simplification, created work measurement forms and devised a new suggestion program, known as the Improved Methods Plan. "Some used to say I was the simp behind the IMP."

"For the first six months I nearly lost my mind," what with very little to do. Considerable home office turmoil surrounded him, a fallout from the aborted reorganization plan a year earlier

The 1929 board: (left to right) A. F. Moon, David M. Odaffer, W. W. Barnsworth, Perry L. Green, George L. Cooley, Murray D. Lincoln, O. J. Bailey, Lee B. Palmer and Harry C. Fast.

"Father of the Farm Bureau," "Uncle" George L. Cooley.

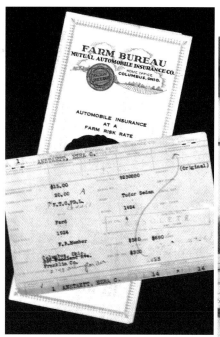

First Farm Bureau Mutual automobile policy was issued April 14, 1926, to Ezra C. Anstaett (seated). Murray D. Lincoln (right) and Lee B. Palmer witness the signature.

Ohio farmers welcomed the lower rates for automobile insurance.

Early Columbus headquarters included the Southern Hotel (top) and 620 E. Broad Street.

At the first annual meeting in 1927, the leadership sat for this portrait. Left to right are: Ezra C. Anstaett, Lee B. Palmer, Murray D. Lincoln, O. J. Bailey and David M. Odaffer.

Commission and Record Department, 1929.

Early pioneers posed on the steps of the Ohio Statehouse for this group photo at the 1928 annual meeting.

"Fair, Frank, Firm and Friendly"
service was a hallmark of the new
company.

The "246 N. High Street" headquarters in 1937.

Correspondents dictated letters to agents and policyholders in 1938.

In 1951, the "246 Building" was renovated inside and out.

WRFD, located between Columbus and Delaware, Ohio, was the companies' first venture into broadcasting. Below is the "modern" transmitter room in 1951.

Murray D. Lincoln enjoys a laugh at the company's Activities Association "What's My Line?" show. John E. Fisher, right, sits next to Lincoln.

Nationwide fought early and often for seat belt laws.

Charles W. Leftwich goes on TV to announce the name change to Nationwide.

Name change broadcast went to closed-circuit TV sites throughout the nation, including the Palace and Broad theatres in Columbus.

Dean W. Jeffers (left) and George H. Dunlap.

President Bowman Doss (second from left) signs Neckura agreement July 15, 1964, with Joseph and Peter Neckermann (right) and attorney Rolf Albern.

John E. Fisher speaks at 1974 ground-breaking ceremonies for One Nationwide Plaza.

One Nationwide Plaza was built across the street from the 246 Building (lower right), providing the anchor for the revitalization of the north end of downtown Columbus.

Nearly 500 feet tall, One Nationwide Plaza was dedicated in 1978.

Civic Action Program employee volunteers have brought political candidates, including President Jimmy Carter in 1980, to Nationwide Plaza.

Home Office employees achieved $1 million in contributions to United Way for the first time in 1985. Pictured with the plaque commemorating the event are Paul A. Donald and John E. Fisher.

The John E. Fisher Nationwide Training Center.

John E. Fisher greets Wausau Insurance employees during that company's 75th anniversary.

Employees have fun while supporting a community food drive called Operation Feed.

Nationwide executives visit a Florida policyholder in the aftermath of Hurricane Andrew in 1992.

D. Richard McFerson introduces the Enterprise Vision at a management meeting.

that resulted in the demotion of Doss. "I began to look elsewhere," for a job outside Nationwide, Fisher admitted.

E.S. "Stan" Jones, the office manager and assistant secretary, invited the unhappy 27-year-old into his office for a chat. "To go into his office would be like making a visit to see God," said Fisher, who described Jones as somewhat of "an elitist" among the home office staff.

"Look, you think you've been hurt," Jones began in a kindly manner. "You shouldn't be concerned. If you make up your mind to stay here for six months more, you'll be satisfied that you've made the right decision."

"There I was, sitting in a job where nothing that I did could go anywhere, so I became the educational director of the Franklin County Mental Health Association," and thus launched some 40 years of community and social service. He also used his excess time to join the local chapter of the Toastmasters organization to improve his skills as a public speaker, for which he became well-known.

Doss failed to implement a significant turnaround for the insurance companies under his first year of leadership, but "I am encouraged," he said. "We were one of the first in the auto insurance business to get clobbered by the upturn in accidents. There are signs this year (1965) that we may be one of the first to recover."[9]

The casualty and fire insurance companies had a combined operating loss of $19.2 million in 1964, only $700,000 less than the record loss the previous year. Even after investment income, which partially offset the deficit, the net operating loss was $8.9 million. Nationwide Life, on the other hand, concluded its best year with record sales and a net operating profit of $2.9 million.

What the Ohio Department of Insurance took away from Nationwide Mutual's surplus as a result of its directive the year before, it all but returned in 1964. It approved the auto company's request to value its holdings of Nationwide Corporation Class B stock at market value, the same as the publicly traded Class A stock. After all was said and done in the reevaluation, the surplus of Nationwide Mutual increased $44.6 million to $103.7 million by year-end.

Falling back on his original theme, Doss told the insurance boards in the fall of 1965, "Yesterday's mistakes are a part of today's problems, and these must be solved first; these have priority."[10] As for reducing the losses, he said "appropriate steps" had been taken, such as increasing rates, reducing operating costs and becoming more selective in the people the companies insured. About 80 percent of the deficit from the auto company, Nationwide Mutual, was the result of "more accidents, greater property damage, more injuries and deaths, and constantly rising costs of everything that goes into the repair of bodies — vehicular or human," Doss said.[11]

He instituted the Automobile Insurance Committee not only to improve profitability in that area of insurance but also to work for the passage of safety legislation, such as seat belt laws, stronger licensing programs and better traffic law enforcement. Nationwide long has been an industry-leading advocate of these and other issues pertaining to automobile safety.

Although still far from acceptable, the operating loss dropped to $9 million in 1965. Doss said the only consolation from the successive years of losses "is that not many companies can stand losses like that and still be solvent."[12] By the end of the following year, Nationwide Mutual recorded its first operating gain in four years — $196,000. After two years of decline, the number of Nationwide Mutual policies in force increased 10 percent in 1966 and premium income, stagnant for the same period, rose 6.5 percent. Then, for the first time since 1962, the auto company posted both an operating gain and a surplus increase in 1967.

"We're turning red ink into black," Doss said, but some 20

years later he admitted "the seriousness of the situation. It was more serious than you knew — and I knew it."

In the mid-1960s another key indicator, namely losses or benefits paid, also increased as a result of what Fisher described as Doss' "ill-advised expansion plan that brought in a lot of business — not profitable business — that soon got us into difficulty." For four years, beginning in 1966, the losses either matched or surpassed the increases in premium income.

"Bowman knew that he wanted to double the size of the company," said Robert M. Culp, reinsurance director in the mid-1960s, "but he wanted to do it the way sales agents always want to do it, and that is with less stringent underwriting rules, a lower price and, on the agent's part, a higher commission."

The year of the 40th anniversary of the founding of the insurance enterprise, Doss launched his ambitious "New Nationwide" program at the first Combined Management Conference October 28, 1966. It marked the beginning of the end of decentralization, the plan instituted in the 1950s by Lincoln.

"I hope no one jumps to the conclusion that the 'New Nationwide' means that the old Nationwide is dead; It is most emphatically alive," Doss said in a two-hour address after several hundred managers dined on prime rib and broiled whitefish in the home office cafeteria. "These are the same people-oriented companies with the same democratic and cooperative beliefs, principles and objectives that have helped us become one of the most unusual, most respected and most influential insurance organizations in the world."[13]

A concerted effort to improve Nationwide's agency force through more effective recruiting, better training and incentive compensation was a key element of the plan. "In order to attract good prospective agents, we must be competitive with the practices of other companies," Dean W. Jeffers, then vice president of marketing, said.

At the second Combined Management Conference January 28, 1968, Doss told the managers, "We are going all out on one of the boldest, most daring, most ambitious campaigns in our history. We are going to double our policies in force in five years and at the same time reduce our expense ratio by several points. We're setting out to make insurance history. We're blasting off on a new era of Nationwide growth, services and profit."

Such was the enthusiasm generated by drums and brass at the closing night banquet that "the whole room was swinging and rocking," reported Bob Krause in the employee newspaper, *The Dividend*, with "Nationwiders swaying, clapping, singing. People who don't even smile all year were seen laughing."[14]

The "year of the great Nationwide leap" began in August 1968 with the introduction of the "Superstep" plan, developed over 18 months by the Corporate Planning Group chaired by Dr. Robert A. Rennie, at the time vice president of planning, finance and systems. Doss said it "excited me more than any piece of business news I've heard or read about in a long time. ... All of us are standing on the threshold of something big ... "

The purpose of Superstep was to "catch up with the leading companies in the insurance business today," namely chief rival State Farm, said Rennie. He described Superstep as "a big, ambitious move," which included expansion of business insurance operations by combining property and casualty with group insurance.

"More and more businessmen are demanding ... adequate and complete insurance protection along with such related services as safety and engineering," Rennie said. The Nationwide agency force was told it could elect to handle either business or family insurance or sell in both markets. The agents also had a choice of becoming a Nationwide employee or remaining an independent contractor. Superstep also attempted to make

Nationwide less dependent on automobile insurance.

Doss revamped his management, effective January 1, 1969, to accommodate the New Nationwide operations under two umbrellas — family insurance and business insurance. Ashley T. McCarter became vice president, business insurance; Chilcott became vice president, family insurance, and Fisher succeeded him as vice president, public relations, reporting to Doss.

"I was asked by Bowman to take over the responsibility of implementing the new plan," recalled Jeffers. "He ended up our conversation by saying, 'I don't know what we ought to call you. Oh, sure: vice president of implementation.'"

"Let's not do that," Jeffers pleaded, but that's what he became. He concluded that "Bowman was doing it for orneryness more than anything else." When Jeffers succeeded Doss as president, "and I *really* had the responsibilities of implementation at that time ... I changed the name so fast it wasn't even funny."

In Fisher's opinion the all-out expansion program Doss mapped out "was really the seed, the real reason why Bowman was asked to step down as president." As Doss turned to a high-powered growth effort to unlock Nationwide's future, he failed "to control it with some very disciplined risk selection practices and pricing," Fisher said, which got the company into difficulty. As a result, Doss began to lose favor with the directors. He and Chairman Dunlap grew further and further apart as each tried to exert power over the other.

Management found itself caught in the middle, "trying to figure out who's running the show and wasting too much time figuring out where their loyalties should go. That can tear a company apart," said J. Richard "Dick" Bull, vice president and assistant to the president throughout the five years Doss held the presidency.

Outwardly Doss and Dunlap were cordial to each other, until the spring of 1969 when at board meetings it would get "ugly" between them, according to one observer. Each suspected the other of undermining his position. For example, Senior Vice President Charles W. Leftwich spoke to the board in favor of an issue Doss also supported. Dunlap cut him short, accusing Leftwich of taking sides. The highly respected senior executive, who had been with the company since 1927 — longer than anyone present — was deeply hurt. He eloquently defended his position and strongly took offense to the suggestion that he favored any individual.

According to Bull, both Dunlap and Doss perceived plots lurked in every conversation. If Doss spied Dunlap and Jeffers together, it had to be to his detriment, he thought. At the same time, when Doss invited a group of board members to join him for a few days at The Beach Club, a Nationwide-owned hotel property in Fort Lauderdale, FL, Dunlap suspected skullduggery was afoot.

What really was afoot was a plan to force the "retirement" of Doss. The board's unhappiness with the president began with the constant bickering with Dunlap, according to Sollars, who also felt Doss "didn't have the horsepower" to run the insurance companies. Beyond that, however, "the number one thing that he did that really kicked me over to make the decision was Doss' plan to 'drastically' increase premium income ... and take in way more risk than we could afford. ... He wanted to pass State Farm."[15]

Dunlap lined up several board members — Sollars, Carl H. Stitzlein, a Loudonville, OH, farmer, and Leslie E. Woodcock, of New York, among others — hired outside counsel and enlisted the aid of Edward F. Wagner, vice president of the Nationwide subsidiaries, who was a board confidant. Over several weeks they secretly put together their plan, which included another reorganization of management post-Doss.

The axe fell the afternoon of April 3, 1969. Doss completed his report to the boards of the Nationwide Insurance Companies and was excused. As he left the boardroom to return to his 7th-floor office, Woodcock touched his arm. "I'd like to come down and see you in a few minutes," he quietly told the president. Doss felt "something was cooking."

About 10 minutes later he received a visit from Dunlap, Stitzlein and Woodcock. Stitzlein closed all the doors of the office, including the common one to Bull's office. At the time Bull thought that strange: Doss literally maintained an open door policy at all times.

"The board has decided you should resign because of the lack of harmony between you and the board," Woodcock began.

Doss stared at the delegation. "I have friends on the board," he thought to himself, "but I know Dunlap has over the years politicked enough support to oust me."

"I don't know if I will resign," the chief executive replied, fighting back anger.

"We have the votes," Dunlap said coldly. Doss knew it to be true, but that didn't make the words any softer to his ears. "They could fire me," he thought.

Doss did have an option, Woodcock explained: He could retire early and close out a 37-year insurance career with all his benefits intact. However, the board wanted an answer before the day was done.

"I will consult with Hallie (his wife of 34 years), and I'll let you know tonight," said Doss, rising from his chair.

"By eight o'clock?" asked Dunlap.

"I'll let you know tonight." A very small victory, Doss thought.[16]

After the board delegation left, he walked into Bull's office. "Dick, they just fired me," he said.

Bull was stunned, and "Bowman obviously was surprised. ... I think he was surprised as hell, after five years in office and relatively youngish. ... Both of us were in kind of a state of shock."

Doss left almost immediately for his home in Bexley, a

Columbus suburb, and for a tearful talk with his wife. By late afternoon they decided early retirement would be best, but, whether out of spite or not, Doss kept the board waiting for his decision until after 11 p.m. Even at that late hour it reconvened to vote on the management changes.

Besides serving as chairman and president of the Nationwide Corporation, Dunlap acquired the new and imposing title of general chairman and chief executive officer of the Nationwide Insurance Companies. Jeffers succeeded Doss as president and general manager, and Wagner was rewarded with a promotion to president of the Columbus-based subsidiaries.

According to Gordon E. McCutchan, executive vice president, law and corporate services, no job description existed for general chairman, so several days later "George and I sat down at the Columbus Club and wrote some big job description."

When Doss returned to the office the following day to pick up personal things, he wrote in his unpublished notes for his autobiography that he "found Jeffers' car in my (parking) place. Can you beat that, I said." Then, as Doss cleaned out his office, "Jeffers came in and sat at my desk." It upset Doss, as did the absence of his portrait in the board room alongside those of Lincoln and George L. Cooley. At Dunlap's direction, Doss' portrait was never painted, Sollars said.*

"All of us are going to miss Mister Doss," said Jeffers in *The Dividend.* "He gave us a new vision of Nationwide, and it will stand as a monument to him as we successfully implement it.

"I'm not naive enough to think this major change could be made without a ripple, but I do believe this institution is a bedrock for all of us, and it's founded on such principles that a ripple will simply wash us a little cleaner."[17]

---

*Doss died of cancer April 23, 1986. He was 78.

13

ON THE MOVE AGAIN

In the final year of the 1960s the nation watched in wonderment as an American astronaut took "one small step for man, one giant leap for mankind." Nearly 239,000 miles away, American GIs left their footprints on the war-ravaged landscape of Vietnam. In the skies above, jet fighters engaged in combat, unmoved by the introduction of the Boeing 747 and the era of commercial jet aviation. New York sports fans discovered dreams do come true: The Amazing Mets won their first pennant and World Series, and Jets quarterback Joe Namath delivered on his promise to whip the Baltimore Colts in Super Bowl III.

Over the next 13 years Dean W. Jeffers delivered on his promise of a better and greater Nationwide Insurance Enterprise, although he knew he was starting from a deep hole. The tough, ex-Marine corporal had been in tight spots before; on Iwo Jima during World War II, for instance, but this battle was different. It was against the negative numbers Nationwide Mutual and Nationwide Mutual Fire posted each year since 1963.

His predecessor, Bowman Doss, who also faced an uphill fight to reduce underwriting and operating losses when he became president in 1964, believed high volume sales would turn the deficits around. His solution was to woo customers through lower rates, but in doing so, the companies attracted a high-risk element that haunted the initial years of Jeffers' term.*

Shortly after becoming president, Jeffers told the sales force he was "totally dedicated to the New Nationwide program" unveiled by Doss. "I am convinced that our greatest years are immediately before us," the 52-year-old president said in a rousing address to the four multi-regional sales conventions in the spring of 1969. By the end of the following year, however, the New Nationwide plan all but disappeared from view, and the family and business insurance operations reunited into one office. "We're not going to talk about the New Nationwide anymore," Jeffers said softly.[1]

At the outset of his term, Jeffers realized he would need a top management team to reverse the sagging fiscal fortunes of the Nationwide Insurance Companies. However, those associated with Doss, and who remembered his house cleaning four years earlier, feared for their jobs. Perhaps no one was linked closer than J. Richard "Dick" Bull, assistant to the president under Doss as well as Murray D. Lincoln.

"I fully expected to be gone," Bull said. "I didn't know who was going to call me — Dean or George Dunlap," the newly elected general chairman and chief executive officer. The week following the departure of Doss, it was Dunlap who called, "and I thought, here it comes," Bull said. "Lay your head on that block."

He walked into Dunlap's office to find Jeffers sitting there,

---

* Nationwide Mutual produced an operating gain of just $115,000 in 1968, or $1.5 million below target. The life company again was the bright spot. It had its best year with a $6.5 million increase in premiums and a $371 million increase in insurance in force, bringing its total volume to nearly $4.3 billion.

too. All the color rushed from Bull's face, becoming "just as white as can be," Jeffers recalled.

The two senior executives tried to allay Bull's worst fears, apologizing for the sudden turn of events a few days earlier and telling him he still had a job at Nationwide if he wanted to stay. Jeffers then got to the point: "Dick, I would like for you to help me become a president." A much relieved Bull accepted immediately and served as vice president, assistant to the president, until 1970 when Jeffers gave Bull the job he really wanted, that of vice president, public relations.

Bull succeeded John E. Fisher, whom Dunlap tapped to serve as a vice president in his Office of General Chairman. Until then, "I never gave any thought to the possibility of serving as the president of anything," Fisher said. "There were those who thought that when I took the position in the office of the general chairman, I probably was becoming a lifetime assistant" and assuming yet another in a series of "dead-end jobs ... not likely to lead to a higher office."

However, Dunlap explained to Fisher that the position would be a learning experience, not just an assistant. To prove the point, he gave Fisher two assignments in the first week — one to study the possible merger of two subsidiaries, the other to help him evaluate several computer proposals for the life company.

Another key Jeffers appointment in his effort to turn the red ink into black was the naming of Dr. Robert A. Rennie as vice president, investments. "Dean told me, 'We're losing money on underwriting of insurance. Your job is to make enough money from our investments to offset the losses that we're suffering on the underwriting.'"

That was music to Rennie's ears, not only because he had a clear assignment after having drifted under Doss, but it was his opportunity to put the whole investment function on a professional plane.

"Up to that point, some members of the board had their pet hobbies, their pet subsidiaries, and they all wanted below-market rates of interest for communications, for development or something," Rennie said, practices that resulted in "some lively sessions" with Lincoln several years earlier.

"As an economist, I felt that the return on investment, the interest rate is the price of money, and you can't really know how well you're doing in the subsidiaries unless you charge them a market rate of interest. You're just concealing the losses you're suffering if you lend money from the insurance companies to the subsidiaries at below market rates of interest."

In the 12 years he had the responsibility for maximizing investment income, Rennie said he went "flat out." Never once did Jeffers try to influence the direction of the investments or to make unwarranted loans to cooperatives, subsidiaries or pet projects, Rennie said. As a result, net investment income jumped six-fold over the dozen years, from about $50 million to about $300 million annually. By the end of 1993 it totaled $2.3 billion annually.

The losses of the 1960s continued into 1970, "running well ahead of the heavy losses we experienced in 1969," Jeffers said, "and this trend must be reversed if we are to avoid severe financial problems." The rising number of automobile accidents and thefts significantly added to the cost of doing business, and threatened to exceed Nationwide Mutual's ability to handle the load. In September 1970, Jeffers ordered a moratorium on the writing of all new automobile policies except those generated by existing policyholders. The moratorium lasted six months, and then was lifted only to a limited degree.

"I don't care if a man could walk on water, we couldn't write his car insurance," said Robert Black, an agent in Broadway, VA, since 1956.

Unfortunately, some agents reacted irrationally, Fisher remembered. A Dayton, OH, agent told an applicant

Nationwide Mutual was not writing any more automobile insurance. Acting on a tip from the applicant, the *Dayton Daily News* ran a story to that effect and the news spread across the land, including in *The Wall Street Journal.* It took weeks for the story to fade away.

The *Challenger*, the monthly publication for the sales force, reported that "the company was heading for another severe setback similar to the $19 million loss experience in 1969," but as a result of the moratorium on "green," or new, business it only lost $3.7 million.[2] The ratio of written premiums to surplus was 3.3 to 1, still far too high but down two-tenths from 1969.

"We can't be satisfied with operating losses, even if they are less than we expected them to be," Jeffers told the board.

Fisher put the difficulties of the time in perspective. "I think sometimes people ... don't realize what a fragile business this is," he said shortly before his retirement as general chairman in 1994. "We deal with large numbers but if you get under-priced on large numbers or under-reserved on large numbers, you can create massive losses in short periods of time."

Throughout the industry concern for the rapid growth in automobile claims grew as more and bigger cars, as well as thieves, hit the road. According to the *Journal of American Insurance*, "auto insurers as a group had an underwriting loss of more than $660 million on auto insurance coverages" in 1970, and during the previous 10 years "the industry paid out $2 billion more in automobile claims and expenses than it has collected in premiums."[3]

Jeffers and his top executives attacked the problem on every possible front, often leading the industry in the assault. For example, in late 1969 Jeffers went to Washington to fight for improved traffic safety and for design changes that would result in safer vehicles. He also unveiled Nationwide Mutual's plan for a 50 percent rate hike on the so-called "muscle cars." In testimony October 8 that set the standard for the insurance industry, Jeffers told the U.S. Senate Antitrust and Monopoly Subcommittee that "superpowered cars are producing, on the average, 56 percent more losses than standard-powered cars" namely those with hundreds of horses under the hood and four-on-the-floor.

"It boils down to the fact that the amount of money paid for insurance on these cars has been insufficient to pay for losses they cause," Jeffers told the senators. "Nationwide is plainly sacrificing its competitive position ... because the company is going it alone with higher rates, but in this case, we feel competitive position is of secondary importance."[4]

Many other insurers adopted Nationwide's position, and in 1970 demand for new "muscle cars" dropped 50 percent. In addition, federal and state lawmakers introduced legislation to set standards for automobile design. Nationwide campaigned for safer, less fragile cars that "could bring substantial savings" to the industry and the policyholder.[5]

Although the Nationwide Insurance Companies paid out a record of nearly $1 million a day in claims and benefits in 1970, the enterprise improved its financial position, posting a combined underwriting loss of but $2.1 million. A year earlier the underwriting loss was $20 million. In the 1970 annual report, Dunlap and Jeffers attributed the improvement in part to the "muscle cars" campaign.

The effectiveness of such campaigns can be attributed largely to Jeffers and Fisher, both charismatic public speakers, and later to D. Richard McFerson, who succeeded Fisher as chief executive officer of the Nationwide Insurance Enterprise. They and dozens of other executives, past and present, worked tirelessly for highway safety. One of the major debates of the 1970s revolved around air bags and whether they should be mandated.

In the face of considerable opposition and lengthy debate,

Fisher undertook a media blitz in January 1973 to declare the air bags a totally reliable safety device that promised a significant reduction in crash casualties. A month later the company leased the first 36 of 1,000 Chevrolet Impalas equipped with air bags and assigned them to executives in various regions to demonstrate the life-saving value of the device. Today in Nationwide's fleet of several thousand vehicles, all have air bags.

Even though few automobiles had air bags as original equipment in 1975, Nationwide joined Allstate in launching the industry's first price discounts on first-party medical coverage to owners of cars so equipped to increase the demand.

"If there's ever a program that we know statistically that we have saved a specific number of lives, boy, that one is it," Fisher said. The air bag advocacy program is one of which he was most proud.

Other milestones in Nationwide's automobile safety program included:

- 1950 — First to offer discounts to policyholders who successfully complete a driver training course.
- 1963 — Pioneering steps to provide at no charge 50 percent more in medical benefits as an incentive to policyholders using seat belts.
- 1970s — A series of campaigns against roadside hazards, such as dangerously-placed guardrails, unguarded and immovable light poles, and hazardous roadside signage.
- 1972 — Advocacy of mandatory seat belt use laws, a lonely position widely condemned at the time, but today an international reality. In 1982 only 12 percent of the seat belts were used; 10 years later use jumped to 62 percent nationally. Also in 1972, Nationwide offers discounts for owners of cars whose bumpers prevent damage in 5-mph collisions, or double the industry standard.
- 1974 — First insurer to demand that hazardous roadside fixtures be replaced with safe equipment to qualify for

claims payments for damaged fixtures.

- 1983 — The doubling of the benefits introduced to policyholders in 1963 and the addition of $10,000 in death coverage, again to encourage seat belt use.
- 1986 — An expanded range of discounts for policyholders whose cars had air bags or automatic safety belts. Nationwide led the industry in this regard.

Jeffers, who loved to take the controls of the company's planes on business trips, had a habit of dropping into an office and department and then just wandering about, talking to employees. He usually shunned senior management on these visits because he wanted to *really* find out what was going on.

"Dean had just an inestimable amount of charisma," in the opinion of W. E. "Fitz" Fitzpatrick, who closely worked with Jeffers throughout his time as president and later general chairman. "I mean, he could walk into a room and even if you didn't know it, you'd see him come in and you'd figure, here's the boss.

"Dean would give you something to do and then unless you had a problem, he'd just forget about it. He expected it to be done, and you'd do it just because you didn't want to disappoint him."

Neither Jeffers nor Fisher remained in their elected positions for more than three years because of the retirement of Dunlap February 29, 1972. Despite having witnessed how long it took to get Lincoln to retire, Dunlap didn't want to pack it in at 65, either. The board agreed to a 12-month extension, after which Jeffers was elected general chairman and chief executive officer, Fisher succeeded Jeffers as president of the Nationwide Insurance Companies, and John L. Marakas, whom Dunlap had hired 14 months earlier as a vice president of Nationwide Corporation, was elected its president.

Retired Vice President Patrick L. Doyle believed "Dean and John started somewhat far apart. ... They had some sparks between them" initially, but "over time they became friends because Dean is a decent, good person and so is John."

The two senior executives were fortunate in that their promotions came as Nationwide, and the industry, came out of its long slump. The casualty company reported a record operating gain of $27.3 million in 1971 and the fire company posted a gain of $3.4 million. Jeffers was cautiously optimistic.

"You will remember that it was just three years earlier that the companies lost almost as much as they made in 1971, and that we have suffered operating losses in six of the last 10 years," he said. "Those are among the reasons we must continue to be watchful of expenses."[6]

One of the real problem areas both Jeffers and Fisher tackled in the mid-1970s was the New York metropolitan region, specifically New Jersey. Nationwide lost more than $35 million in the 25 years it did business there, but there were numerous efforts to save it. Eugene E. Sherer, who retired in 1983 as vice president, line operations administration, was among those dispatched to get it cleaned up.

Although Sherer felt he never had staff support from headquarters in Columbus, he devised a reorganization plan. "It was our last hope," so Jeffers approved it. "All he said was, 'Good luck.'" Sherer needed it, too, because he found New Jersey operations were "just rotten every place you looked": Rampant auto theft, fraud, kickbacks, high employee turnover resulting in poor productivity, and even personal threats. "The situation was so tense that I sent my wife back to Columbus" for her protection, Sherer said.

Although he found it to be "a very painful decision," Fisher felt it was time to pull out of New Jersey. Jeffers was reluctant to do so, "but one thing about Dean Jeffers was that when he agreed to back you on something, he did not backpedal," Fisher said. On October 13, 1977, Nationwide Mutual announced it would phase out New Jersey operations "because of chronic operating losses in that state and because there is no prospect for improvement there in the foreseeable future." The company had nearly 137,000 policies in force in the state. Three-and-a-half years later, Nationwide Mutual turned in its license to do business in New Jersey and never returned.

To move the company forward with less reliance on automobile insurance, Nationwide placed greater emphasis on diversification into life and business insurance and eventually, financial security services, such as annuities wrapped around mutual funds. The changes initially did not go down well with the agency force, Fisher remembers. "You might even say they were somewhat resentful," particularly about the business thrust.

As president of the insurance companies, Fisher said he tried "to make it crystal clear that to take a new initiative into the business insurance world didn't mean in any way, shape or form that we were going to neglect our prominent position in the family insurance business." Still, there was considerable skepticism.

Fisher acknowledged that for many years, "commercial insurance was a stepchild (because) we started out as a family membership organization." In recent years more agents became specialists in the field of small business insurance and the Wausau group, which affiliated with Nationwide in 1985, had the expertise to write the very large risk business, he said. As for the western movement, the retired general chairman said Nationwide reached out "a little far" in establishing regional operations as early as the late 1950s, affiliating with state employee associations.

A part of the early "go west" movement was the acquisition of Northern Life Insurance Company of Seattle in January 1963. Nine years later that led to one of the more bizarre incidents in Nationwide's history. It involved the sale of Northern Life in August 1972 to Equity Funding Corporation of America, Los Angeles.

Marakas, president of Nationwide Corporation, wanted to merge Northern Life and West Coast Life, a plan proposed eight years earlier by then Executive Vice President Louis E. Dolan but rejected by Dunlap. Before Marakas moved on his plan, however, Equity Funding offered to buy Northern Life.

Through previous business dealings, Marakas knew Equity Funding's chairman, Stanley Goldblum, and came to know the California conglomerate's executive vice president, Fred Levin (a.k.a. Fred J. Evans). Marakas was impressed by Levin, but found him to be "a terribly nervous guy." A nail-biter.

John C. Wagner, senior vice president and general counsel, sat in on the first meetings with the management of Equity Funding, and "they were thorough and appeared completely honest," he recalled. "None of us would have realized that there was anything afoul ... because of the professional way that they went into negotiating and closing that transaction."

Equity Funding offered $39.2 million for the 90 percent of Northern Life held by Nationwide Corporation. Most, $31.2 million, would be paid in cash and the remaining $8 million in one- to three-year notes. Early in 1972 Marakas took the offer to his board.

"Hey, they're willing to pay a price that we think is way too much," Marakas said.

"What do we know about Equity Funding?" a director asked. "What do you think about them?"

"Well, they've got a swinging sales concept. They have been expanding greatly (and) their stock is inflated." Marakas also admitted that he hadn't "studied the company, but we would take a closer look if they were offering their stock. But they didn't want to offer their stock."

"You know Goldblum," another director said. "What can you tell us about him and Levin (pronounced Levine)?"

"Frankly, I don't trust him (Goldblum)," Marakas replied. "However, our dealings have been with Fred Levin, a sharp young guy. I think his word is good."

The board approved the sale but Dunlap urged Treasurer Richard Mader to "sell those notes as quickly as we can." Fisher said "George was *always* more interested in cash than paper."

After shopping the notes to several financial institutions, Mader sold $3 million in notes to BancOhio Corporation and the remaining $5 million in notes to its Columbus subsidiary, Ohio National Bank.* They bought them "without recourse," Wagner said. "That means the buyer couldn't come back against the seller if anything went wrong." Eight months later, "Equity Funding's horrible situation came to light and those notes looked like they were practically worthless." He was right.

The "horrible situation" involved overstating the life insurance sales of Equity Funding Life Insurance Company by about $2 billion. From these overstated results the parent corporation, Equity Funding, went from about a $54 million general insurance agency in 1967 to a $6.5 billion conglomerate five years later. After the scheme collapsed in 1973, both men were charged with securities fraud. Subsequently Goldblum served about half of an eight-year prison term and Levin served 2 1/2 years in prison.

March 14, 1975, BancOhio and Ohio National Bank sued Nationwide Corporation in federal district court to rescind the sale, claiming fraud was involved. "It wasn't a nice way for them to sue us," said Gordon E. McCutchan, executive vice president, general counsel and secretary of the Nationwide Insurance Enterprise. "As you can imagine, that really made Jeffers mad ... and when he got mad, his neck got red." His indignation "probably was exceeded only by mine," said Marakas.

"We prided ourselves on our ethics and our reputation," Fisher said, "and anytime anybody would accuse our top

---

* The notes were sold August 2, 1972, five months after Dean W. Jeffers succeeded George H. Dunlap as general chairman and chief executive officer of all Nationwide companies.

management of fraud and misrepresentation ... I mean, that was unthinkable, that we should put up with that."

Three weeks after the filing of the suit, Jeffers ordered an armored car to Ohio National Bank on a quiet Saturday morning in Columbus. It loaded up more than $600 million in securities, which represented everything the bank held for Nationwide, and under tight security trucked the funds to The Cleveland Trust Company, a Federal Reserve bank in Cleveland. As a result of the transfer Fisher believed Nationwide improved its cash flow and saved a considerable amount of money, but Ohio National lost one of its largest accounts.

In January 1976, Walter C. Mercer, president of Ohio National Bank, visited Jeffers to introduce the new chairman, president and chief executive officer of BancOhio Corporation, Robert G. Stevens. When Stevens asked politely, "Is there anything we can do for you?" Jeffers replied, "Well, yes, there is. You can drop that ___ suit." BancOhio and Ohio National did so the following month, but 10 years passed before the financial institutions won back Nationwide's business.

In the 1970s Marakas struggled with a number of complex regulatory, tax, investment and internal issues that he felt hindered the progress of Nationwide Corporation. Already it had the complexities associated with two classes of shareholders, "A" and "B."* That put almost half of the ownership in the hands of the public, which elected half of the directors. From time to time, dissension arose between the two classes of directors because of their different interests.

In addition, the interests of the corporation and those of its subsidiaries were not always compatible, Marakas noted. For example, Nationwide might tell a subsidiary such as Michigan Life that it couldn't sell a particular insurance product in an

---

* "A" stock was publicly traded; "B" shares were owned by Nationwide Mutual and Nationwide Mutual Fire. Each class elected an equal number of directors — six.

area where a Nationwide agent already was doing business. "Well, that's not the best solution for that little subsidiary with private shareholders," he said. Therefore, it would be far better if Nationwide Corporation owned all the stock in its subsidiaries, rather than just a majority interest, Marakas believed. "I felt we should not have minority shareholders out there with different interests."

Then there was the relationship with Nationwide Life, a company under the supervision of Fisher even though the corporation owned controlling interest in the life company. Nationwide Corporation had only an advisory relationship with Nationwide Life. As the price of the corporation's stock fluctuated, however, it affected the financial base of the insurance companies. A dollar up or down in the price of the stock affected Nationwide's surplus by several million dollars.

The 1970s also saw numerous corporate takeovers, the prime targets being companies perceived to be undervalued. Some were sitting up and taking notice of Nationwide Corporation. "Nationwide appears to be one of the most undervalued stocks in the insurance group," said *Dow Digest* in its December 1972 issue. "The shares appear undervalued relative to current earnings ... and future growth."[7] Later in the 1970s, American General Corporation of Houston, an insurance holding company, acquired a substantial 11.42 percent interest in the corporation, snapping up shares at bargain prices.* The board became concerned that due to the decline of its stock, Nationwide Corporation could be targeted. "We didn't want that to happen to our company," said Dwight W. Oberschlake of Hamersville, OH, retired chairman of Nationwide Mutual.

Since it was founded, Nationwide Corporation was basically a holding company without much intervention in the activities

---

* After the reverse merger that took Nationwide Corporation private in 1983, published reports estimated American General Insurance realized a profit of $4 million on the sale of the stock.

of the eight subsidiaries it held.* That changed in 1972 when Jeffers and Marakas introduced "a new corporate operating plan and philosophy ... which changed our role from a passive to an active nature. It is our belief," Marakas said, "that the proper role of a holding company is to control and coordinate the direction our companies are taking and to integrate the activities of each company into an overall master plan that will optimize results for the corporation shareholders."[8]

Thus continued the centralization process, primarily affecting investment operations, pricing and product development, and marketing. As Marakas told Cleveland analysts and brokers in 1972, the corporation "is now a financial services holding company." At one point consideration was given to changing the corporation's name to reflect that.

An important part of the shift in the corporation from a passive player to an active one came as a result of its acquisition in 1969 of Heritage Securities, Inc., the investment advisor and distributor of two mutual funds — the Mutual Investing Foundation Fund and the Mutual Investing Foundation Growth Fund.[†] The corporation paid $2.5 million to buy all the Heritage shares from the Nationwide insurance companies and the Nationwide Foundation.

"This acquisition is part of the new growth plan for Nationwide Corporation," Dunlap said in June of 1969. "It will add impetus to our efforts to diversify into areas of finance and money management that complement our present operations."

Heritage was the outgrowth of Mutual Income Foundation, a shell of a Detroit-based mutual fund management company acquired in 1951 by Approved Finance, Inc., a Farm Bureau Mutual subsidiary. MIF's assets totaled $2.5 million; by 1969

---

* Nationwide Life, Michigan Life, Northern Life, West Coast Life, National Casualty, GatesMcDonald, Heritage Securities and National Services, Inc.
† See Chapter 7.

assets in the two funds totaled $177 million.

To obtain additional expertise in the fledgling mutual fund field, Approved Finance exchanged 49 percent of its MIF stock in 1956 for the same percentage of stock in Galen Van Meter & Company, Inc., a New York investment advisory firm, and its namesake became MIF's investment advisor. The marriage did not go well because, in Van Meter's opinion, "the idea that there is no profit in the distributing end of the mutual fund business is deeply embedded in Columbus."[9]

Three weeks after making that observation in November 1962, Van Meter died. Approved Finance acquired all the outstanding shares of what had become Heritage Securities, plus 90 percent of Van Meter's firm, which also had changed its name to Basic Economics Corporation. On May 28, 1963, the Nationwide insurance companies and the Nationwide Foundation bought all the common and preferred stock Approved Finance held in Heritage and Basic for a total of $650,000.

Even though the focus of Nationwide Corporation had shifted to a financial services holding company, Jeffers had his eye on buying back all the outstanding shares of Nationwide Corporation and taking it private. Many years before he had voiced his opposition to the initial public offering because he felt it would adversely affect Nationwide Life, which was tucked into the corporation only to sweeten the stock offering for Wall Street investors.

Marakas agreed with Jeffers. Trading in the stock was light, yet the corporation had the expense of maintaining shareholder relations. Furthermore, because the life company's management remained with Nationwide Mutual, it raised such questions as expense allocations, investment and management policies, and the rights of shareholders versus the policyholders in the mutual company. There also were the complex regulatory entanglements.

In the fall of 1978, Marakas and other senior officers

recommended to Jeffers a plan to buy the corporation's "A," or public, stock. The Nationwide property/casualty companies owned all the corporation's "B" shares, which represented nearly 54 percent of all the outstanding "A" shares.

"Let's take it private!" said Jeffers, who considered it "a very, very important decision." The process began December 12, 1978, with Nationwide Mutual making a $20 cash tender offer for 2.5 million of the 4.7 million outstanding shares of corporation "A" stock. The previous week the over-the-counter issue closed at $18.50.

At the time the offer expired, some 4.1 million shares were tendered, including the large block held by American General. However, Dr. Robert A. Rennie, senior vice president, investments, recalled "it was like the *Perils of Pauline*. As we got down to within a few minutes of the deadline, American General had not tendered its stock. We were all very concerned." At virtually the last minute, it came in.

Four years later, after Fisher succeeded Jeffers as general chairman and chief executive officer, Nationwide Mutual acquired the remaining outstanding shares of the corporation for $42.50 per share in a reverse merger. Fisher hailed the $33.6 million transaction, which made the corporation a wholly-owned subsidiary of Nationwide Mutual, as one of "considerable financial and historical significance."[10]

Of equal financial and historical significance was the arrival on the Nationwide scene of Massachusetts Financial Services (MFS) of Boston, purveyor of mutual funds. MFS is the nation's oldest mutual fund group, having established America's first mutual fund, Massachusetts Investors Trust, in March 1924. Fifty years later, in 1974, it hired consultant John David Davenport* of Oklahoma City, OK, to find an insurance partner to sell annuities, hoping to give the MFS group a lift in

---

* See PEBSCO, Chapter 16.

what then was a sagging mutual funds industry.

Davenport pitched Marakas on the idea of wrapping a Nationwide Life annuity* around an MFS mutual fund at a time when Nationwide Corporation officers were working independently on wrap-around annuities. "We were looking at it to see if we could use (annuities) in one of our small companies," Marakas said. "We were intrigued about the possibilities of hooking up with MFS. It had great potential.

"I took it to John Fisher, and I wasn't too optimistic that he wanted to get Nationwide Life involved ... but he also thought that this had tremendous potential for development of premium income."

Proper distribution consumed many hours of discussion, but in Marakas' opinion, it was unlikely the exclusive Nationwide agency force could become specialists in the variable annuity line. "So, it was structured as a group product," he said, to be distributed primarily outside the agency force, through brokers. Nationwide Life was the product manufacturer and MFS the distributor through their own network of wholesalers and brokers throughout the country. This would require a fundamental, and significant, shift within Nationwide.

"This was an extremely important step. I would characterize that decision made by John, with Dean Jeffers' approval, as one of the most important he has ever made. ... Dean, always very close to the agency organization, had his doubts, as others did, about us getting involved with different distribution forces, but Dean OK'd that decision."

"I suppose I had my neck out about as far as anybody in taking us into an area in which not too many people even knew how to spell 'annuity' back when we started doing it," Fisher said, "and that included me."

As the MFS joint venture went together, Joseph J. Gasper,

---

* An annuity is a contract sold by life insurance companies that guarantees a fixed or variable payment to the annuityholder at some future time.

in charge of marketing tax-sheltered products for Nationwide Life, said that if it hadn't been for Fisher, "we'd be dead. He was a staunch supporter. Every time we needed money, he found a way to support us."

Nevertheless, Marakas spent many a night, lying in the bed and staring at the ceiling, unable to sleep. He kept thinking about the millions of dollars spent in enlarging the annuity business, setting up the systems and buying the field forces. Over the years, he estimated, the amount of statutory surplus expended totaled more than $40 million.

Finally, on February 17, 1979, the MFS/Nationwide Spectrum Annuity product, combining into one contract a variable and fixed annuity, went on sale. Buyers seeking tax-deferred shelters had the choice of investing in either a variable account made up of eight mutual funds managed by MFS, the general account assets of Nationwide Life, or a combination of both. Three months later the Securities and Exchange Commission halted the sale of the fixed annuity on a technicality, but sales began again by the end of the year.

Late in 1981 MFS Chairman Jack Barnard called Fisher to inform him that MFS had agreed to be sold to Sun Life Insurance Company of Canada. Jack A. Gulick, at the time vice president of sales-financial services, spoke to Barnard the following morning, just a few hours before the public announcement in Boston.

"I was sick," Gulick said. "It was a blow," agreed Marakas, who immediately sat down with staff to see whether Nationwide could, or should, match the $70-plus million Sun Life offer. "We concluded they were paying way too much; we didn't want to bid that high," he said. "That shows what tremendous experts we were, because that was one of the best investments Sun Life ever made. ... What looked like big sales in those days were peanuts a few years later. ... Today I think they are approaching $150 million a month premium income figure. No one ever dreamed of that in 1981 and 1982."

In hindsight, Fisher said he regretted not having made a counter offer for MFS. "It was sort of snatched from under us. … On the other hand, we almost had exhausted our capacity to grow. … In some ways it was timely to separate. … We needed to go that much further in our own internal corporate development and not rely so heavily on another group of that sort (MFS)."

"If we had bought MFS, we'd be sitting here today big in mutual funds *and* annuities," Gasper said. "We didn't buy them, and we're big in annuities, not in mutual funds."

Nationwide's modest mutual funds family in the early 1990s consisted of "plain vanilla products," said Marian Trimble, president of Nationwide Financial Services, Inc., which is investment manager for the Nationwide Investing Foundation and Nationwide Investing Foundation II.

NIF is the direct descendant of Mutual Investing Foundation, Inc., the Detroit-based fund investment manager acquired by Farm Bureau Mutual in 1951.* NIF II, another diversified, open-end investment company, was founded by Nationwide October 5, 1985.

NIF funds include two common stock funds, a corporate bond fund and a money market fund. NIF II includes a tax-free, income fund and a U.S. government securities fund. All are sold only through the Nationwide agency force unless an annuity is wrapped around the fund. Then brokers also sell the product. In 1993 the assets of these funds reached nearly $3.5 billion.

With MFS and Spectrum gone (both sides agreed not to use the name Spectrum again), Nationwide found itself without an annuity product. "I went to Wall Street, to Merrill Lynch, and I said, 'Hey, we're going to be in business,'" Gasper recalled.

---

* See Chapter 7.

" 'We're coming out with a new product.' "

"You're crazy," Wall Street replied.

Gasper gathered a group of brokers and asked what the best product in America would look like. The ideal, they said, would be for the annuity to wrap around any number of mutual funds owned by different mutual fund companies, not just one mutual fund group, "but you can't do that."

Yet Nationwide did exactly that, creating the Best of America* variable annuity product. Because it was not proprietary, it wrapped around several funds, such as Twentieth Century Fund and Fidelity's group of funds. Best of America became the number one variable annuity in the nation in the 1990s, offering a fixed account and 22 different mutual funds from eight of the nation's leading fund groups.

Through the late 1980s and in the 1990s, assets grew at a compound growth rate of more than 20 percent a year, Marakas said, "and that growth came principally from business produced by distribution forces — outside the Nationwide exclusive agency force — that were not in existence until the late 1970s."

Another extremely important thrust in the early days of the Jeffers administration was to improve Nationwide's relations with the Columbus business community. Lincoln made very little effort to become a part of it; he focused on global concerns. Doss made a half-hearted stab at improving community relations, joining the Columbus Area Chamber of Commerce, for example, but he "didn't attend meetings," Jeffers recalled. "He didn't become involved. I saw to it that I became very much involved, and I had no difficulty ... working with the leadership" of the community, including the powerful Wolfe family that had its differences with Lincoln and his cooperative approach to business.

Since his earliest days at Nationwide, Fisher maintained an

---

* Dan Perkins, a Merrill Lynch executive at the time, is credited with coming up with the name, Best of America.

active role in many community activities, particularly United Way, which honored his years of service upon his retirement in 1994. Fisher saw himself as "the primary representative of Nationwide in the community."

Jeffers was just as active, helping to reorganize the community's Chamber of Commerce and then spreading the wings of Nationwide executives by urging them to take leadership roles in state, national and international industry groups. "That had an impact on all of us in terms of trying to be sure that we did our fair share," Fisher said.

"As I've said many times over the years, I've learned Nationwide is more than a business."

14

GOIN' FISHERING

In jest, John E. Fisher "campaigned" to have the lobby of the new One Nationwide Plaza named the "Halls of Montezuma" in honor of the former Marine who headed the Nationwide Insurance Enterprise and who was instrumental in the development of the new headquarters complex.

"Dean wouldn't quite go for that," said Fisher. Nor did Jeffers, general chairman during the planning phase for the 40-story main building, accept Fisher's idea for a much shorter building but with wider floors. Fisher did not favor a new building "as a monument," but Jeffers, still trying to mend local fences, seized the opportunity to make a bold statement to the Columbus community that here was a strong, vibrant contributor to it.

Groundbreaking took place July 12, 1974, two years after Jeffers appointed the Space Committee, first chaired by J.R. "Rudy" Koenig, senior vice president in the office of President Fisher, and later by Charles W. Fullerton, retired president of the affiliated companies. Many studies followed, including one proposal to build north of the city on land now occupied by the John E. Fisher Nationwide Training Center. In the end, it was the will of the employees and corporate citizenship that swayed the decision.

"Staying downtown was a very big financial commitment on the part of Nationwide," Fullerton said, as well as a bold move in selecting a rundown, depressed area of the city's inner core instead of the green meadows of Delaware County. It also was the catalyst for the remarkable rebirth of the entire area of Columbus known as the Short North, attracting hotels, convention facilities, restaurants, art galleries, retail and general restoration.

Jeffers told Fullerton to get the 1,328,000-square-foot tower built and President Fisher and John L. Marakas, then president of Nationwide Corporation, to raise the $80 million for it. "I used to tell people that my job was to open the mail, clean the restrooms and get lunch," Fullerton said.

Designed by the New York architectural firm of Harrison & Abramovitz,* One Nationwide Plaza went up in 42 months with nary a more serious accident than a broken leg. An accountant, working in a construction trailer, stepped out its door and fell flat on his face. He forgot that a foreman had told him earlier in the day the stairs had been moved to the trailer's second door.

The first Nationwide employees moved from 246 North High Street[†] into the new building across the street December 6, 1976, although the dedication was held until 1978. In 1981, just before Jeffers retired, workers completed the 18-story Two Nationwide Plaza. Seven years later Three Nationwide Plaza, a 27-story office facility, opened, giving Nationwide more than 2.6 million square feet of owned office space in downtown Columbus.

---

* The Harrison & Abramovitz architectural firm had a worldwide reputation for major projects, such as the United Nations Secretariat and Lincoln Center for the Performing Arts.
† The State of Ohio bought the 246 North High Street building for $17 million, October 4, 1985.

While not stomping around the One Nationwide Plaza construction site in galoshes he kept in his office for his once-a-week inspection, Jeffers forged the initial plans for busting through on commercial lines insurance, which never had received much attention at Nationwide. As Fisher noted, many at the time viewed commercial insurance as "a stepchild." Every few months or so there would be a big push under a new plan, but never a long-range, concentrated effort to penetrate the market.

Carved out of the agency force to sell business insurance were some of the company's best agents, those with large personal lines portfolios and an interest in enlarging them through commercial production. The regions, and morale, often suffered as a result because the regions no longer could count on their top producers to help meet personal lines quotas and goals. Furthermore, even small gains in commercial lines at the outset were hailed as major victories and lavishly rewarded, much to the consternation of other agents. In the late 1980s the business agents were put back into the regions.

The "stepchild" languished until the mid-1980s when Nationwide aggressively renewed its efforts into commercial lines and its push westward to meet up with a group of Nationwide pioneers who reached the Pacific shores 25 years earlier.

In 1957 the Nationwide trailblazers hitched up the wagons and hit the Oregon Trail. Upon arriving in Portland they intended to sell group automobile insurance through labor unions, government agencies and others. Before they could circle the wagons, however, hostile companies native to the area secured legislation — the Fictitious Fleet Law — that prevented the writing of group insurance without common ownership of the property.

Undaunted, the Columbus pioneers devised a new course of action. "The experiment out west" introduced a direct marketing concept: Individual members of groups could insure directly with Nationwide, by mail, without involving an agent. It was a major departure from the company's traditional distribution channel, namely the exclusive agency force, and gave policyholders a distinct rate advantage by not having an agent's commission add-on.

As a result, the plan's lower rates, convenience and service gained favor among public employee groups in Oregon, then Washington and Idaho. Within 10 years Nationwide was conducting direct-sales operations in eight Western states, adding homeowners, boat and family accident coverage besides automobile insurance.

In 1968 Nationwide joined with the Colorado Association of Public Employees in the first payroll deduction plan for premium payments for association members. Three years later the region turned its first profit. By the 20th anniversary of the western operations in 1978 nearly 250,000 policies were in force and Nationwide was the eighth largest insurer in Oregon. Three years later, headquarters turned up the sales burners to significantly improve market share in personal lines as part of an upcoming western development plan.

This successful foray west led to a promise of future success in the 1980s. California, then Texas were the prime targets. For his vice president of western development, Fisher picked Paul A. Donald, whom Fisher first met in the mid-1950s in the Annapolis, MD, Tri-State regional office.

Donald joined Farm Bureau Mutual's regional office as an underwriting trainee in October 1954. The Annapolis native was hired by a young assistant personnel manager, Edmond Coughlin, with whom he raced sailboats in earlier days. Donald got to know Fisher better, too, after they performed volunteer work together on the local United Way campaigns. They also worked side-by-side to paint the cafeteria in the Annapolis office, first in mauve and peach. "When we were through with it," Fisher recalled, "it looked like an abandoned cocktail lounge." So, they repainted everything "an old industrial green," as Donald remembered; Fisher maintained the color was "eye-ease green."

When Fisher took in 1968 what even he perceived to be a "dead-end" job as vice president, public relations, he wanted Donald in Columbus, too, as his director of policyholder relations.

"I was clearly not interested in that job," Donald said, "because I thought it was a dead-end street." He went through the interview anyway, at the end of which Fisher asked:

"Paul, if I were to offer you the job, would you take it?"

"Frankly, I don't think so, John."

"What do you mean?"

"Well, I don't know how to say it other than candidly," Donald replied. "I think the job's a dead-end street. ... I would hope one day that I would be a vice president, regional manager, and I don't think that job would enhance my credentials for that."

"You're probably right," Fisher admitted, but he clearly was disappointed. "Well, maybe some day I'll be promoted and certainly you would be a prime candidate for this job."

"I understand that, John, and that would be a very good job. But, if I were making the decision now, I would have to say no, I don't think I want that."

Ten years later, when Fisher was president, he brought Donald back to the home office as his vice president, property and casualty marketing, then into the western development job for about a year. Early in 1981 Donald became Fisher's vice president, administrative assistant. "I didn't know it then but John was grooming me, or at least considering me ... to take his place when Dean Jeffers retired."

It happened just that way. Fisher succeeded Jeffers as general chairman and chief executive officer of the enterprise October

1, 1981, and Donald succeeded Fisher as president of the Nationwide Insurance Companies.

Planning for the commercial and western expansions went forward, but this time, unlike the late 1970s, the agents were new to Nationwide, recruited from other companies specifically to sell commercial insurance. Still, there was considerable debate as to the efficacy of the entire strategy.

In the opinion of William P. DeMeno, who briefly served as vice president of western development in 1984 before heading up the Farmland Insurance Companies, Nationwide led with the wrong lines in the two prime target states of California and Texas. "We should have been selling personal insurance in those markets, because if you looked at industry data, the personal lines were more profitable than the commercial lines, particularly in Texas."

Supported by a study by outside consultants, McKinsey & Company, Donald became convinced that "commercial products were the right way to go," DeMeno said, despite the voices of warning, including his. At the time, 80 percent of Nationwide's business lived east of the Mississippi and 90 percent of premiums came from personal lines. The 10-year plan aimed at reaching a 70/30 mix of personal to commercial premium.

"The hot buttons at the time were write commercial insurance, write life insurance, reduce the expense ratio and go west," Earl F. Peitz remembered. "So, Paul put the four hot buttons together and said, 'Let's go do those.'"

Trucking company president Arden L. Shisler of Dalton, OH, was excited, as were others. At only his second meeting as a new board member in 1984 the growth plan was implemented. "You couldn't help but be excited, (being) brought in to be a part of this great, big, strong organization." He was delighted to be named to the board's audit committee.

Peitz, in the mid-1980s vice president, markets development, believed the consultants "led us down the path to believe we could do some things that really were incompatible," such as commercial and life insurance. "You can't reduce the expense ratio by writing commercial because it is a higher expense-ratio product. And we had no ability. We were going into new markets leading with our weakness."

In Peitz's opinion, the effort was ill-prepared, lacking adequate support and accounting systems, proper reserves and proper claims procedures. "It turned out to be a disaster. Those guys (agents) who had been writing small accounts — $5,000 or $10,000 — suddenly started writing $50,000 to $100,000 to $250,000 to $300,000 to $1 million accounts," and larger still.

The losses mounted, due in part to the tremendous up-front investment. As the new business flowed in, the claims increased, too, creating a major problem for the company, DeMeno said. At the same time, eastern operations were allowed to increase automobile policies in force from 4 million to 5 million. "There's no way you can have a claims structure handle a 20 percent increase in business in two years unless you really planned for it," said Peitz.

Fisher recalled that in 18 months, Nationwide wrote "about a million new automobile policies (and) more than a billion dollars of commercial insurance, which is more commercial insurance than Wausau had written in 75 years. ... Our growth was somewhere between out of control and suspicious."

California was very expensive and very difficult, too, not only because of the start-up costs but because the market was so competitive; the only way to compete was on price. However, the most damaging aspect, DeMeno believed, "was the price war that was going on. It was in the middle of the cash flow underwriting days, when investment income was fairly high, so companies were willing to write business at underwriting losses to generate cash flow."

Donald agreed. "We can't realistically expect to produce

commercial growth with rates significantly higher than the competition's," he told the directors in November 1984. Month after month new commercial sales set records. In commercial auto lines, such as truck fleets, "several millions of dollars of premium are literally looking for a home," Donald reported to the board in April 1985, "and we're attracting a lot of this business because of marketplace presence."

"We wanted strong growth in the commercial insurance area, and we got it," Fisher reported to Nationwide Mutual's annual meeting April 4, 1985. Five months later, though, Donald noted for the first time that premium growth in commercial lines may have become overheated, adversely affecting the premium-to-surplus ratio.

"You could write anything you wanted," Hornell, NY, agent Lee Ryan remembered. "I mean, it was open season. We were just taking everything that came down the pike. ... Then they left (the gate) open too long."

Donald informed the board as much. Too much of a good thing "has put us in a position where a need to dampen growth, mainly in the commercial lines, is necessary to preserve our service capabilities," he said.

Shisler, who went on to chair the audit committee and then to chairman of the parent company, understood at the outset "our ratio could go to 3 to 1 ... and it wouldn't cause any problems; that was the cost of growth." However, as the amount of premium approached three times the surplus, the outside auditors were banging on his door.

Donald remembered the strategic agreement, as had Shisler: a 3-to-1 premium to surplus ratio was deemed acceptable, but when the ratio reached about 2.75, Donald said, "we began to get all kinds of noises from the financial side of the company. ... The board began to get nervous about that and when the board got nervous, John Fisher got nervous, and he sent that message down to me."

By early spring, 1986, Donald told the board, "I can assure you there is no reason to panic," yet the word went forth to the sales force: de-emphasize, and virtually halt, sales in commercial lines until there is a measure of control — and cut out the special incentives to agents for commercial premium production! In anticipation of the cut-off, however, some agents raced to get as much business on the books in the first quarter as possible.

"Just two years ago we were stretching to reach the $100 million mark in new commercial sales," Donald reported to the board. "Today we're struggling to contain sales to four times this level."

After Donald, then Fisher instituted a series of moratoriums, it took nine months to process the backlog of premiums, Shisler said. This pushed the ratio close to 3.5 before it came back down. A workaholic before the crisis, during it Fisher worked even harder, often late into the night only to return to his office as early as 5 a.m. Despite his best efforts, he could not get the giant ship turned around fast enough. So, he made the tough decision: He got a new crew. Several of Donald's senior officers received new assignments and others were dismissed.

In September 1987 Fisher promoted D. Richard McFerson to executive vice president of property-casualty insurance operations, a new position. Six months later he succeeded Donald as president of the Nationwide property/casualty companies. Donald was named assistant chief executive officer and president of the property/casualty affiliates, such as GatesMcDonald, Neckura, Scottsdale and Wausau. He retired April 7, 1989, at age 59, ending a 35-year-career with Nationwide.

Fisher believed "bouncing back" from those darkest hours represented his most difficult challenge while at Nationwide's helm."I am somewhat embarrassed that we really had to go through a turnaround in 1985," he said. "I always felt that I should have caught that earlier."

Many agents wrote to Fisher, angry at the severity of the cutbacks and at the 26 percent increase in premium prices. Their ire he defused in a videotaped message to them in the spring of 1987. "I do understand and share the frustration you feel," he said, and "I clearly recognize that our containment actions ... are in conflict with responsibilities you feel to your policyholders and to your families." However, he said he applied "a tourniquet to halt some very severe bleeding. ... Our losses have become intolerable.

"The simple, hard truth is," the chief executive explained, "we have lost money ... on our property/casualty business in three of the past five years. We haven't had an underwriting gain for seven consecutive years."

Longtime agent Will DeSain of Liverpool, NY., remembered the difficult time well, but when "the crisis came, we kept our jobs (and) Nationwide came back. It hurt; it hurt like the devil," he said. "My income went down $60,000. I lost 480 automobiles. (Others lost considerably more than that.) It took me four years to recover ... but we stayed in business through John Fisher's leadership. (He) found a way to curtail everything, yet save the institution."

In the midst of the crisis, Beaver Pacific Corporation and its subsidiary, Beaver Insurance Company, entered Nationwide Mutual's tumultuous picture. Beaver's president, William T. Waste, approached Nationwide in February 1985 after he heard the Columbus insurer was in search of a California workers' compensation company. Nationwide had been in negotiations with Western Employers Insurance Company, but "Beaver wasn't burdened with other lines of insurance; almost all of it was in workers' compensation," Donald explained. "They were the cleanest of the candidates that we looked at that met the size criteria."

Nationwide Mutual hurt for a workers' compensation outlet

because of a law known as California Form 46 surplus. Briefly, California's lawmakers, and the state's insurance industry, wanted to preclude out-of-state companies "creaming" workers' compensation business in California. The Form 46 legislation said an insurance company's workers' compensation business must grow and policyholder dividends be paid from profits made in workers' compensation in California, not from profits earned in other states.

On September 1, 1985, Nationwide Mutual acquired San Francisco-based Beaver for $33 million. From the start, however, the newcomer created problems Nationwide didn't need.

"In the first place," Fisher explained, "management ... looked upon the arrival of Nationwide as a great source of financial capacity, and the amount of new business that they wrote in the first year was a shock and a drain on the company's surplus."

In workers' compensation, Beaver increased its gross premiums written in 1986 to $115.1 million, up from $63.3 million the previous year. In its property/liability line of business, gross premiums written reached $36.9 million, more than three times its 1985 amount.

Beaver's management, intent on diversifying, also engaged in several enterprises, involving nearly 20 corporations, that took Nationwide more than a year to unravel, shut down or transfer, and write off at $7.5 million. One involved an off-shore reinsurance operation in the Grand Cayman Islands that "had the potential to be a pretty serious financial hit to us," said Robert A. Oakley, senior vice president and chief financial officer. He perceived it as "a lot of off-shore wheelin' and dealin' activity."

The California company also engaged in numerous small claims management operations in Nevada, handling claims for other companies. According to Donald, Beaver was "making money on one side of its ledger and losing it on the other, (which is) something we didn't discover" until later.

"It was just one of those things that after two years of owning it, we were not sure what we had, we didn't trust it (and) we didn't know what they were doing," Oakley said.

In February 1988 Donald reported to Fisher that Beaver's 1987 performance was "unsatisfactory" but that an effort would be made to bring "the strategic focus back to California workers' compensation." The intent was to improve Beaver's results and enhance its marketability because it was on the block. The decision to sell Beaver was quietly made in the fall of 1987, [1] about two years after the Wausau group affiliated with Nationwide in November 1985.* Nationwide really didn't need Beaver inasmuch as the much larger Wausau organization covered the same workers' compensation territory. Thus, Beaver became a financial liability. It was sold January 3, 1990, to Pacific Compensation Capital Corporation of San Bruno, CA, for $31 million.

"Probably our investment in Beaver Pacific was ill-advised," Fisher said. "It was really one of the more unsuccessful things that we ever did (but) at least we had the good sense to get out of it."

While Beaver Pacific was not as rewarding as Fisher might have hoped, the performance of the Nationwide Insurance Enterprise as a whole far exceeded expectations. Even the visionary Murray D. Lincoln could not have foreseen the enormous growth, especially during the two decades Fisher served first as president of the insurance companies, then as general chairman and chief executive officer of the entire enterprise.

In 1993, just before Fisher retired, assets of the enterprise surpassed a major league $42.2 billion, up from $2.1 billion in 1972. Net written premiums jumped from $832 million to $12.8 billion in the same period. Policies in force were 11.3

---

* See Chapter 15.

million, more than twice what they had been 21 years earlier, and investment income produced spectacular returns to reach a healthy $2.3 billion, up from $88.6 million in 1972. It also took 32,600 employees and agents to get the job done, nearly triple the number two decades earlier.

Gordon E. McCutchan, executive vice president, law and corporate services for the enterprise, looked back on the Fisher years. "If you analyze the 1980s, we grew rapidly until about 1986 in the property/casualty business and then we suddenly realized we had grown too rapidly ... so we were in a no-growth period for the second half of the 1980s, when the property/casualty business actually declined. So our market share today — about 3.5 — is about what it was about five or six years ago. The growth was in the life insurance side of the business." With $25.4 billion in assets in 1993, Nationwide Life ranked 16th among 2,150 U.S. life insurance companies.

Fisher said he found "great satisfaction in the life company's growth, particularly in the field of annuities and deferred compensation and other means of managing people's long-term savings." Throughout the nation public employee deferred compensation programs experienced tremendous growth, but none could point to greater success in the past decade than the enterprise's Public Employees Benefit Services Corporation. Fisher knew it was right for Nationwide and successfully fought for it, despite considerable opposition and the administrative and financial strain at the outset. However, it turned out well: In 1993 PEBSCO managed nearly $8 billion in deferred compensation assets for 726,000 state, county and municipal employees.

"John Fisher kept that alive ... even when it appeared to be a losing proposition," said Joseph J. Gasper, senior vice president, property and casualty operations.

James E. Brock, the senior vice president for investment product operations, looked upon Nationwide's leaders as pioneers in the large forest. "The guys at the top — Fisher, McFerson — allow things to get done. All are absolutely critical in cutting down the trees to make a path ... The inclination is not to do bold new things in large companies. It takes a real effort on the part of the people at the top to permit change, encourage it (and) nurture it."

The selling of Nationwide's mutual funds required considerable nurturing. As retired Vice President Patrick L. Doyle observed, most Nationwide agents do not actively pursue mutual funds for their customers.

"They are a very creative sale," agreed agent Bob Pierce of Annandale, VA. "You have to convince the people to save money, to take away their disposable income that they have today and put it away for tomorrow ... which is very hard sometimes."

"The big deal in my opinion," Doyle continued, "was the wonderful adroitness of Fisher and Jeffers to get our exclusive agency force to accept that we'll distribute our products through brokers and banks and savings and loans as we do on the life side. That was a remarkable sales job."

On numerous occasions, Fisher would step into the role of an agent inasmuch as he always kept his home number listed in the telephone book. That engendered calls at all hours but mostly at night and sometimes collect. His wife, Eloise, said if the caller didn't reverse the charges, they really needed help.

Shortly after he became president, Fisher received a collect call from a vociferous policyholder in California who threatened legal action and worse because Nationwide told him he did not have coverage.

"I found out by talking to this young man's mother in Cincinnati (where the policy was issued) that he had been involved in some bad checks and then had taken his father's car to California. There he had an accident and in responding to the claim, the Portland, OR, office discovered his new California address, so they billed him under the California rates."

Meanwhile, Fisher said, the young man moved again without a forwarding address, continued to write bad checks and ignored Nationwide's bill. "So, we canceled him," the president said. "The gentleman was so obnoxious when he talked to me on the phone that the next morning, 7 o'clock my time and 4 o'clock his time, I called him and told him that I was pleased to confirm that he really didn't have any coverage. If he wanted to complain to the insurance department or a lawyer or anybody else, I said he was free to do so.

"All he said was, 'I was afraid you'd say that.'"

Fisher's associates recognized his "unbelievable discipline" in his work habits. They also described him as a "plodder," "perfectionist," "workaholic," "pragmatic," and "avid reader." Officers have said, "Don't send John something to read unless you expect that he will read it, because he will." Eight large briefcases beside his desk quickly filled with his reading for the evening. One could well have been filled with his seemingly unending supply of corny jokes, for which he was infamous. He always had a new one for the board meeting.

"I have, I think, a natural, inborn tendency to laugh at myself," Fisher said, "and not take things too seriously. That always has led me to have a positive attitude. I've told the board on several occasions that I try to be cheerful, even when I'm unhappy."

What most board members seemed to remember about Fisher was his good humor, his keen perception of the issues and the power that lay behind them, his steadiness even under fire, and his always being thoroughly prepared. He was a great leader, said Chairman Shisler.

"I feel a great sense of fulfillment," Fisher said upon retirement.

15

'W-A-U-S-A-U. WARSORE.'

While the camera crew prepared to film a new Wausau Insurance television commercial, veteran character actress Doris Belack rehearsed her three lines, making sure she exaggerated just enough the strong Eastern accent called for in the script. When she stepped before the camera as a hotel desk clerk, she was ready.

"Oh, Warsore Insurance," she smiles, handing the salesman his hotel bill.

"That's Wausau," he replies, without looking up.

A mite miffed, she spells it out for him: "W-A-U-S-A-U. Warsore."

"We're the business insurance experts — from Wausau," comes the salesman's reply — and correcting her pronunciation once again.

"Whateva," she says, getting the last word.

The thrust of the 30-second "Where's Wausau?" television spot was to highlight the name and headquarters location of the Wausau Insurance Companies. Between takes Belack got the ear of Robert W. Gunderson, vice president of corporate advertising for the company.

"Just where *is* Warsaw, Bob?" she asked.

"In Wisconsin," Gunderson replied, "like it says in the script," but it didn't say it in Belack's portion of the script.

"Oh," said the actress, who evidently knew the whole Midwest only as a fly-over between New York and Hollywood, "that's near Seattle, right?"[1]

The commercial became a classic, comparable to "Spelling Bee" produced four years earlier. In it, a young girl wins the spelling contest on the word Wausau, adding that "There's a U-S-A in the middle ..." On the air from September 1980 until the end of 1988, it well may hold the record as the longest-running commercial in television history.*

In 1984 "Where's Wausau?" was the only television spot produced for what was a foundering insurance company, although few knew it. The previous fall Gunderson was told to "hold the line" on advertising at 1983 levels, which totaled some $7 million, the highest in the company's history. By February 1984, Wausau's President, John Schoneman, told Gunderson he had to reduce the advertising budget by another $1 million. Gunderson, a Wausau veteran of 41 years before he retired in 1991, was concerned. So was Thomas E. Kryshak, but for a different reason. The senior vice president of financial services continually spoke out against what he believed to be excessive advertising expenditures in the early 1980s. "Advertising just got out of hand, and we spent way too much money" given Wausau's revenue base at the time and the overall proportion of advertising dollars to total expenses.

Although he knew the cutback demand had to be met, that didn't make it any easier for Gunderson to pare at its peak one of the nation's most successful advertising campaigns, a

---

* During the eight-year run of the commercial, only three viewers correctly pointed out to the company that the youngster should not have won the bee because she failed to capitalize Wausau.

campaign that put the Wisconsin business insurance company into the homes of millions of Americans. A large share of the campaign's success is attributable to the immense popularity of *60 Minutes,* which has had Wausau Insurance as a sponsor since 1969, the show's second year on the air.

Previously Wausau Insurance was a name virtually unknown to the general public. The name of its headquarters community, Wausau, derives from a Chippewa Indian word meaning something "far away."* Originally known as Big Bull Falls, the community was settled in 1838 by men who built a lumbermill there on the shore of the Wisconsin River. The mill thrived and fostered related and new industries in the early 1900s, including the Employers Mutual Liability Insurance Company of Wisconsin. On September 1, 1911, it wrote its first business and the nation's first workman's compensation insurance policy for the Wausau Sulphate Fibre Company, still in business as the Mosinee Paper Corporation. The policy is still in force, too.

Several Wausau businessmen, known as the "Wausau group" and mostly from the lumber industry, founded Employers Mutual in July of that year, shortly after the Wisconsin legislature passed historic legislation providing for workmen's compensation.

"Workmen's compensation is the greatest social revolution of 20th century America!" Clyde F. Schlueter, president and chief executive officer of Employers Mutual, declared in 1974. "It did not ride through America on cannon wheels as did the abolition of slavery the century before. It did not parade into the 20th century as did women's suffrage. It did not splash in boldface onto the front pages of the nation's newspapers as did the labor union movement. But workmen's compensation legislation was, nevertheless, revolutionary."[2]

---

* There are several different translations of the word.

Hans J. Hagge, the Murray D. Lincoln of Employers Mutual, was its fourth employee. He owned a court reporting business in Chicago when hired in 1911 by the insurance company as assistant secretary. When he professed to know nothing about the industry, the directors told him not to worry. "This is a new thing. We don't want to get old dogs to try to teach them new tricks."[3]

Like Lincoln in his first years with the Ohio Farm Bureau, Hagge (who knew Lincoln) had a tough row to hoe in the early 1900s. He didn't have Lincoln's luxury of a hotel room for an office; he worked out of a converted stock room over a cigar store. Furthermore, he had to contend with the vitriolic campaign conducted by the established stock insurance companies to discredit and undercut Employers Mutual. Hagge admitted "we didn't have a darn thing to sell except an idea."[4] At the end of the first year, however, the company had issued policies providing $85,212 in coverage, posted assets of $21,000 and recorded a $3,000 surplus.

Hagge, described by an associate as "a blood, guts and feathers kind of a guy," became the company's first full-time president in 1931 and served in that capacity for 21 years, longer than any before or since. The board elected him chairman in 1952, a post he held until his death in 1959.

At that time Employers Mutuals of Wausau, a name selected in 1935 to reflect the growing family of companies, had business in all 50 states and assets approaching $500 million. In 1972 the company's assets broke through $1 billion; $2 billion in 1978, and $3 billion in 1983.

By then Employers Insurance of Wausau A Mutual Company, (the name adopted in 1979) was a troubled company in an equally troubled industry. Beginning in 1979 and extending into the mid-1980s, price wars broke out like measles and all companies had to scratch to keep business. Property and casualty underwriting losses throughout the industry hit a record $6.3

billion in 1981, but these were mitigated somewhat by the unusually high interest rates that fattened investment portfolios. However, record losses followed in each of the succeeding four years and interest rates dropped. By 1985 industry losses weighed in at $24.8 billion.

The industry was badly out of whack. Many blamed an early bout with inflation, the declining rates, record losses from natural disasters, the price wars, dramatic increases in health care costs, and the exploding lawsuits, jury awards and costs of litigating same.

"The mood of our society is to seek a culprit for all of life's mishaps, and look to the insurance companies with the 'deep pockets' to reward victims," John E. Fisher, general chairman and chief executive officer of the Nationwide Insurance Enterprise, said at the time.[5]

At Wausau Insurance the numbers were just as ugly as the industry's, if not more so. In 1984 its underwriting loss totaled $342 million, up from $230.9 million a year earlier. Earnings from its large investment portfolio helped improve the numbers, but the real problem was in the surplus, or the capital a company has available beyond what it holds in reserve for policyholder losses. Some equate a mutual company's surplus to a stock company's net worth.

Wausau Insurance operated at a 4-to-1 ratio in 1984,* considerably higher than the 2-to-1 ratio that often is considered an industry yardstick.

A ratio that high wasn't new for Wausau Insurance, however. A decade earlier the company battled another lengthy and devastating price war that forced it to freeze, and then cut, salaries across the board. To help heal its wounds and shore up its resources, Wausau's board in 1976 brought in a new executive vice president, John A. Schoneman, to head up the shaky

---

* In comparison, Nationwide's ratio hovered around 2.5-to-1 during most of the 1980s.

insurance operations. By design, Schoneman became the company's first outside president and chief executive officer a year later.

Schoneman's experience was as a senior property insurance executive with the Atlantic Companies in New York. He was a mannered, personable and energetic businessman in whom the board placed a great deal of trust. Under his leadership in the late 1970s, the company came out of its crisis, its product was in demand, the return on its investments was excellent, there was capital available for expansion and the company's premium-to-surplus ratio improved to a sturdy 2-to-1.

"So, we felt financially strong … everything was humming along," according to Executive Vice President Lowell H. Tornow.

As the decade came to a close, Wausau's prime business still was in workers' compensation, but Schoneman had begun to diversify into property and casualty insurance to smooth out some of the bumps in the road of the past and to grow the company. The board agreed with the strategy.

"In the insurance industry, the real innovations during the 1980s are going to come in the area of providing coverages for the new exposures faced by American businesses," Schoneman said. "What is left of the traditional way of carrying on the insurance business will fade, and Wausau is committed to not only being a part of this revolution but to being one of its leaders."[6]

First Schoneman established an excess and surplus lines business in San Francisco and called it Wausau International Underwriters. Because it was a somewhat risky segment of insurance, a number of senior officers opposed the plan as well as the company's leadership, but Schoneman "took an independent approach," and proceeded anyway.

More subsidiaries followed. From his days at Atlantic, Schoneman was fascinated with the ocean marine reinsurance business and that resulted in the purchase of American Marine

Underwriters in Miami, FL. Chicago-based Lansing B. Warner, Inc. was acquired in January 1983. The Warner group included Underwriters Insurance Company, a multi-line property and casualty insurer, and management of Canners Exchange Subscribers and Warner Reciprocal Insurers, two well-known reciprocal* insurers primarily serving the food processing industry.[†]

Most of these, and several other new business ventures, Schoneman knew something about through previous business dealings — a friend, an associate, etc. — and for a time it all looked very good on the company's books. Very quickly Wausau went from about $20 million in property and casualty business annually to 10 times that amount. Early on Schoneman was "rewarded" by the board with a promotion to chairman in 1981; Executive Vice President Gerald D. Viste moved into the president's chair, a seat he coveted prior to Schoneman's arrival.

Although the prices paid for these and other enterprises were not extravagant, Gunderson refers to them as "distressed merchandise (that) required millions of dollars to rehabilitate. We had neither the current funds nor the time to make them profitable. It was a dilemma."[7]

The new ventures also put pressure on the parent company's surplus. Additional strain came as interest rates descended in the early '80s from their record heights. As a result the return on investments and the amount of capital available for growth declined significantly. Furthermore, the price wars were back.

"In my opinion," said Tornow, "had we not had all these extra companies to manage, which were spawned by John Schoneman's thirst for diversification, we would have been better fortified to handle our mainstream business." In the

---

* In reciprocal insurance two insurers cede insurance to each other, usually in near-equal amounts, and share in the profits and losses. It is a form of reinsurance.

[†] While at the University of Chicago for his MBA, Schoneman had written a paper on the two reciprocals, hence his interest in them.

process, Schoneman lost the confidence of his senior managers.

At the November 1983 board meeting in Boston, a degree of concern surfaced in the form of a question from Thomas Hancock, a crusty 14-year member of the board who had been chairman of The Trane Company of La Crosse, WI.

"Is Wausau Insurance in a precarious position?" he asked Schoneman.

"I don't believe we are in a precarious position," the chairman replied.[8]

With declining performance came additional questions. At the board meeting in Scottsdale, AZ, the following February, it was Ralph Moore, chief executive officer of Owens Steel in Columbia, SC, who asked Schoneman to estimate what the operating losses would be in 1984. Schoneman said he thought they would be between $75 million and $100 million.

Moore then turned to Kryshak, the company's chief financial officer. "Tom, what do you expect from your forecast of what the loss is going to look like?" Kryshak said $200 million.

"After that meeting, I was told directly by both Schoneman and Viste that my comments were inappropriate," said Kryshak. It may have been one of the few times Schoneman and Viste agreed on anything in the mid-1980s. As the company's situation worsened, each badmouthed the other to company executives without ever openly confronting each other.

Despite the warning flags at the Scottsdale meeting, top management still received half of their annual bonuses. In a view shared by others, Tornow saw the bonuses "as a signal that we were really kidding the board about how serious our situation was."

By the time of the annual meeting in May of 1985, senior management knew Wausau Insurance was in deep trouble. All the officers gathered at the company's training center up the hill from its headquarters to hear Schoneman announce that "Tom Hancock was going to help us out of our financial problems," said Tornow. "We knew when we saw Tom Hancock standing on that platform with Schoneman that this was deadly serious."

Everyone knew Hancock as a hardened, demanding administrator who had led Trane through some difficult days before retiring in 1978. He had just left the Wausau board as director emeritus in 1984; now he was returning to see what could be done about the downward slide. At 72 he assumed the chair of the executive committee.

Although many in the company knew times were tough, only a very few knew how tough. It wasn't until the spring of 1985 that senior officers were told A.M. Best, industry rater of financial stability, planned to publish an "omit" rating for Wausau. (A year earlier it dropped the company from "A" to "B+.")

"An 'omit' means you are not rated; it's bad news," said Tornow, "and that's when we sort of knew we were in a crisis situation."

Initially Best was reluctant to consider a less damaging "deferred" rating until Wausau showed some action toward correcting its problem. The same could be said for the State of Wisconsin's insurance regulators, who were deeply concerned with Wausau's unstable position and Schoneman's apparent inability, or unwillingness, to deal with it.

For some time the state regulators pushed for action, but the company chairman all but ignored them. "He apparently felt that the insurance department was unduly concerned, and we could work our own way out of our financial difficulty," said Leslie J. Baumer, retired executive vice president.

Late in May 1985, Deputy Insurance Commissioner Lou T. Zellner* led a delegation to Wausau for a showdown meeting. Also around the board room table sat Schoneman, Hancock,

---

* Zellner won praise from all parties concerned for her efforts to save Wausau.

board member San W. Orr Jr., Viste, Kryshak, Baumer and other senior executives.

"They were really ticked off," said Baumer, recalling the state's attitude. "They mentioned a letter they had sent to John that he hadn't responded to. 'Well, I've been traveling,' Schoneman said. Apparently he was just sort of winging it as far as trying to give them definite answers and action plans."

The Sunday following the meeting, June 2, 1985, the *Milwaukee Journal* published a long article about Wausau in which Schoneman said he expected the company to be profitable by the third quarter of the year and show "a substantial profit" in 1986. The article concluded with another Schoneman quote: "See me in two years, and we'll throw a party."[9]

Two days later the following bulletin went out to all employees: "The executive committee of the Wausau Insurance Companies board of directors today accepted the resignation of John A. Schoneman as chairman and chief executive officer." It was signed by Hancock, who assumed Schoneman's duties.

Schoneman's indifferent performance in the meeting with the state was the final straw for Hancock and Orr. Immediately thereafter they took a recommendation to the board that the chairman be relieved of his post. Schoneman passed it off to *The Wall Street Journal* as "a friendly difference of opinion with the executive committee as to the road to recovery."[10]

Hancock's road certainly was different. It was bumpy but necessarily so for the survival of the company. He set up his command post in the chairman's office, made Kryshak his chief-of-staff and gave a select few senior executives marching orders for saving the company. Viste, blocked again from the top job or from even having a hand running the company, hung on for a couple of months until Hancock suggested he move on.

At a June meeting with his senior executive team, Hancock admitted the extent of the company's problems surprised even him. "He didn't know how ... such an apparently capable management team could let such a thing happen," said Bill D.Wymore, a former regional manager who returned to the home office in May of 1985. Hancock tried to pump up his in-shock troops.

"We've got to work hard; discipline ourselves," Hancock told them. "You have my sympathy, but not my pity. … We've got to know where we're going: We need objectives. The problem is how to get people to buy our product. We've got a stinking Best rating, (and) we've got problems with brokers and buyers. We've got good products, good organization, good reputation, good service, and we back up our promises.

"Don't spend your time worrying; get the job done. Do it the same old way you've always done it: You work your butt off. We'll preserve the things that made us great (and) perform as always. Maybe with fewer people, but that's life."[11]

As the team then realized, the situation for the insurer was "desperate," although still most of the more than 7,400 employees did not have the whole story — and those who did couldn't tell the rest. The surplus declined to $268 million in the first quarter of 1985 from $303 million in fiscal 1984 and $511 million the previous year. The ratio of premiums to surplus was pushing 6-to-1. Major customers, such as Xerox, were bailing out and more promised to do so as the time for the January 1 renewals approached. Major brokers of Wausau's business — the giant Marsh & McLennan and the Corroon & Black organizations for example — pulled back their support.

"Effective immediately, no new or renewal business should be placed with the Employers Insurance Company of Wausau or its affiliated fire and casualty companies," declared a June 11 memo sent to all M&M offices by John W. Foley, head of the broker's security committee. To do business with Wausau would require a signed disclaimer from the client, Foley said.[12]

This was just one of the damaging fires that Hancock and his team had to put out. Even with Schoneman out of the picture, much work remained to turn the corner with A.M. Best and the Wisconsin regulators, and to stop the internal bleeding.

The recovery plan included cutting directors' fees in half, selling corporate aircraft and the New York apartment, culling out certain lines of business, reducing its risk through reinsurance,* increasing rates, slashing travel and advertising budgets, instituting a hiring freeze and longer work hours, and whacking off 10 percent of the workforce almost overnight. On a Tuesday Hancock's staff reduction order was made; the following Monday nearly 700 people knew they no longer had a job. At the end of 1985, the workforce totaled 6,000.

By June 21 Hancock had made enough progress to issue a press release. "The management is convinced that the aggressive recovery actions we are taking, which affect all elements of our business, will accelerate our return to profitability and improve our capital base," his statement read.

Hancock and Kryshak continued to concentrate on the biggest problems. They had hired New York insurance consultant Richard Stewart to help shore up relations with the Wisconsin insurance department, which began an intensive, internal audit. Hancock, Kryshak and Ronald C. Retterrath, senior vice president, commercial property underwriting, met with Marsh & McLennan's security committee and obtained some relief from the harsh tone of the June memo.

Much depended on which way Best would go with its rating of Wausau, however. Board member San Orr and Kryshak were forthright in their approach to Best, admitting the mistakes of the past but emphasizing the steps the company had taken to

---

* Wausau reduced its exposure to risk by obtaining an aggregate excess of loss with North American Reinsurance and USF&G for accident year 1985, thus improving its surplus by about $60 million. At the same time Wausau's lead property and casualty reinsurers, New England Reinsurance and Kemper Reinsurance, agreed July 1 to renew the contracts.

improve the situation, which included the firing of Schoneman. Finally, on June 24, Wausau received the "deferred" rating it preferred.

Several insurance companies in the Midwest made a pass at the distressed merchandise, but they were just passes. In the hope that a viable "white knight" would suddenly appear to save Wausau, Hancock pushed for Orr to secretly appeal for help from Goldman Sachs in New York.

Overnight the investment banking firm had a team at Wausau's headquarters. Certainly Tornow was surprised by the swift turn of events. He walked into his office to find a conference table set up at one end of the room, stacks of records everywhere "and strange people sitting around the table."

Throughout the summer Goldman Sachs introduced to Wausau five or six suitors,* some of whom flew into Wausau to take a look. Each time the rumors started about this company or that taking over Wausau. One day someone saw the Oscar Mayer weiner van drive by, and the rumors started anew.

Wymore remembers one meeting with an interested party and the uneasiness he had with "the big hotel room, the cigars, big dinner. These guys were obviously venture capitalists representing all sorts of money," he said, "and they're trying to pump you for information. … It was very obvious to me that these people cared nothing about our culture … philosophy … employees … policyholders.

"All these people were interested in, very clearly, is what they could get out of Wausau in the very shortest period of time if they could get control of you."

Management's greatest fear was that Wausau would be broken up and, in the process, the pieces moved out of Wausau. Community leaders shared the same concerns inasmuch as the insurance company was the city's largest employer, by far.

---

* The names of those with whom there had been discussions have not been made public.

Goldman Sachs sought out Nationwide's interest very late. Peter F. Frenzer, executive vice president, investments, received the first call from the investment banking firm late in September 1985. He immediately put in a call to Fisher, general chairman and chief executive officer of the Nationwide Insurance Companies, who was attending a Beaver Pacific Corporation board meeting in California with Paul A. Donald, president and general manager of the insurance companies. They returned to Columbus to review documents Goldman Sachs provided Frenzer.

After a hurried examination of Wausau's situation, the Nationwide group met the Wausau people for the first time October 10 at the Hilton O'Hare,* Chicago. It was a very chilly day for the second week in October, Donald remembered.

The Nationwiders were D. Richard McFerson, senior vice president, finance, Donald, Frenzer, Gordon E. McCutchan, senior vice president and general counsel, and Leon J. Weinberger, vice president of Nationwide's property and casualty insurance subsidiaries. Kryshak, Baumer, Wymore, Ronald Retterrath, senior vice president, underwriting, and Mark Fiebrink, actuary, represented Wausau's position.

Also around the table were Dan Johnson, a partner in the accounting firm of Peat, Marwick, Mitchell & Company, and Judith Kirby, a vice president at Goldman Sachs who had been active in bringing investors to Wausau.

Following an all-day meeting, Donald characterized Wausau's situation as "desperate," yet he felt a strong camaraderie emerge between Nationwide and the Wausau management team. "I

---

* Originally a Howard Johnson's Motor Lodge, the $8 million hotel was financed in 1972 by the Buckeye-O'Hare Company in which former Ohio Gov. James A. Rhodes and some of his associates were general partners. Nationwide Life Insurance Company was a limited partner in Buckeye-O'Hare and provided $1.06 million in mortgage loan money for the hotel. Nationwide and Rhodes also hooked up on hotel developments in Dallas and St. Louis.

think they wanted to find a way to make this work," he said.

Wymore remembered Wausau's reaction. "We walked out of there saying, 'These are our kind of people; they've got the same values we have,' and actually praying that if anything could happen, let it happen with these people."

Nationwiders felt much the same way. Even before the Chicago meeting, it appeared to be a marriage made in heaven. Nationwide wanted to develop business west of the Mississippi; Wausau already was well positioned there. Nationwide wanted to expand into commercial insurance; that was Wausau's traditional strength. Nationwide had a strong work ethic; so did Wausau.

"When we came out of that meeting," Donald said, "there is no question that we left there thinking, you know, unless we discover some ghost or skeleton in the closet we hadn't imagined could exist, we think we are going to go with this."

Both sides met next the following Sunday evening, October 13, at the Radisson Hotel in Madison, WI. Donald was the only one missing from the original Nationwide team; Kryshak, Orr and Hancock represented Wausau. The seven sat around one small table in the middle of a large room.

"It had an eerie feeling of a dark and suppressed Russia almost," McFerson recalled.

The Nationwide team laid out its plan, including: the core business would stay in Wausau; an infusion of up to $300 million in surplus notes; the promise of an improved A.M. Best rating, and no golden parachutes for key executives.

The Wausau group asked for time to consider the offer, so the Nationwide delegation went to the lobby and mingled with the guests at a wedding reception, nibbling on the food in the process. Within 20 minutes, the Wausau group had made its decision: "We'll take it," they said.

More Nationwide meetings in Madison, Chicago and Columbus followed in rapid order, but it wasn't until October

24 that McFerson, Frenzer and McCutchan first visited Wausau's headquarters — and undercover, too. So as not to alert anyone as to their presence or purpose, they left the Nationwide jet in Madison in the morning and flew into Wausau on Wausau's King Air. Posing as reinsurance managers, they toured the facility, including the training center.

Built in 1982, the expansive Westwood Conference and Training Center became what some regarded as a monument to the company's excesses. It has accommodations for 76, numerous dining rooms, 35 training centers, including a state-of-the-art fire protection training laboratory, and several auditoriums.

Nationwide made two creative, and critical, moves toward affiliation with Wausau, neither of which came out at the initial Chicago session. The first involved the financing. Nationwide transferred $250 million from its surplus into Wausau's surplus and took a 10-year, 9.7 percent surplus contribution note in return.* In a peculiarity of accounting, the parent company improved its affiliate by $250 million without diminishing its own wealth because it held the note. It was as if it had created $250 million out of thin air.

The second creative maneuver involved "a sequential resignation" of the Wausau board, which Nationwide first successfully employed to gain control of a small mutual insurance company in Texas. As W. Sidney Druen, senior vice president and general counsel at Nationwide, explained: "One group of eight Wausau directors resigned, and eight Nationwide nominees replaced them, thus maintaining a quorum. Then nine more Wausau directors resigned as a group and six Nationwiders replaced them." The bylaws were amended to

---

* By the end of 1992 an additional $150 million in notes had been issued at rates of 9 percent and 6.7 percent, maturing December 1, 1998, and December 1, 2002, respectively.

reduce the number of directors from 17 to 15: 14 from Nationwide plus San Orr, the only Wausau director retained on the new board.

The entire Wausau transaction, including the surplus notes and board election, had the approval of both the Wisconsin and Ohio insurance departments.

Frenzer saw the affiliation as "a unique opportunity to bring a leading commercial company into the Nationwide family with limited risk relative to the potential benefits." Furthermore, he said, Nationwide could realize its strategic objectives, i.e., western expansion and commercial lines development, at substantially less cost than if it had to build a duplicate organization.[13]

On November 6 both parties joined in the announcement of the affiliation and the creation of the nation's fourth-largest property-casualty group.* Donald became chairman of the new affiliate and Weinberger was elected president. Hancock returned to retirement, Kryshak eventually moved to Columbus as Nationwide's executive vice president, finance, and Best's "A" rating returned to Wausau December 9, 1985.

After a very hectic 27 days — one of the most momentous periods in Nationwide's history — McFerson wrote in his notes, "What do I do now?!!"†

What Fisher, Donald, Weinberger and other senior officers did was to talk up all that was right with the company rather than focus on the past and the negatives. The "Thank You, Policyholders" message in the 1985 annual report appeared to be directed to the employees as well as the company's customers.

---

* The affiliation was confirmed after the news leaked to the *Columbus Dispatch,* which published articles November 5 and 6. The pact was concluded November 26 with the election of the new Wausau board.
†McFerson's humorous notation was in reference to a line delivered by Robert Redford in the motion picture, *The Candidate* (1972), after he, as the lead character, wins election to the U.S. Senate.

"Relationships can be strengthened by adversity," it began. "The last year has not been an easy one for our company. We are well on our way to recovery, but this would not have been possible without your loyalty."

The recovery process also included cutting back on the expansion that got Wausau into trouble initially. Nationwide sold some companies and merged others into other Wausau or Nationwide organizations. By the end of 1992 eight of the 12 major companies operated by Wausau eight years earlier had passed from view, one way or another.

At the helm during the restructuring and resurrection period was Weinberger, who once worked "down the road" from Wausau as an executive vice president and director at Sentry Insurance at Stevens Point, WI. After an acrimonious falling out with Sentry Chairman John Joanis in late 1979, Weinberger joined Colonial Insurance Company, Anaheim, CA, a Nationwide affiliate. In 1984 he moved to Columbus as vice president of Nationwide's property and casualty subsidiaries and to Wausau the following year.

In the fall of 1992 Weinberger told employees that Wausau's losses had accumulated to $1.6 billion, or at least three times what Nationwide had anticipated. "I am convinced," said Galen Barnes, a veteran Nationwider who succeeded Weinberger in May 1993, "that none of the key people ... involved in that decision in November of 1985 knew how deep" the problem was.

"And, to be honest with you, it's not done yet," he said at the end of 1993. "We still have another $500 million to $600 million to get done — on top of the $1.6 billion." That, he said, will take another five or six years to work off.

W. Barton Montgomery, who retired in April 1994 as chairman of Nationwide Life Insurance Company, thinks Employers Insurance of Wausau and its problems kept the parent company from earning an A++ rating from A.M. Best in the early '90s.* "Our Wausau affiliation has ended up costing us more than we ever figured," the Washington Court House farmer said. "It was one of those things 'probably too good to be true.'

"It's a little bit like, you know, I bought a couple of farms here at the wrong time. They're going to work out, but hindsight sure is better than foresight."

---

* In 1993 the Nationwide Insurance Enterprise enjoyed a very strong A+ rating from A.M. Best.

16

THE ENTERPRISE'S ENTERPRISES

A t the time of John E. Fisher's retirement as general chairman in the spring of 1994, the Nationwide Insurance Enterprise encompassed nearly 100 companies. The majority of these engage in some aspect of the insurance industry, but there are a few exceptions.

Among the more catatonic is the Beak and Wire Company, one of many entities that just sit and wait for the appropriate time for activation. Steven P. Berger, president of Nationwide Communications, chose the unusual name to be free of duplication anywhere else in the nation.

Berger said "Mr. Fisher got great pleasure and great amusement at the annual meeting of calling the meeting to order once a year because he is the chairman of the Beak and Wire Company. ... It's quite the joke in the company. ... I am the president, (so) I have to get up and elect the officers and go through the whole thing. It's a great sport."

Of course, Nationwide management actually has taken a very serious view toward the subsidiary and affiliated companies in the enterprise. As Nationwide matured, a number of general principles developed in acquisition philosophy. For one, after the early Lincoln acquisition battles, there was general agreement to forego unfriendly (and unproductive) takeover attempts. There was a realization that the enterprise should build on its strength and this included staying in the mainstream of business services and not exposing policyholders' assets to exotic risks. Peripheral companies that came with acquisitions or affiliations that did not contribute to the central business mission were usually sold or dissolved.

Many of Nationwide's acquisitions were aimed at broadening its strength in life insurance, the commercial markets, and the west. In the broadcasting business, there was a strategy to develop a "critical mass" that could afford professional management, provide opportunities for advancement, and then "trade up" into major markets. Nationwide has attempted and generally succeeded in becoming an important player in whatever markets it has served.

So entities other than the Beak and Wire Company have had active roles to play at Nationwide. Chapters 10 and 15 detail the German subsidiary, Neckura, and the Wausau Companies, respectively. Among the other major affiliates are:

Colonial Insurance Company of California, Anaheim, CA:

Nationwide's entry into nonstandard automobile insurance through the purchase of Colonial Insurance Company of California was the direct result of a "revolt" of sorts by Nationwide agents.

Shortly after he became president of the Nationwide Insurance Companies in 1972, Fisher attended a zone sales meeting in Cincinnati. There he heard firsthand from Nationwide agents that because the company did not provide a vehicle for writing nonstandard, or high-risk,* automobile

---

* In general terms, anyone denied insurance by at least two companies is considered high risk. The insured pays considerably higher premiums.

insurance, the agents placed such business with other insurers. Fisher recalled that one Ohio company alone, Progressive Insurance in Cleveland, raked in as much as $25 million in premiums annually from business placed by Nationwide's agents.

Furthermore, if Nationwide failed to establish its own outlet for nonstandard automobile insurance "some agents were thinking of starting their own company," Fisher said, "and I must say that interest on their part kept me stimulated to try to see if we couldn't solve the problem."

Both he and General Chairman Dean W. Jeffers approached the matter cautiously, not wanting to unduly emphasize "a category of business that we were not really going to build the future of the company on," Fisher said. On the other hand, both men were eager to find a way to fulfill the need that was causing the agents to broker business elsewhere.

In the mid-1970s, Robert M. Culp, vice president-business insurance; Dr. Robert A. Rennie, senior vice president-investments, and Raymond G. Smith, vice president-treasurer and controller, formed an acquisitions committee to find a high-risk automobile insurer. This was not an easy task, given the oft-cloudy arena in which such companies operated versus Nationwide's decidedly conservative bent.

Enter Stuart H. Struck, a jolly, 54-year-old former university professor and innovator, who founded Dairyland Insurance Company in Madison, WI, before selling it to the Sentry Insurance Group. With the proceeds he subsequently bought for $1.75 million an inactive corporate shell, Colonial Insurance Company of California in Anaheim, and began in 1977 to sell nonstandard auto and motorcycle insurance through independent agents. Culp, who had business with Struck at Dairyland 10 years earlier, tracked him down in Carefree, AZ, where he was raising thoroughbred horses. In December 1977 the two men got together in Carefree and, in Struck's parked pick-up truck, talked about Colonial for almost six hours.

Nationwide Mutual paid Struck $2.5 million for Colonial*
and bought $10 million in preferred shares of the company,
which was very small in 1978. Struck continued as president
and was allowed to continue his entrepreneurial ways, although
he "could get carried away," Fisher said.

On an early visit to Anaheim, Fisher caught wind of a plan
by which Colonial was going to develop agency computer
service systems for several West Coast insurance companies that
were not in Nationwide's family. Struck was going to charge
these companies for the computer development to defray the
cost of developing his own computer system, Fisher recalled.
He paid Struck a private visit, closing the door to Struck's office
behind him.

"Let me understand this, Stu. Am I right that you have
decided to take the Nationwide Insurance Enterprise into the
field of software development, which we normally avoid, and
put our name on the line with these various other insurance
companies? And you are going to do this with the resources of
this very infantile or embryonic insurance company? And you
haven't even talked to your board chairman about it? Is that
so?"

Struck leaned back in his swivel chair and put a big, friendly
but sort of guilty grin on his face. "Yeah. I guess that's right!"

"Stu, I can tell you that if we wanted you to go into the
software business, we would have told you!" Fisher said. The
project was shut down, then and there.

When Struck's wife died in 1981, "he seemed to lose all
interest in the whole idea" of running an insurance company,

---

* Nationwide Mutual kept the Colonial name primarily because neither Dean
W. Jeffers nor John E. Fisher wanted the parent company to be tainted by the
nonstandard insurance industry.

Culp said. "I proposed to Paul Donald (president of the Nationwide Insurance Companies) that he send me out there to run the company for a while," which Donald did. Culp served as Colonial's president in 1982 and 1983.

At the time of Nationwide's purchase in 1978, Colonial posted about $15 million in revenues. Then Nationwide's agents began selling Colonial alongside other high-risk carriers, such as Progressive in Cleveland, and in five years Colonial became a $60 million company. In March 1983 Nationwide told its agents they no longer could broker with competing companies, With the aid of an aggressive marketing campaign, Colonial sales took off again. When it became apparent in the summer of 1986 that premiums for the year would reach $350 million, Galen R. Barnes, who succeeded Culp as president, received a visit from his boss, who was concerned about the rapid growth.

"Do you remember when you agreed that you were going to write $225 million (in insurance) for 1986?" asked Donald. Barnes agreed he did. "Well, that's what it is going to be — $225 million and no more," said Donald.

Barnes took his foot off the accelerator and applied the brakes, "but we did some damage, because in 1987 we went down to $210 million," he said. "We put the brakes on so hard we irritated a lot of our agents, and they said they didn't want to use us anymore."

The damage was only temporary. Colonial is today one of Nationwide's most profitable enterprises, having posted an underwriting profit for its seventh consecutive year in 1993. "In our business," Barnes explained, "it is unusual for us to make money on underwriting. We generally make most of our money on investment income."

Scottsdale Insurance Company, Scottsdale, AZ:

Within a dozen years of its start-up March 29, 1982, the Scottsdale Insurance Company was the nation's second largest excess and surplus lines* insurance company with $623 million in written premiums in 1993.

Originally known as The Scottsdale, the Arizona-based company was born out of Fisher's desire to create a better balance for Nationwide Mutual through more points of entry in the field of business insurance. "That had an impact on our decision to form Scottsdale," Fisher admitted.

Colonial's Struck again was the catalyst, introducing Culp to Rolland L. Wiegers, president of Great Southwest Fire Insurance Company, a Scottsdale-based excess and surplus lines insurance company owned by the Sentry Insurance Group. Wiegers and Leon J. Weinberger, who was to head both Scottsdale and Wausau in future years, both worked for Struck at Dairyland. According to Wiegers, Sentry never felt comfortable with E&S business — "they were scared to death of this stuff we were writing" — and therefore gave Wiegers and Great Southwest half-hearted support and imposed numerous controls.

"A company should never be in the excess and surplus lines business unless it is willing to grant its officers the freedom to make quick decisions and go with their best hunch," Wiegers said.[1]

Because, like Sentry, Nationwide had no experience in E&S lines, making a move from Great Southwest concerned Wiegers, but he said Culp and Donald "said all the right things" during their talks. Still, Nationwide was operating under "a little bit of a misconception in thinking that our own agents could readily handle E&S lines business," Fisher said. "We then realized we would have to write this business through experienced managing general agents (because) it was not the type of business that Nationwide agents would normally be experienced in."

In any case, Scottsdale, a wholesaler of insurance rather than

---

* Excess and surplus lines insurance provides coverage for unusual or unique perils and specialty business, such as medical malpractice and police liability.

a retailer, is not equipped to accept business directly from a large agency force like Nationwide's. The more than 100 managing general agents throughout the country, who are underwriters and work on commissions from Scottsdale and other insurers, package the business.

Nationwide Mutual's board approved the expenditure of $10 million to capitalize Scottsdale and sent Wiegers a simple admonition: "You've got a tough insurance operation; just don't go broke."[2]

Wiegers hired his first employee, Barbara Nasworthy, who had been a marketing administrator at Great Southwest. Initially their "office" was in the lobby of the Sheraton Hotel in Scottsdale, then a 1,000-square-foot office suite furnished with folding tables and chairs, a leased copier, one electric typewriter and an orange crate for a table.

Before leaving Great Southwest, Wiegers knew who in that office he'd like to have in on the start-up, besides Nasworthy, but Nationwide made it clear it didn't want to "raid" Great Southwest's personnel. So, it attempted to notify Great Southwest in advance of "anybody that showed an interest in our operation. But that didn't work out very well, because by the time we gave notice, why, we found out that those people were getting fired," Fisher said.

Scottsdale grew rapidly, not only in business but in personnel and office space, with Wiegers as president and Weinberger as chairman. It moved into a 6,000-square-foot office, doubled that shortly after and eventually had 25,000 square feet leased before moving again into double that space in September 1986. "Six months later we maxed out," said Nasworthy, vice president-corporate services. Finally, after Scottsdale reached more than 100,000 square feet under lease, Nationwide agreed to construct and develop an office complex for Scottsdale's more than 900 employees, all at its headquarters location in Scottsdale.

Excess and surplus lines business creates a balance for commercial business because it can run wide open when the rest of the market is "tight as a drum," Culp said. "Scottsdale also enabled Nationwide to become a factor in insuring segments of the insurance-buying public that normally you couldn't write because of rate regulation on the standard market, such as police legal liability, medical malpractice and the more exotic risks like a circus or carnival."

"The craze in the early 1990s was bungee jumping," said Wiegers. "We were inundated with calls to write that, and I refused; just too hazardous. We've never done them, and that's proven to be a good move," but the company has issued policies for holes-in-one, basketball shots, rain delays and fishing tournaments.

Big prize money brings out the fraudulent operators, according to Vickie Kartchner, who succeeded Wiegers as president in May 1994 when he succeeded Weinberger, who retired. In one fishing contest, the big payoff went to anyone catching a premarked fish, which someone did. Something seemed fishy about the catch, however, and a careful examination proved that the fish had been previously frozen.

At the outset Scottsdale stuck to fairly low limit policies — maybe $1 million — so it would not get itself out on a limb with a lot of exposure. Today it is still conservative, rarely topping $5 million liability on a casualty policy and $1 million liability on property.

One of the company's market strengths is in law enforcement and public officials liability coverage. With a whopping 35 percent of the market (in 1993), Scottsdale led the industry. The market, which includes law enforcement groups, public officials and school boards, represents better than $60 million in premiums annually, according to Kartchner.

"It's a tough class to underwrite because it's very dynamic," she said. "It's one of those lines that you better know what you are doing from an underwriting and a claims handling perspective because you're not just dealing with local law. You are also dealing with federal constitutional law, and it's very complex."

Kartchner recalls the lean and hungry days for the company in the early 1980s, but then the market turned in the mid-1980s "and I thought, I'll never live through this. The work was phenomenal ... Mountains of paper ... We probably will never experience a growth like that again. ... What we really are talking about in terms of putting Scottsdale on the map took place in a five-year period (1982-1986)."

Public Employees Benefit Services Corporation (PEBSCO), Columbus, OH:

A hard-driving entrepreneur, John David Davenport, is credited with introducing Nationwide to the multi-billion-dollar world of tax-deferred savings plans for public employees. His business began in 1963 in Oklahoma City, OK, under the name Davenport-Dillard, Inc. (DDI). The mass-marketing sales company sold retirement savings programs to such organizations as the National Tire Dealers Association, the Florist Transworld Delivery Association and some 200 other trade organizations.

Other customers included the American Oil Company and the Shell Oil Company, which established DDI retirement programs for their independent franchised dealers and distributors. "These types of programs were the forerunners of what later became the HR10/KEOGH legislation, creating new tax incentive savings plans for small businesses," Davenport said.

From these early efforts, Davenport founded PEBSCO in 1973 and was joined three years later by Charles B. "Bud" Wilkinson, former head football coach at the University of Oklahoma. Wilkinson became chairman and Davenport served as president and chief executive officer until 1982 when Wilkinson's son, Jay, succeeded him.

PEBSCO's first customer as a third-party administrator of governmental deferred compensation programs was the State of Oklahoma (although DDI initiated the business). As enabling legislation and regulation moved across the land, the company picked up additional contracts. By 1976 PEBSCO had more than 15,000 employee participants with annual payroll deferrals of $12.6 million.

Davenport and PEBSCO linked up with Nationwide in the early1970s. At the time, Fisher was engaged in sponsor/endorser discussions with a number of affiliates of the Assembly of Governmental Employees, among them the Maryland State Employees Association. Independently, Nationwide Corporation's chief actuary, Robert Powell, had been approached by Raymond Krappo, an actuary, and his friend, Davenport. The three talked about PEBSCO's deferred compensation programs.

When they learned of Fisher's talks with the Maryland group, Powell and Davenport spoke to Fisher about PEBSCO and Nationwide joining forces to introduce to the public sector deferred compensation variable annuities. The Columbus insurance company would underwrite the products and PEBSCO would market them to the state employees. Maryland's program involved about $3 million in premiums, but Nationwide did not have any way to administer deferred compensation programs. With PEBSCO assuming that role, it relieved Nationwide of what could have been a major problem.

Still, convincing senior management and the directors was difficult, and Fisher came under heavy fire. Why are we doing this? they wanted to know. Everyone recognized the difficulties the plan presented: It was an untried departure for Nationwide; Nationwide's agency force would not be involved, at least initially, and it could be an expensive start-up.

"This was a pretty big step for us," recalled Dean W. Jeffers, then Nationwide's general chairman and chief executive officer.

"It was unplowed ground, and we weren't equipped to do it."

Fisher stoutly defended his position and put Paul B. Johnson, his vice president, business sales, in charge. Johnson, in turn, hired Robert Sharp, director of tax sheltered products, and several others for the start-up, but it was a bumpy road for Fisher. Powell, who later became president of West Coast Life Insurance Company, and Fisher teamed up to convince the board of the program's efficacy. PEBSCO would act as independent adminstrators that represented the state organizations and Nationwide would underwrite products and services administered by Davenport's group.

"It was a hard sell" for Fisher, Jeffers agreed, "but I can assure you it would not have gotten to the board level without my approval. ... I always have believed that if you really don't know anything about something, then you should be very careful ... and hire the people who *do* know."

Davenport sought and received from Nationwide a loan of some $400,000 to buy out his DDI partner and finance his exploding PEBSCO operations. By 1980 PEBSCO operated in 33 states through 250 licensed field representatives. It was the exclusive deferred compensation representative for five state governments and 67 cities or counties: Within a year those numbers jumped to 10 and 661, respectively. As 1982 came to a close, PEBSCO counted 951 public jurisdictions as clients.

"He signed up contract after contract, got production underway, hired agents and finally got to the point where he was completely out of funds," recalled John L. Marakas, retired president of Nationwide Life. Senior Nationwide management agreed with Marakas' assessment: "David was a tremendous entrepreneur and salesman, but when it came to administration, he was drowned with volume."

The lack of administration was the one thing that really concerned the board's audit committee in the winter of 1981-82, especially after having put several hundred thousand dollars into PEBSCO. Nationwiders visited the company in Oklahoma City to try to put the stopper in the drain. Following the assessment, it became obvious to D. Richard McFerson, vice president of individual life and health operations, that the only way to stop the bleeding was for Nationwide Corporation to buy PEBSCO.

"I was convinced all along that we absolutely had to acquire PEBSCO," he said. "Our assets were at risk administratively. PEBSCO was not able to keep up with the business. Their service was poor; we had to take over the servicing of the business."

It took McFerson "the better part of a year to convince John Marakas to (acquire PEBSCO and) to allow us to take the matter to the board for a vote." When finally the time came to make the pitch to the board, it was McFerson who made it.[3]

Several directors and members of senior management felt that not only had too much money been poured into PEBSCO but that $9.7 million was too high a price to pay for it. Frank B. Sollars, longtime chairman of Nationwide Mutual and a director of the corporation, was particularly vociferous in opposition to the cost of the buyout. "I thought we could buy it for a lot less," he said.

Davenport himself didn't think the price was right, either: He wanted more, and so exasperated everyone at a May 1982 Nationwide conference to complete the agreement that Peter F. Frenzer, then executive vice president of investments, nearly walked out of the meeting. He would have, too, had not J.A. Gulick, vice president of sales and financial services, urged him to stay.

Even after the sale, for more than $4 million in cash plus a percentage based on asset growth for 10 years, the board had second thoughts on what it had approved: "At least, we let (management) think we were having second thoughts," Director Dwight W. Oberschlake said, but "I guess you could say we were probably a little nervous. We wanted to make sure (management) kept paying attention to it." Sollars led the board's charge "to keep Dick McFerson's feet to the fire on the project," he said.

In his report in the 1993 Nationwide Insurance Enterprise annual report, Nationwide Life President Frenzer noted that together Nationwide Life and PEBSCO created the nation's market leader in sales and administration of public employee deferred compensation programs. They administered the plans of more than 726,000 state, county and municipal employees. The total assets of the programs were $7.9 billion, by coincidence, exactly 1,000 times the price paid for PEBSCO 11 years earlier.

"We are still probably far from being one of the very top groups in pensions," Fisher admitted, "but we have gained a great foundation in this entire field of retirement products … sophisticated products that give consumers choice on the investments that underlie their financial security.

"I take a lot of pride in this. It was a team effort, but I suppose … I had my neck out about as far as anybody in taking us into an area not too many people knew when we started doing it. That included me."

Nationwide Communications Inc., Columbus, OH:

Peoples Broadcasting Company, the forerunner of Nationwide Communications, was the first affiliated, non-insurance enterprise. After several false starts, its first station, WRFD, went on the air Sunday, September 28, 1947, broadcasting from studios in the Henri Boyd Inn, Worthington, OH.* The 5,000-watt station broadcast from 7 a.m. to 6 p.m. Edgar Parsons was the station's first manager.

Peoples acquired its second station, WOL Radio in

---

* See Chapter 5.

Washington, DC, in February 1950, then sold it three years later. In 1953 and early 1954, the company acquired WTTM, Trenton, NJ; WMMN, Fairmont, WV, and sold both in 1963.

Certainly the purchase of WGAR, Cleveland, in 1954, was Peoples' most interesting. With the radio station came a majority 35 percent interest in the Cleveland Browns and a vice presidency in the professional football team, a position filled by Peoples President and General Manager Herbert E. Evans. There also were 20 box seats for every game for guests of the broadcast and insurance companies, and all the shrimp you could eat at the pre-game buffet luncheon. For seven years, every Sunday the Browns played at home senior officers, directors and dignitaries flew to the game in the company's DC-3, weather permitting.

It crushed the many who eagerly looked forward to these fall outings when Peoples* and its fellow investors sold the Browns in 1961 to New Yorker Art Modell. The company realized a significant profit from the sale — more than $1 million. "Not a bad deal for a bunch of farmers," Murray D. Lincoln commented.[4]

With the proceeds, Peoples built Green Meadows Country Inn on the land acquired in 1947 for WRFD. Lincoln wanted to build an entire old-fashioned village, much like his hometown of Raynham, MA, with a church, a general store, an inn, a picnic park, a summer playhouse, etc. "We're going to build this inn (in a dry township), by golly, because there's not a restaurant in Columbus where you can go and not have liquor served," said Lincoln.[5] On January 15, 1962, Lincoln, Evans, and Peoples Chairman James H. West officiated at the opening of the attractive facility on Route 23, a few miles north of Columbus.

The Green Meadows Country Inn was somewhat less than a success. Despite every effort to make it a profitable restaurant

---

* Although the parent company names changed to Nationwide in 1955, Peoples did not become Nationwide Communications until 1967.

and motel operation, the ban on liquor sales proved to be its downfall. In 1973 Nationwide Mutual bought the inn and turned it into a training facility, since renamed the John E. Fisher Nationwide Training Center.

KVTV in Sioux City, IA, became in 1953 the first television station acquired by Peoples, followed by the powerful WNAX in Yankton, SD, a farm station that covered five states. Its program director, Clark Pollock, later became president of Nationwide Communications.

Over the years many other radio and television stations came and went, in New Jersey, West Virginia, Tennessee, Virginia, Maryland, North Carolina, Florida, Ohio, Minnesota, Washington, Pennsylvania and Wisconsin. NCI's entry into the latter state came through the purchase of WBAY-TV in February 1975. The sellers were the Norbertine Fathers, a Catholic order that realized owning a commercial television station was not a religious endeavor.

Among the pre-1980s deals that never came to pass were ownership of the highly respected WQXR-FM, *The New York Times*-owned station in New York; the Outlet Company, owner of radio and television stations, and Storer Broadcasting Company. Storer was a multi-million mouthful for Nationwide: Jeffers said he "believed in thinking big, but perhaps not quite that big."[6]

Pollock engineered one of the largest NCI acquisitions, Western Cities Broadcasting, in March 1985. The $43.5 million package included eight radio stations, in Phoenix and Tucson, AZ, Las Vegas, NV, and San Jose and Sacramento, CA. "Everybody thought we were nuts," said Steven P. Berger, who succeeded Pollock as president in 1989.*

---

* In 1993 NCI paid $15 million for just two Columbus radio stations, WCOL-AM and WCOL-FM. The third NCI station in Columbus is WNCI-FM. It is one of the three most-powerful FM stations in the nation with 175,000 watts transmitting from atop Nationwide's headquarters.

Berger arrived at NCI in 1979 as general manager/radio, which entitled him to a company car but not a loaded one, as he discovered.

"I went down to the garage to get my car and ran into Hank Turner, who was in charge of company cars. 'They told me to come down here and get my car,' I said."

"Oh, you're the new radio guy," said Turner. "Well, you can't have power door locks."

"What?"

"Well, you're not an officer, so you can't have power door locks. You can have power steering and any radio you want because of what you do, but you can't have power door locks."

Berger went out and bought his own car. "McFerson had come in at the same time, in 1979, and he and I had the only two two-door cars in the garage, and eight wire wheels between us. We became kindred spirits because of the cars." When he became a vice president three years later, Berger got power door locks.

In mid-1994, NCI decided to sell off its three remaining television stations and concentrate on radio. At the time it was the nation's 19th largest radio broadcasting company, with 13 stations in nine markets. "We examined our options and decided it was unlikely that we could assume a dominant position in television through mergers and acquisitions," said Berger.[7] Still, NCI claimed 850 employees and about $100 million in annual revenue.

Farmland Insurance/Nationwide Agribusiness, Des Moines, IA:

Farmland Insurance is the second oldest affiliate in the Nationwide Insurance Enterprise. It incorporated as the Farmers Cooperative Elevator Mutual Insurance Association in Aurelia, IA, in 1909 to protect against the loss from a grain elevator fire. In the 1920s the farmer-owned cooperative association changed its name to a mouthful: The Farmers National

Cooperative Elevator Mutual Insurance Association of Iowa to reflect its planned national expansion.

Immediately after World War II, it again changed to Farmers Elevator Mutual Insurance Company, which formed a casualty company, Farmers Elevator Mutual Casualty Company, in 1946. The two companies merged 10 years later, retaining the earlier name. In 1961 Farmers Life Company was formed.

Hard times brought on by excessive claims losses hit the association in the late 1960s. It needed an immediate $3 million capital infusion, which came in the nick of time from Farmland Industries, Inc.,* a Kansas City-based farmer cooperative founded in 1929 under the name Union Oil Company and six years later the Consumers Cooperative Association. Its first interests were in cooperative oil refineries in the Midwest, then fertilizer plants. The Farmland Industries name was adopted in 1966, a year before it acquired the stock of Farmland Insurance Companies.

"In the late 1960s, when I was in policyholder relations, I began visiting Farmland Industries to see if they would sponsor Nationwide in the West," said Fisher, who also had his eye on acquiring the Farmland Insurance Companies. On some of his trips Dean W. Jeffers, Bowman Doss or Frank B. Sollars would accompany him to the Kansas City, MO, headquarters of Farmland Industries "to add a little credibility."

Fisher said one of the reasons for an interest in Farmland, aside from the fact that it was western, was that "they had a great reputation in insuring farm elevators and other farm co-op exposures that we had never been able to gain expertise in. ... Despite some difficulties, they really had expertise in that field."

---

* The founder of Farmland Industries, Howard A. Cowden, and Murray D. Lincoln were both active in the cooperative movement, although not always on the same side. For a time, Cowden also served as a consultant to Nationwide.

The difficulties included getting into the field of reinsurance, which several years earlier also had created considerable problems for National Casualty, and automobile insurance when "they really didn't have the internal talent to manage it," said Fisher. In addition, inflation in the early 1980s took its toll with many enterprises throughout the nation, including Farmland Industries, which searched for a way to sell off its insurance operations.

"They began to move away from their expertise, which was commercial property casualty products for agribusiness and (into) a very price competitive market they did not understand," said William P. DeMeno, a longtime Nationwide senior executive who served as president and chief executive of Farmland Insurance from October 1984 to October 1989. Furthermore, the company tried to grow too quickly into auto insurance, he said, and, "as a result of their unbridled growth, their products were outdated and their prices were inadequate — and they got into deep trouble." Bankruptcy was near at hand, he felt.

DeMeno discovered after examining the company that Farmland's President and Chief Executive Officer William L. Balliu and his chief operating officer, Alden Brosseau, were "married" to the expansion concept, "which already had proven to be a mistake. They would not change."

In August 1982 Nationwide Mutual announced it had agreed to buy control of Farmland Life Insurance Company and its wholly-owned subsidiary, Farmland Insurance Company,* for $24.2 million. In addition, Nationwide paid $1.7 million for the debt obligations of Farmland Mutual Insurance Company and $2.8 million for the headquarters facility in Des Moines.

At the time, the three companies comprising the Farmland Insurance Companies posted combined premium income of

---

* In an effort to improve its market position, Farmland Insurance was renamed Nationwide Agribusiness Insurance Company June 1, 1986.

$73 million, assets of $135.8 million, more than 450 employees and nearly 170 agents. Farmland Life had nearly $1.4 billion of insurance in force. "We were possibly six months from going out of business," DeMeno said, so severe was the drain on the company's surplus.

Under the agreement Farmland Industries also became a Nationwide sponsor. In return for access to Farmland's nearly 500,000 members, Nationwide paid $10 million to Farmland over a 10-year period. Nationwide has similar sponsor relationships for the marketing of insurance and the promotion of a wide range of policyholder, safety and communications issues with six other sponsoring organizations. They are: Harvest States Cooperatives of St. Paul, MN; Maryland Farm Bureau; Ohio Farm Bureau Federation; Pennsylvania Farm Bureau; Ruralite Services Inc. of Forest Grove, OR, and Southern States Cooperative, Inc. of Richmond, VA.

Acquiring Farmland was "our first step in taking on a mutual insurance company without buying or demutualizing it," Fisher explained. It also bolstered Nationwide's position in the co-op agribusiness insurance market, established Nationwide in the middle of the nation as it moved westward, and helped fertilize "the kind of commercial insurance business that Nationwide wants to cultivate."[8]

However, the start-up was rocky, what with Balliu and Brosseau still in office to smooth the transition with Nationwide's newest sponsor. DeMeno and his Nationwide associates prepared and adopted in January 1983 a five-year marketing plan to put the companies back on their feet, but "Balliu and Brosseau refused to implement it," DeMeno said.

The new chairmen of Farmland Mutual and Farmland Life, Dwight W. Oberschlake and Leonard E. Schnell, respectively, were both Ohio farmers who long had been directors of Nationwide. They thought, as did the management team, that they were committed to keeping Balliu in place as part of the deal. ... "It became obvious to Leonard and me that he didn't have the horses to do the job."

Stymied by a false assumption, Oberschlake and Schnell met with Farmland Industries board members and the chairman, Vaughn Sinclair, at an October 1984 dinner at the Peppercorn Duck Club at the Hyatt Regency Columbus, across the street from Nationwide's headquarters. "*They* were wondering why *we* were keeping this fellow," Oberschlake said, "and we were under the impression we *had* to" for the sake of the sponsor relationship. "I think we all learned a lesson (in communications) from that experience."

The next day Fisher called DeMeno into his office. "Bill," he began, "since you are the architect of the marketing plan, and since we believe it's the right way, we're going to give you the opportunity to implement it."

DeMeno's heart sank.

"We want you to go there as the new president and chief executive officer," Fisher said.

"I appreciate the confidence you have in me, John, but I really don't want to go," replied DeMeno. Promoted to vice president-western development only months before, he was happy in his job with no interest in heading up an agribusiness company. The 47-year-old executive also didn't want to tell his wife that they would be moving for the 13th time since joining Nationwide in 1960.

"You really don't understand," Fisher continued, turning up the heat. "It's an opportunity to lead three companies. It's a real growth opportunity ... to deal with an investment portfolio, a life company, a board of directors. It will be a broadening experience ...

DeMeno still resisted, but then relented. Balliu was voted out October 4, 1984, and DeMeno voted in four days later. Later he would say, "John was exactly right. It was a terrific experience."

What DeMeno followed was a bad year for the Farmland Insurance Companies in 1982, "'83 was a worse year and '84 was worse than the other two," he recalled, with a 20 percent loss in surplus, or equity. "They were bleeding to death."

He put on the brakes while he took stock, then began restructuring the company. The 170 agents, most of whom were hired during Balliu's expansion days, were pared back to 40. The shift was to insuring the local co-ops, Farmland's strength; today it insures more than 30 percent of the nation's co-ops.

The very large, regional co-ops with the larger risks went to Nationwide National Accounts. In 1992 McFerson approved DeMeno's recommendation that these accounts be disbursed back to the individual companies in the enterprise, such as a now-healthy Farmland, for greater efficiency.

DeMeno noted that by 1994 Farmland had increased its premium almost five-fold, to more than $200 million, since Nationwide's acquisition in 1982.

"They are back to serving the customers that we believe they should have targeted in the beginning, and they do it more effectively than anybody in the market."

West Coast Life Insurance Company, San Francisco, CA:

The first significant event following the founding of Nationwide's oldest affiliate April 2, 1906, occurred 16 days later when the offices of West Coast Life burned to the ground.

The San Francisco company, established to provide Californians with an alternative to the East Coast life insurance giants, was reduced to ashes by the city's infamous earthquake and fire. Founder Henry Crocker and his associates picked up the pieces, and "with fighting spirit," established new offices. The next year the company opened a general agency in Honolulu, followed by branch offices in Oregon, Washington, Idaho, Utah, Nevada and Arizona. Later West Coast Life became the first American life insurance company to operate in the Philippines, China and Hong Kong.*

Through the 1920s and 1930s the insurer rapidly expanded operations in the Far East, an area which represented more than 30 percent of the company's income. With the advent of World War II and the imprisonment of some of its officers and employees, West Coast Life suffered tremendous losses. As a result, the company discontinued its Far East operations.

The second public offering in Nationwide Corporation stock in the summer of 1964 provided Nationwide sufficient funds to buy 61.5 percent interest in the 49-year-old West Coast Life for $26 million.† At the end of 1963 the company had $876 million of insurance in force, and almost three quarters of its direct premium income originated in California. West Coast Life also operated in all states west of the Continental Divide and the territory of Hawaii. All were of interest to Nationwide and its desire to expand westward.

Unlike many Nationwide insurance operations, West Coast Life writes most of its insurance today through independent agents, or the American agency system.

Nationwide Corporation paid $12.5 million for Dallas-based Gulf Atlantic Life Insurance Company and transferred its insurance business‡ into West Coast Life in 1990. A year later Investors Equity Life Holding Company, a California holding company, bought the shell and the name of Gulf Atlantic.

GatesMcDonald, Hilliard, OH:

"There is no other entity under our corporate blanket which

---

* Between 1915 and 1920 the company was known as West Coast-San Francisco Life Insurance Company as a result of a merger.
† Nationwide Corporation eventually paid approximately $50 million for West Coast Life's outstanding stock.
‡ At the time of the purchase, Gulf Atlantic had about $700 million of life insurance in force and admitted assets of more than $27.5 million.

has greater profitable growth potential than does GatesMcDonald," Fisher told the company's management meeting in April 1985. Yet, despite establishing itself as an industry leader in the administration of unemployment compensation programs, GatesMcDonald "has a low profile"[9] in the Nationwide Insurance Enterprise. That is changing.

Maryland passed the semblance of a workers' compensation law in 1902 and during the next 20 years all but six states followed with similar, but stronger, legislation. Many states took action after the Triangle Shirt Waist Company fire in New York that claimed the lives of 146 workers March 25, 1911. In general, the revision of labor laws included making the employer responsible for on-the-job injuries to employees, without regard to fault. "As a result of the new laws millions of dollars were soon paid out each year in benefits to injured workmen or their families."[10]

Auditing, administering and managing the growing number of claims appeared to Columbus Realtor Charles McDonald to offer an opportunity. In the summer of 1929 he teamed up with his neighbor, actuary Frank Gates, and together they convinced clients they could save them money through a comprehensive review of workers' compensation programs and lower rates. Gates sold the first four accounts for as little as $50 annually, but McDonald captured the big prize — the Ohio Electric Power Company in Marion, OH — at an annual fee of $600.

"The 1930s were a scary time to be in business, let alone to begin one," said Gloria Chapman, McDonald's daughter. "Dad had a lot of guts. People would ask me what my father did. … When I told them he was a consulting actuary, no one ever knew what I was talking about (so) I instead began telling people he was a doctor!"[11] Mrs. Chapman's husband, Donald, succeeded McDonald as president of the company in 1965.

Gates, McDonald & Company flourished, even during the

Depression. When Ohio's unemployment compensation law was enacted in the mid-1930s, clients asked the company for help in that area, too. Specialized divisions to provide safety, tax and Social Security services were established and the company branched out beyond Ohio's borders.

Nationwide Corporation acquired the privately held company for $6.5 million in September 1969 to use it as a vehicle to sell Nationwide insurance products and services to GatesMcDonald's high-profile clients. By then GatesMcDonald was the nation's largest professional cost-control service in the fields of unemployment and workers' compensation, serving clients in 44 states. The executive vice president of Nationwide Corporation, Howard Hutchinson, became the first president of GatesMcDonald following the acquisition. He made it clear expansion of the company was just around the corner.

Under its new owners GatesMcDonald entered a decade of rapid growth. It acquired such companies as Associated Safety and Claims, New York City; Delta Claims, Baton Rouge, LA; the E.I. Evans Company, Columbus, OH, and Southwest Safety and Claims, Tulsa, OK. Also, it established a presence in nearly a dozen major cities, from Seattle and Los Angeles to Philadelphia and Atlanta. By the early 1990s GatesMcDonald served all 50 states from more than 30 offices. It employed 800 associates who served nearly 18,000 companies, including many of the *Fortune* 500 giants.

Jack Gulick, who served as president of GatesMcDonald from 1985 to 1989, described the service company as "a gem in Nationwide's crown" despite some difficult years in the 1980s. For example, in the workers' compensation market there were an increasing number of large companies that switched to self-insurance. As DeMeno, vice chairman of GatesMcDonald, explained it in Nationwide's management newsletter, *Issues*, "We went through a period when there was a flurry of activity, a number of organizational changes, high employee turnover, realignments of operating territory, office closings and unprofitability."[12]

Part of the new strategic direction for the company came with the move from Nationwide's headquarters complex in downtown Columbus to a new office building in suburban Hilliard, OH. "When we were in Three Nationwide Plaza, you never knew GatesMcDonald was a tenant unless you were on our floor," one executive complained, yet "our competitors had their own headquarters." The new building solved that problem.

DeMeno also pointed to an improvement in customer service, a strengthening of management, the leveraging of GatesMcDonald's client list to Nationwide's benefit, and having the company take advantage of Nationwide's financial strength, support and managerial services.

"With all the changes that have taken place at GatesMcDonald, the mission hasn't changed," DeMeno said. "We are returning it to the fundamentals of providing high-quality claims and risk management and providing good service to our customers to give them a competitive edge."[13]

17

MORE THAN A BUSINESS

"You can find Nationwide people involved in almost every important community undertaking, from social services, the arts, the chambers of commerce, sports: You name it, and I'll show you our people in it. They tend to be doers and builders. Some even say they are competitive!"[1]

In a 1981 address to The Newcomen Society in Columbus, General Chairman Dean W. Jeffers neatly summed up a remarkable record of service by employees of the Nationwide Insurance Enterprise. The ledger is overflowing with achievements for the good of their fellow man, from gathering food to feed the hungry to saving lives on the highway through vigorous support of safety programs.

"Most people go into business to make money," said Edward F. Wagner,* vice president of the affiliated companies in the late 1960s. "We went into business to serve people and ended

---

* Wagner often recalled Murray D. Lincoln's reaction when he told Lincoln of his plans to to take some insurance courses. "Don't do it, Ed," said Lincoln. "You'll become another half-baked insurance man, and the world has too many of those already."

up making more money than the guys who were out to make it in the first place."[2]

John E. Fisher credited Wagner with Nationwide's first significant community efforts. He participated in urban planning studies for Columbus, including highway development, and in national and international relations. "People need big solutions, not small ones," Wagner said. "There's too much to be done to allow us to waste any of our resources on insignificant affairs."[3]

Nationwide's commitment to broad-based citizenship took on formal structure in June 1959 with the founding of the Nationwide Foundation, which later became the Nationwide Insurance Enterprise Foundation. Its first president, Murray D. Lincoln, said its purpose was to support charitable, religious, scientific and safety programs. Thirty-five years later 60 percent of the contributions from the tax-exempt foundation went to health and human services related functions, followed by education and the arts.

"It was very, very wise and insightful when Nationwide moved to establish a private foundation," said Stephen A. Rish, vice president, public relations and chairman of the foundation's contributions committee. Its first contributions the following year totaled $5,000 and supported the United Negro College Fund, the National Council of Churches, an educational fund at The Ohio State University in Columbus, among other organizations. In 1994 awards and grants totaled $8 million.

The initial endowment of $363,000 from corporate funds blossomed into assets of almost $33 million. In terms of giving, it was the nation's 24th largest company foundation by 1994. The foundation's assets are replenished by not only interest on the principal but also through contributions out of profits from each of the Nationwide companies.

Through the years the foundation enabled Nationwide to continue its level of philanthropy in good years for the company as well as the lean ones, although the income did not always equal the contributions. For example, in 1989 Nationwide distributed $2.2 million but the foundation's income fell $300,000 short of that.

A sizable percentage of annual funding funnels through United Way. In 1993 United Way received more than $3.1 million from the employees and another $3.1 million in matching corporate funds.

Rish said funding priority goes to organizations that have active Nationwide involvement. "If we have Nationwiders out there identifying with truly quality organizations, then as employer and corporate citizen, we should listen to that and respond with our corporate financial support," he said.

Employee participation in outside organizations shifts from year to year, but one foundation survey revealed some 800 different organizations were represented among 1,200 employees. Discovery of this information was "mind-boggling," Rish said, but helpful later in determining financial support. Almost 80 percent of the funding remains in central Ohio, the area with the greatest concentration of Nationwide employees.

The $290 million payroll in 1993 for more than 8,000 Nationwide employees made a significant impact on the Columbus metropolitan area. Their city income taxes alone topped $5.8 million, to say nothing of the millions in sales and real estate taxes. In addition, the enterprise paid more than $4 million in real estate and equivalent taxes and spent in central Ohio some $68 million on office supplies, equipment and the like.

Within Nationwide there was a noticeable and "dramatic culture shift" with the promotion in 1972 of Jeffers to general chairman and Fisher to president of the insurance companies. In the previous decade, 1961-1971, under Lincoln and Bowman Doss, the charitable gifts from the foundation more than doubled to $92,000. During the first 10 years of the Jeffers/Fisher administration, however, contributions increased more than 13 times, to $1.2 million.

The tremendous difference reflected the change in attitudes toward the community and its needs. "Dean (Jeffers) energized our corporate foundation," said J. Richard "Dick" Bull, who served as administrative assistant to Jeffers and later as vice president, public relations.

Throughout their careers, Jeffers and Fisher volunteered their time, financial resources and leadership to numerous community and industry organizations, a role that D. Richard McFerson now plays.

Probably no senior executive in Nationwide's history was more committed to community service than Fisher. From his earliest days at the company, he found time to volunteer for his industry, his company and his community.

Fisher followed Richard G. Chilcott as vice president, public relations, a position Chilcott broadened in scope. "So, just as Dick had been willing to represent himself (to the community) as Nationwide ... that's the way I handled it. I'm Nationwide," Fisher said. In the succeeding 25 years at the company, he also vigorously supported other officers becoming involved in community and industry activities.

"If you look at what Dean Jeffers did, what John Fisher has done, I don't think that can be repeated by Dick or whoever is chairman 20 years from now," said Peter F. Frenzer, in 1994 president of the Nationwide Life Insurance Companies. "There is just not enough time to do it. ... I think the companies' corporate involvement will continue to expand but the individual involvement will be less. You will have to spread it to more people."

Although the enterprise board recognized and totally supported the contributions made by senior management to a variety of community and industry affairs, it shifted ever so slightly following Fisher's retirement. Arden L. Shisler, chairman of the Nationwide parent company, and others felt that as the enterprise grew, it became "more of a challenge for him (Fisher) to do it all. ... He just got to spreading himself too thin," serving on so many boards, councils, task forces and the like.

"It has been said, jokingly ... that if you work at Nationwide you have to give your blood as well as your sweat," Jeffers told The Newcomen Society in his 1981 address, and he was right. Over the years there has been considerable blood-letting at Nationwide but for good cause. Between 1970 and 1994, enterprise employees gave 20,250 gallons of blood. The American Red Cross Blood Services also confirmed that the 10,300 donations in 1993 at Nationwide's Columbus headquarters established it as the largest single corporate site blood donor group in the U.S.

Group blood donations began December 7, 1948, when the central Ohio civilian blood donor center opened its doors in Columbus and accepted 65 pints from company employees. Then everyone still worked for the Farm Bureau Insurance Companies. Some men and women continue to contribute annually, even though they retired some years earlier. Many are members of the Gallon Club for which the dues are at least a gallon of blood.

Operation Feed is yet another community program in which enterprise employees consistently outstrip other corporate groups in Columbus. In 1994 the employees collected enough money and canned goods for 345,767 meals for central Ohio's hungry. It marked another record for Nationwiders, who set one year after year.

Since 1966 Nationwide has processed Medicare Part B payments for Ohio and West Virginia under a nonprofit contract with the federal government. Claims payments for 1994 were an estimated $1.7 billion and claims payments processed hit a record 30.5 million.

Nationwiders at all levels are encouraged to volunteer their support of the political and civic process that favors the goals of the enterprise, such as local, state, and federal legislation. Two organizations most active at Nationwide are the Civic Action Program (CAP) and the Nationwide Political Action Committees (PAC).

More than 3,600 PAC members, working through home office, regional and federal PACs in eight states, contributed more than $203,000 to 1993 candidates. The figure represented almost half of the funds contributed to the PAC funds during the year.

As McFerson said in his report to the 1993 membership, their contributions "have enabled the Enterprise to support those legislators who best understand the needs and concerns of the insurance industry."

Beyond the monetary contributions, however, are the letter-writing campaigns on important issues. The importance of these campaigns was recognized by Gerald D. Keim, professor of management at Texas A&M University, in an article he wrote for the *California Management Review.*

"Since the company carefully avoids postcards, form letters, and other mass mail techniques that are viewed as little more than harassment by many politicians, the individual letters generated by Nationwide's efforts are an indication of serious concern by voters," he wrote. "This feedback is political intelligence of value to elected officials, and the comments from politicians are usually very favorable."[4]

Nationwide's long association with all manner of highway safety programs* came to the fore once again at the 1994 annual meeting where Fisher recognized his successor for his work in safety and loss control and prevention. Fisher cited McFerson's "vigorous campaigns" against drunken driving, the development of the Vehicle Research Center in Ruckersville, VA, and his promotion of air bag installation and seat belt use. "All in all,"

---

* See Chapter 13.

he said, "these are some of the most pragmatic safety accomplishments any insurer ever recorded."

McFerson, a fierce advocate of all aspects of highway safety, co-chaired the board of Advocates for Highway and Auto Safety and served as board chairman of the Insurance Institute for Highway Safety, both active national organizations. Nationwide and the institute forged a five-year alliance in 1993 to establish North Carolina as a model state for seat belt use through the "Click It or Ticket" program.

One of the most successful of the safe driving campaigns McFerson initiated in 1989 was Prom Promise. High school students across the nation are encouraged to pledge to avoid drinking and driving on prom night as well as the other 364 nights of the year. Some 1.1 million students signed pledges in 1994. The rapidly growing program had plans for 3,500 schools as participants in 1995, supported by more than 2,000 Nationwide agents.

The success of Prom Promise prompted McFerson to add "a new twist in the partnership between parents and teens" with Family Pledge Day March 23, 1994. "It is just as important for parents to sign the pledge to show their support of the program as the teens."

Beyond these two significant, nationwide programs, McFerson ordered a special issues radio, television and billboard advertising program, arranged for the donation of some 1,600 alcohol detectors to law enforcement agencies and co-sponsored with Mothers Against Drunk Driving the National Sobriety Checkpoint Week during the July 4th holidays.

Fisher continued to pursue Nationwide's long-standing interest in cooperative affairs, both in the United States and abroad. In 1994 he joined five other Nationwiders in the Cooperative Hall of Fame, Washington, DC — Lincoln, George H. Dunlap, Dwight W. Oberschlake, Frank B. Sollars and Leslie E. Woodcock. It is the highest honor bestowed by the National Cooperative Business Association's Cooperative

Development Foundation.

"Murray Lincoln would have been proud of our current capacity to serve national cooperatives," said Fisher, such as the NCBA, the National Council of Farmer Cooperatives, several state-wide co-op councils and others with interests in finance, housing and other endeavors. Among the cooperatives on the global scene in which Nationwiders actively participated were the Americas Association of Cooperative/Mutual Insurance Societies, the International Cooperative Alliance, the American Cooperative Enterprise Center in Prague, Czechoslovakia, and the International Cooperative and Mutual Insurance Federation, which Fisher served as chairman for five years.

Throughout its history Nationwide has maintained sponsor/endorser relations with several cooperatives or cooperatively oriented organizations that share the philosophy and goals of the enterprise. The Ohio Farm Bureau Federation is the oldest of the relationships, of course. In return for an annual, primarily promotional fee, the organizations recommend Nationwide's services to their membership and sponsors may nominate a representative for the insurance boards of the enterprise.

"Nationwide is not a personality," Fisher said. "It is an organization that is based on a strong underlying philosophy and mission. The fact that this company was organized by a group of people to help themselves ... has never been lost in our governance system or our overall philosophy of self-help (and) it has a major bearing on how we approach the charitable projects in which we excel."

Fisher reiterated a favorite theme of his, namely that Nationwide is "more than a business. It is a company that from the beginning had an attitude of professionalism and, at the same time, had a worthy social purpose," such as helping people through cooperatives, insurance services and charities and responding "to things that will really make a crucial difference to people's lives."

18

A VISION FOR NATIONWIDE

D. Richard McFerson couldn't believe his sleepy eyes when he looked at his watch. It said 6:41 a.m. Hardly giving a thought to the hotel employee who had failed to ring his room at 6 a.m., McFerson dashed into the shower, shaved, dressed and hurried into downtown Columbus and the headquarters of Nationwide.

At 7:15 a.m. he straightened his tie one more time, just before the elevator doors opened on the 37th floor of One Nationwide Plaza. Jeanne Pence, secretary to the president of the Nationwide Insurance Companies, John E. Fisher, escorted the guest through the double white doors and into the executive offices. McFerson barely noticed the profusion of Currier & Ives prints on the walls of the hallway before stepping into Fisher's office suite, 15 minutes late.

As Fisher rose from his easy chair, where he had been sipping coffee and reading papers, an embarrassed McFerson apologized for his tardiness at their first meeting. "I figured this was going to be a short interview," he recalled. It was, less than an hour, "but I think the chemistry was good on both sides, so he invited me back."

Before leaving, though, the handsome senior vice president and controller from Boston-based New England Mutual Life Insurance Company said: "I really want to talk to you some more about where this company is going and what its objectives are, and strategies. I'm not ready to commit to anything until I have had a chance to have another two or three hours with you." Fisher agreed.

Although the 41-year-old McFerson knew little about Nationwide — "I didn't understand the scope of the operation," he admitted — he felt it was about to enter a major transition. "You could just see the handwriting on the wall. Sixty-five percent of its officers were over 55. ... I thought, this could be an interesting and fun challenge."

McFerson found it all of that, and more, after joining the Nationwide Insurance Companies in 1979 as vice president, internal audits. What he discovered was "an eye-opener," he admitted: A $6.5 billion enterprise with 7.4 million policies in force; $15 billion in life insurance in force and $255 million in mutual funds under management. Little did he realize that by December 3, 1992, when he succeeded Fisher as chief executive officer, the enterprise would top $37.6 billion. Two years later it was $5 billion larger still.

As he took the reins of management, he thought to himself: "The first thing you have to do, McFerson, is make sure you don't screw it up and ruin it."

Future scribes will determine how well he did during his watch over the Nationwide Insurance Enterprise, but there is absolutely no question his promotion to helmsman marked the setting of a new course for the institution. For the first time in 68 years, neither Murray D. Lincoln nor anyone who knew Lincoln steered the venerable yet vibrant insurance organization.

Senior Vice President William DeMeno described McFerson as the "merchant of change," a Marco Polo for the 1990s, perhaps. "I can promise you, it's going to be exciting," DeMeno said. "I expect to see enormous change in the organization."

McFerson, a native of Los Angeles, a graduate of UCLA with a master's degree from the University of Southern California, and a certified public accountant, quickly established his agenda "to get this organization ready for the next century. We need to make some significant changes ... move faster ... get more competitive and become more of a player in the market." Virtually nothing concerned him more than increasing market share.

Even though he acknowledged he didn't have "a total grasp" of the organization, he expressed much the same concern in 1980, less than a year after joining Nationwide. "But as a newcomer, I also have the advantage of objectivity because I am not yet part of the 'woodwork,'" he wrote in a memorandum.

After studying a proposed 20-year plan for Nationwide labeled Image 2000, McFerson concluded it was too ambitious, even for "a sleeping giant with tremendous financial capability and resources." He said the next five years would shape Nationwide's destiny more than a course of action for the year 2000. He urged the immediate focus be on becoming more competitive; on capitalizing on the strength of the agency force; on adding more technology to improve productivity, and on implementing plans for western expansion.[1]

By 1994 he was a solid member of the "woodwork," yet he still held to those 14-year-old thoughts. A number of Nationwide operations had achieved significant market positions, in particular, the entire family of financial security services, especially the individual annuity products that dominate the industry. Farmland Insurance topped its market and both Scottsdale Insurance and Colonial Insurance sat solidly in second against their competition. Nationwide Mutual ranked fourth among automobile insurers across the land and even higher in some individual eastern states.

As a result of the success of the financial services products, Nationwide enjoyed phenomenal growth between 1972 and 1993 under the general chairmanship of Dean W. Jeffers and Fisher. In those two decades the assets of Nationwide Mutual and Nationwide Mutual Fire rose to $18.6 billion from $1 billion and the life company's assets soared to $25.4 billion from $640 million.

In an interview with *The Nationwide Dividend*, the employee newspaper, McFerson pointed to those "significant" results. It would be easy, he said, "to keep doing what we've been doing and enjoy the fruits of our labors. But I felt that was absolutely the wrong approach to take."[2]

The reason it seemed so wrong to him was because in the property/casualty and life insurance lines "our market share has not changed in 20 years, which is awful. ... We had no market share changes at all. It was flat. Our competitive position was deteriorating a little bit at a time and, over time, we allowed ourselves to get more and more noncompetitive. ... You absolutely cannot let yourself become noncompetitive."[3]

In 1993 Nationwide's individual lines of business — automobile and homeowners insurance — represented about 3.5 percent of the market, up a few tenths of 1 percent during the 1980s.

"We have been successful growing these businesses in the past three years, and I expect we'll continue to grow them. By growing them, I mean we will add a few hundred thousand policyholders every year compared to nothing five or six years ago. In absolute terms, that's a 5 percent growth rate in units. ... That's a lot of growth."

He sees State Farm Insurance, the strong, national leader that the Ohio Farm Bureau came within a whisker of buying out in 1930, as "a wonderful, absolutely sensational company, but in the marketplace, they are the competition." However,

McFerson is convinced State Farm intends to maintain its market share without growing excessively. Similarly, Allstate's growth is not as rapid as it once was. The strong, new competition for Nationwide in the 1990s comes from United Services Automobile Association, an aggressive, San Antonio-based giant, and energetic regionals, such as Erie Insurance Group, Progressive Insurance Group and American Family Group.

Because of the competitive environment, Nationwide needs to be creative and flexible, he told Nationwide's managers in 1993 in their periodical, *Issues.* "There is no such thing as making 10-year plans anymore. Markets change too quickly. We can't take forever to get product and systems to the marketplace (or) wait until everything is figured out before we move."[4]

The idea of involving groups of managers in the decision-making process is a McFerson trademark, according to Peter F. Frenzer, president of the life companies, the corporation and chief investment officer for the enterprise. "Dick is comfortable doing that. I would call it a team role: He's emphasizing team."

Galen R. Barnes, a senior vice president McFerson successfully urged to take on the presidency of Wausau Insurance in early 1993 and restore it to health, agreed with Frenzer. "Dick would prefer to engage and conduct his business face-to-face; he's not a memo kind of guy. He would, if he could, spend all his time in the field, with people."

Not everyone felt comfortable with engaging in team behavior, however. Some senior managers in terms of years of service felt threatened by a perceived disintegration of authority patterns, in the opinion of Stephen A. Rish, vice president of public relations. "We are suddenly having people being forced to open up and defend with rationale the decision, and that makes some people uncomfortable," he said.

McFerson appeared comfortable with what Nationwide had

on its plate in 1994, although he wished he had been served a larger portion of the market. Even so, he had virtually no appetite for taking big, or even little, bites out of other companies to achieve growth. His administration focused on growing the business internally rather than by acquisition — unless Nationwide could immediately achieve a strong position in a target market. Such was the thinking when Wausau Insurance affiliated with Nationwide in 1985: It strengthened a pair of Nationwide weaknesses with a stronger presence in the West and in commercial insurance.

However, "for all the strengths of Wausau," McFerson said, "we totally underestimated their reserve requirements. That cost us $1 billion more than we thought it was going to cost us." Coupled with the $500 million he estimated it cost to go west with commercial insurance, "that's a lot of money. I thought to myself, Dick, what could you do with $1.5 billion in your established business that you're good at?"

His thoughts went back even further, to the 1950s, when Lincoln had his sights elsewhere and the company's focus was on eastern states only. "We lost a major opportunity to go west" then, in McFerson's opinion. State Farm, Allstate and Farmers Insurance Group gained dominance in the market instead. "It should have been Nationwide in the West," he said, somewhat ruefully.

Under McFerson Nationwide set a new course for western expansion, first into Texas, Indiana, Illinois, and Michigan, and then perhaps into contiguous states.

Yet, a very disciplined, sophisticated, computer-assisted plan to extend personal lines business into the West was put in place in the early 1990s by retired Senior Vice President Earl F. Peitz. It is a grass roots effort to hire agents, assist them financially in their start-up if necessary, provide them with the latest in demographics to identify customers in the immediate area, and build the western business community agents in a manner similar to new agent development in the East. "It's a little slower this way," McFerson said, "but in the long term, it's just as powerful" as spending a few hundred million dollars for a company that needs fixing.

"You win this game (of market share) by blocking and tackling better than your opponents," he added. "You don't go for the flea-flicker or try to hit a home run. It's back to the basics. You've got to be better than anybody else in the basics of sales, sales management, claims, claims handling, claims management, underwriting — you've got to be tough on your underwriting — and you've got to be willing to price based upon what you earn. You can't subsidize your pricing forever; you just can't afford to do it."

The decision to price Nationwide's products competitively yet provide a return was made in the late 1980s. Previously there were times "when we were so noncompetitive that we would drop the rate to try to satisfy the agents," McFerson said. That approach, without trying to fix the underlying problem, he described as "a disaster." Premiums were increased in a healthy state or region to subsidize losing operations elsewhere in the enterprise. "Today, everybody's got to fix their own problems."

Fixing some of the basic inefficiencies in sales management, underwriting, and claims practices and management allowed Nationwide Mutual and Nationwide Mutual Fire to keep its insurance rates fairly stable during the early 1990s. The claims side received special attention. For instance, a program labeled Accelerating Claims Excellence specifically addressed claims performance; several hundred claims adjusters were added to improve the settlement of claims, and an effective computer operation was dedicated to the area of claims.

McFerson estimated the annual savings will be about $100 million, savings that can be passed along to the policyholder through stable or lower rates. "So, when your rate increases are very, very modest, then you are able to grow because it is a commodity-driven product. People buy auto insurance and homeowners based on price."

Quality business moves to the lowest price points; substandard business moves to whatever is available. That can load up an insurer with substandard business and that gets mixed in with its quality, standard business. Before long, the company begins to post losses "and it's only a matter of time before you have to take some stiff rate increases to keep your financial balance," McFerson said. At that point, the quality business that's still with the company is driven away. "Then you get yourself all messed up." That's why being competitively priced is so important to the enterprise, he said.

Robert A. Oakley,* senior vice president and chief financial officer of the enterprise, confirmed the commitment to driving down the cost of the product. "We have to compete on the basis of price. We are going to be a low cost provider of insurance, which is a powerful strategy.

"If it is properly articulated and understood, it is a very powerful strategic statement and causes us to be extremely conscious of what the competition is doing, to drive the technological changes through the enterprise as a way of reducing cost."

Besides taking a more aggressive, competitive stance, the surplus, or capital of the enterprise must grow, too, McFerson said. "That's a big challenge," one that goes hand in hand with strict, and enforced, cost controls as management streamlines

---

* Oakley feels fortunate he's still on McFerson's team. One of his first encounters with McFerson came in 1983 on the racquetball court. "It was my chance to get some face time with the chief financial officer ... and give him a chance to know me." Less than 30 seconds into the match, "I absolutely drilled him in the back of the head with the ball," Oakley said. "I mean, I really caught him. ... My whole life flashed in front of me. I thought I had really done it now." He said McFerson soon forgot about the lump on the back of his head.

operations and hones its competitive edge.

"Dick is tending to streamline and consolidate ... and I think that's prudent," said his predecessor, Fisher. "A little disruptive, but it's prudent."

Fisher's successor wants to make sure Nationwide's core businesses grow and succeed and place on notice those that do not generate a market share position of significance or importance. "The best payback for us is to invest our excess investment opportunity dollars in those markets where we know how to make a buck." The pruning of the television operations of Nationwide Communications in 1994 epitomizes McFerson's thinking in this regard.

Already on the shelf, just a shell of its former self, is Nationwide Development Company, founded in 1947. At the time McFerson joined Nationwide in 1979, it had nearly 6,000 acres in development property. Today its prime responsibility is the management of the downtown Columbus properties. "I don't think it makes any sense at all for us to go out and develop real estate and do the kinds of things the development company did 15 to 20 years ago," he said.

The processing and administration of Medicare claims is not a profit center for Nationwide, but it never was intended to be one. When the Medicare law became effective in mid-1966, Nationwide was one of the private insurance companies appointed by the Social Security Administration to process claims and pay hospital and medical insurance benefits for senior citizens in need of assistance. Because it is a not-for-profit partnership with the federal government, some senior executives at Nationwide question its value to the enterprise, but not McFerson.

"I believe we almost have a corporate and community commitment" to continue the Medicare operations, primarily to protect the more than 900 jobs it provides members of the Columbus community, he said. Also, "sometimes we can learn some things out of Medicare technology — interesting ways of processing business that will help us in some of our other businesses." However, if a similar "at cost" processing opportunity presented itself to Nationwide, it's likely it would be rejected. "We would not add another 900 people if we had no opportunity to make money out of it," McFerson said.

Spurred by the fast-paced age of high-tech communications, the McFerson administration committed itself to a decentralized field program to put more and more service capability in the agents' offices. Claims adjusters and underwriters, too, need but a car, portable facsimile machine, cellular telephone, and a laptop computer to conduct business. New technology will bring more changes.

He expects the agency force to play an increasingly pivotal role as the enterprise broadens the capabilities of the agents. "It will frighten some, because they are not ready for it, but it's what the customer wants," the chief executive officer said. "More and more agents are beginning to understand that point of service claims have either got to be done by them, or they have to put that policyholder in touch with someone ... who is right out there within 24 hours, handling that claim. That is what we are investing our time, energy and money in right now, so we can give that kind of service."

Oakley noted how Nationwide's claims service has become more policyholder friendly in recent years. All but abandoned is the "Live Wire" system that used a toll-free 800 number. "The customer does not want to call an 800 number," said Oakley. "The customer wants to call the agent. That's the person the payment is sent to, the person who sold the policy. ... So we had to sort of dismantle everything that we had built for 20 years in terms of a philosophy of how you deal with the customer."

Putting more responsibility for servicing the policyholder in the hands of the agent raised questions concerning the commission agents receive. "The only way we can continue to pay current commissions is if there is a value added by that agent," Oakley said.

Nationwide's agency force also has been encouraged to play a much larger role in the area of retirement savings and asset accumulation among individual policyholders. Many agents resist selling annuities and funds, and even life insurance, because of the longer time it takes to sell such products versus standard automobile or homeowners' policies. That attitude may have been acceptable in the past, but today people are concerned about living too long and running out of money, McFerson believes. That's why "we are trying to help our agents understand that they have to pay attention to the financial services side of this business, not just the auto and homeowners insurance."

All the companies in the enterprise were required to set their own goals to fit the Vision McFerson unveiled December 9, 1993. "First, this is my vision," he said. "Second, it is a vision calling for change. And third, all employees have to get involved."

The Vision announcement clearly signaled the changing of the guard, from Fisher to McFerson, as well as challenging the 32,500 employees and agents to "get ready for the revolution that is coming. Business as usual is not acceptable," the new CEO told them.

McFerson encouraged his inner circle of senior executives to push him, to challenge him. "I love to be pushed. I don't want people around me who think the same way I do and won't question me," he said. "I love to get people who will challenge me and question me."

"I don't plan to work until 65 ... but I will give it my best shot for six or seven years. By then, I will have failed miserably if I don't have several good people to step in because I am a firm believer in management development. ... That's the one thing I am going to make dead certain happens around here, that we have a lot of bench strength (so that) when we have major appointments, we have two or three candidates from which to choose."

Whether McFerson would see the challenges met before his time is up as Nationwide's CEO was unknown, but impregnating the organization with the goals can be realized, he believed. "My job is to get the ball on the green. ... That's a lot; that's a big assignment."

His analogy to golf was not out of character. Next to spending time with his family, particularly the grandchildren, McFerson enjoyed playing golf best — and as a fierce competitor. The oft-told story around headquarters concerns a round of golf with his former vice president of systems and data processing, Virgil L. Pittman. As Pittman approached his ball in the fairway, he rolled it slightly with his clubhead to improve the lie. Although the act violated the rules, many amateur players take such liberties in non-tournament play.

"Virgil, let that be the last time you ever roll your golf ball," McFerson said. Word quickly spread through the executive ranks: When on the course with the boss, play strictly by the rules.

He, of course, would prefer the stories that endure around Nationwide will be those about the competitiveness he instilled in the enterprise. In a quiet, reflective moment, McFerson said:

"When the dust settles, and McFerson is gone, they'll say, 'What did he do while he was here at Nationwide? What was his contribution?'

"I hope they would say:

"'He aggressively expanded these companies into new markets in America;

"'He made the companies competitive,' and

"'He put in place an organization full of excellent, talented men and women of all colors, each capable of assuming leadership positions.'"

Finally, McFerson said, "I hope they would say, 'Here was a good, honest man.'"

In a letter that outlined the Vision to Nationwide directors, McFerson recognized Murray D. Lincoln as "the father of Nationwide's heritage (whose) values are central to what defines Nationwide and differentiates us from other insurers." In conclusion, McFerson wrote:

"As we continue to move forward, our challenge remains the same — we must successfully manage our culture to ensure the future success of the enterprise and the continuation of the cooperative values and heritage that Nationwide embodies."[5]

Appendix A

LEADERSHIP THROUGH THE YEARS

NATIONWIDE INSURANCE DIRECTORS

Service as Director

Oscar J. Bailey	Tacoma, OH	1925-41
George L. Cooley	Dover Center, OH	1925-38
Harry C. Fast	Napoleon, OH	1925-41
Clarence Henry	Hebron, OH	1925-26
David M. Odaffer	Bucyrus, OH	1925-46
Lee B. Palmer	Pataskala, OH	1925-30
A. C. Robison	Proctorville, OH	1925-26
A. S. Thomas	Mount Sterling, OH	1925-26
Gomer C. Evans	Jackson, OH	1926-28
Murray D. Lincoln	Columbus, OH	1926-66
A. F. Moon	Conover, OH	1926-43
Perry L. Green	Mantua, OH	1927-57
W. W. Farnsworth	Waterville, OH	1928-39
Harry A. West	Leesburg, OH	1930-44
Harrison S. Nolt	Columbia, PA	1934-54
Arthur H. Packard	Burlington, VT	1934-35
C. E. Wise, Jr.	Baltimore, MD	1934-50
		1962-65
Milo L. Porter	Jeffersonville, VT	1935-55
C. S. Younger	Columbus, OH	1935-43
Roland N. Benjamin	New Cumberland, PA	1938-40
		1955-69
George H. Dunlap	Columbus, OH	1939-75
E. M. Shaulis	Holsopple, PA	1939-61
William E. Stough	Mansfield, OH	1939-60
Leslie E. Woodcock	New York, NY	1939-72
John M. Hodson	Pioneer, OH	1941-53

Everett Rittenour	Piketon, OH	1941-49
E. C. Darling	Nellie, OH	1943-46
M. G. Mann	Raleigh, NC	1944-49
Max M. Scarff	New Carlisle, OH	1944-72
Frank L. Cooperrider	Glenford, OH	1946-60
James H. West	Perry, OH	1946-66
Paul D. Grady	Kenly, NC	1950-70
Harry R. Metzler	Lancaster, PA	1950-65
Harold P. Richards	Strongsville, OH	1950-59
Roy C. F. Weagley	Hagerstown, MD	1950-62
Ralph H. Varian	East Canton, OH	1951-65
David H. Scull	Annandale, VA	1952-83
Herman Walther	Goshen, CT	1952-64
Roy W. Wood	Pittsford, VT	1955-70
H. D. Heckathorn	Forest, OH	1959-68
Rex Long	Loudonville, OH	1959-77
James M. Lewis	Orient, OH	1961-85
Ferris S. Owen	Chevy Chase, MD	1961-85
Curtis B. Wachsmuth	Mechanicsburg, PA	1961-75
Bowman Doss	Columbus, OH	1964-69
Noah E. Kefauver, Jr.	Middletown, MD	1965-90
Robert H. Leslie	Gibsonia, PA	1965-68
Wendell Weller	Urbana, OH	1965-89
Carl H. Stitzlein	Loudonville, OH	1966-85
John W. Galbreath	Columbus, OH	1967-72
Howard Hutchinson	Columbus, OH	1968-72
Frank B. Sollars	Washington Court House, OH	1968-89
Charles L. Fuellgraf, Jr.	Butler, PA	1969-
Dean W. Jeffers	Columbus, OH	1969-81
Charles W. Leftwich	Columbus, OH	1970-73
Young D. Hance	Prince Frederick, MD	1971-73
Thomas J. Gorman	Trenton, OH	1971-72
William G. Greenlee	Marion, NC	1971-86
Gerry J. Dietz	Syracuse, NY	1972-84
John E. Fisher	Columbus, OH	1972-94
Dwight W. Oberschlake	Hamersville, OH	1972-92
Robert W. Summer	Tiffin, OH	1972-84
G. Willard Oakley	Salisbury, MD	1973-86
John K. Pfahl	Columbus, OH	1973-94
Harry P. Metz	Belleville, PA	1975-84

Leonard E. Schnell	Applecreek, OH	1975-90
Paul A. Donald	Columbus, OH	1981-89
Wallace E. Hirschfeld	New Bremen, OH	1981-89
John L. Marakas	Columbus, OH	1981-91
Keith M. Voigt	Eagle Grove, IA	1983-88
Robert H. Rickel	Bayview, ID	1984-
Arden L. Shisler	Dalton, OH	1984-
David O. Miller	Newark, OH	1985-
W. Barton Montgomery	Washington Court House, OH	1985-94
Henry S. Holloway	Darlington, MD	1986-
Nancy C. Thomas	Louisville, OH	1986-
D. Richard McFerson	Delaware, OH	1988-
Vaughn O. Sinclair	St. James, MN	1988-94
James F. Patterson	Chesterland, OH	1989-
Robert L. Stewart	Jewett, OH	1989-
Harold W. Weihl	Bowling Green, OH	1990-
Peter F. Frenzer	Powell, OH	1991-
Fred C. Finney	Wooster, OH	1992-
Lewis J. Alphin	Mount Olive, NC	1993-
Willard J. Engel	Marshall, MN	1994-
C. Ray Noecker	Ashville, OH	1994-

NATIONWIDE INSURANCE OFFICERS

Most Senior Position Attained and Years of Enterprise Service

Lee B. Palmer, President	1925-30
George L. Cooley, President	1925-38
David M. Odaffer, President (Fire)	1925-46
Charles S. Younger, President (Life)	1935-43
Murray D. Lincoln, President	1925-66
Bowman Doss, President	1934-69
George H. Dunlap, General Chairman & Chief Executive Officer	1939-72
Dean W. Jeffers, General Chairman & Chief Executive Officer	1940-81
John E. Fisher, General Chairman & Chief Executive Officer	1951-94
Paul A. Donald, President (Property/Casualty)	1954-89
John L. Marakas, President (Life)	1971-91
Peter F. Frenzer, President (Life)	1974-
D. Richard McFerson, President & Chief Executive Officer	1979-

EXECUTIVE VICE PRESIDENTS

Thomas E. Kryshak, Finance	1959-93
Gordon E. McCutchan, Law & Corporate Services	1964-

SENIOR VICE PRESIDENTS

Galen R. Barnes 1975-
Jack A. Baughn 1949-86
J. Christy Beall 1953-73
James E. Brock 1969-
Enus A. Burigana 1951-91
Richard G. Chilcott 1936-81
Edmond Coughlin 1959-86
Richard D. Crabtree 1965-
Ohmer O. Crowell 1952-89
Harry W. Culbreth 1952-63
William P. DeMeno 1960-
W. Sidney Druen 1970-
Mark E. Fiebrink 1993-
Willard E. Fitzpatrick 1960-89
Harvey S. Galloway, Jr. 1969-
Joseph J. Gasper 1966-
Bernard E. Guinan 1952-90
J. Richard Harmon 1960-90
W. Kenneth Howell 1937-72
Howard Hutchinson 1935-67
Richard A. Karas 1964-
J. R. Koenig............................... 1940-73
C. Eugene Lacey 1951-82
Charles W. Leftwich 1927-69
Ashley T. McCarter 1946-80
Robert A. Oakley 1976-
Jack F. Olson 1954-89
Robert H. Ourant 1947-87
Earl F. Peitz 1951-94
Robert A. Rennie...................... 1955-82
Carl J. Santillo 1993-
Raymond G. Smith 1943-81
P. L. Thornbury 1935-63
Wendell D. Turner 1951-82
John C. Wagner........................ 1951-82
W. E. West................................ 1952-66
Raymond L. Wilson 1956-91
Robert W. Woodward, Jr. 1964-

VICE PRESIDENTS

Jerry C. Allen 1962-
Robert L. Arnold 1939-66
Douglas E. Arthur 1949-86
Brett K. Avner 1981-93
Richard Backus......................... 1938-77
Henry S. Ballard 1946-50
Bruce C. Barnes....................... 1992-
James W. Barnett 1946-66
George E. Bell, M.D. 1967-88
William R. Birkhimer.............. 1949-85
Raymond B. Blake.................... 1964-
Michael D. Bleiweiss 1971-
Donald L. Bowman 1970-90
James M. Buckalew 1962-
J. Richard Bull 1954-89
Alonzo M. Burdge 1937-73
Joseph A. Bushek 1978-87
Wallace J. Campbell 1960-63
William M. Carpenter 1980-
Grady M. Chesson 1944-74
Joseph F. Ciminero 1968-
Darrel E. Clauson 1947-86
Dennis W. Click 1960-
Sidney W. Coe 1960-65
Norman L. Cowgill 1936-64
Roy Croop 1953-91
Thomas L. Crumrine 1966-
Robert M. Culp 1947-83
Herbert E. Cunningham 1961-89
Jerry D. Daughtry 1965-
A. Robert Davies, M.D. 1985-
Byron L. Davis 1946-71
Dwight E. Davis 1985-
Ernesto del Rosario 1961-77
Kenneth E. DeShetler 1976-93
David A. Diamond.................... 1988-
Leslie L. Diehl, Jr. 1951-86
Thomas W. Dietrich................. 1977-
James J. Doherty 1939-77

James M. Doherty	1948-81	Donald E. Johnson	1939-77
Patrick L. Doyle	1951-94	Marvin A. Johnson	1986-
Lyle F. Drake	1951-77	Paul B. Johnson	1951-81
Matthew S. Easley	1982-	R. Steven Johnston	1990-
C. W. Eberhard	1929-63	Ralph Jordan	1946-83
James O. Emert	1982-	Robert E. Kaiser	1947-81
Ronald L. Eppley	1962-	J. E. Keltner	1926-60
Herbert E. Evans	1942-66	Bradley D. Kirk	1969-82
E. M. Erickson	1943-71	Calvin Kytle	1950-63
Maurice H. Evans	1972-75	William A. Lee	1969-
Harry C. Eyre	1958-79	Rueben Y. Leonard	1958-92
Walter W. Falck	1942-73	Forest Lombaer	1957-63
W. W. Farnesworth	1928-38	Enrique A. Lopez	1963-94
Harry C. Fast	1939	James J. Lorimer	1954-91
Alan N. Ferguson	1994-	Joe F. Lowe	1975-84
Fred J. Fietkiewicz	1963-	Philip J. Lucia	1963-90
Michael A. Flack	1984-	Stephen M. Lundregan	1981-
Mark A. Folk	1993-	Carl J. MacDonald	1953-86
Marion E. Foltz	1927-52	William E. Mabe	1978-
George W. Frink	1952-88	Albert E. Macino	1981-86
Gerald G. Frost	1951-85	William F. Maidlow	1942-66
Charles W. Fullerton	1953-81	Edward J. Matulich	1975-92
Danny M. Fullerton	1984-	David L. Maynard	1978-93
Reuben A. Gainey	1961-	Lynn E. McCall	1956-83
Philip C. Gath	1972-	Merle W. McCartney	1939-79
Lance Greene	1950-78	John B. McClintock	1949-81
Robert W. Griffith	1937-77	James P. McCormick	1960-
Jack A. Gulick	1955-89	Audbert L. McMorrow	1951-88
Kyleen Knilans Hale	1975-	Robert H. McNaghten	1987-
Gary M. Hall	1985-	Charles D. Metz, Jr.	1952-89
John R. Harper	1969-	Paul S. Metzger, M.D.	1955-90
Robert W. Heffner	1937-69	Jeffrey G. Milburn	1972-
Will Hellerman	1951-80	David D. Mooney	1963-
John Hogan	1968-76	James C. Morrow	1982-89
Calvin L. Hudson	1971-	Richard E. Munro	1975-
Ronald E. Hunt	1966-	Hugh G. Murphy	1964-
Harold T. Jackson	1937-78	Timothy E. Murphy	1975-
Paul H. Jacobson	1989-	Paul S. Nash	1950-89
David L. Jahn	1972-	Peter Neckermann	1977-
Gerald J. Jerabek	1976-90	Lawrence K. Nightingale	1958-92

R. Dennis Noice 1971-
Bernard H. Parker 1950-88
Curtis M. Parker 1977-93
John T. Perta 1955-88
Virgil L. Pittman 1981-86
John G. Powles 1986-
James W. Pruden 1962-
William P. Ramsey 1954-
Joseph P. Rath 1977-
Herman W. Reeder 1955-66
Ralph A. Rhodes 1953-91
Stephen A. Rish 1968-
Nigel K. Roberts 1989-
Patrick S. Roberts 1967-
Douglas C. Robinette 1986-
Larry M. Robinson 1980-
Elmer A. Rule 1952-75
Robert W. Saik 1982-
Ruth A. Saylor 1975-
Michael J. Schaub, Jr. 1981-88
Frederick D. Schaaf 1940-79
Harry A. Schermer 1965-
George W. Schmidt 1957-87
James E. Schultz 1976-
Stephen A. Sedlak 1969-
Robert W. Selfe 1940-63
E. E. Sherer 1951-84
Waldo V. Siegfried 1967-81

George Sonnemann 1978-84
C. Thomas Starr 1969-
Raymond Tatham 1949-90
James A. Taylor 1966-
L. A. Taylor 1939-44
John X. Teevin 1965-
Paul A. Thompson 1968-
Alan A. Todryk 1985-
William O. Trucksis 1943-78
F. B. Van Newkirk 1938-62
George G. Varga 1955-74
Richard M. Waggoner 1977-
Edward F. Wagner 1950-76
Warren H. Wagner 1953-87
Charles D. Weaver 1969-
Leon J. Weinberger 1980-94
Richard K. Wendt 1956-93
Harry A. West 1938
W. Robert White 1982-93
William A. White 1951-71
Stanley J. Wiemer 1938-74
Gerald W. Woodard 1961-89
Susan A. Wolken 1974-
Charles D. Wollenzien, Jr. 1969-
Donald Yochem, M.D. 1943-68
Eldon A. Ziegler 1987-
W. Craig Zimpher 1983-

SUBSIDIARIES AND AFFILIATES

COLONIAL INSURANCE

Stuart H. Struck	President & CEO	1978-82
Robert M. Culp	President & CEO	1982-83
Galen R. Barnes	President & CEO	1984-87
Jack G. Shea	President & CEO	1987-89
Richard M. Waggoner	President & COO	1990-93
Stephen M. Lundregan	President & COO	1993-

FARMLAND INSURANCE

William L. Balliu	President	1982-84
William P. DeMeno	President	1984-89
William A. Lee	President	1989-92
James M. Buckalew	President	1992-
Carl J. Santillo	President (Life)	1993-

FINANCIAL HORIZONS

Timothy E. Murphy	President	1991-

GATESMᶜDONALD

Howard Hutchinson	President	1969-72
James R. Davis	President	1972-79
Richard O. Mader	President	1979-85
Jack A. Gulick	President	1985-89
Donald J. Sternisha	President	1989-91
Robert W. Witty	President	1991-93
David K. Hollingsworth	President	1994-

NATIONWIDE COMMUNICATIONS

B. S. Van Gorden	President	1946
James H. West	President	1947-49
James R. Moore	General Manager	1948-50
Murray D. Lincoln	President	1950-58
Herbert E. Evans	President	1959-66
George W. Campbell, Jr.	VP & General Manager	1966-72
Edward F. Wagner	President	1969-72
Charles W. Fullerton	President	1973-81
Clark Pollock	President	1982-88
Steven P. Berger	President	1989-

NATIONWIDE DEVELOPMENT COMPANY

Murray D. Lincoln	President	1949-63
Carl R. Frye	VP & General Manager	1951-57

Bowman Doss .... President 1964-68
James T. Foley .... VP & General Manager 1967-80
Edward F. Wagner .... President 1969-72
Charles W. Fullerton .... President 1973-81
George W. Miller .... President 1982-88
Robert J. Woodward, Jr. .... President 1989-

NATIONWIDE FINANCIAL SERVICES
Murray D. Lincoln .... President 1957-59
                                                                                 1963-65
George S. Hough .... President 1959-63
Paul Sebastian .... VP & General Manager 1965-76
J. F. Lowe .... VP & General Manager 1976-78
Marian A. Trimble .... VP & General Manager 1978-81
                                                                President 1981-

NEA VALUEBUILDER
Duane C. Meek .... President 1991-

NECKURA
Ernest H. Klepetar .... President 1966-76
Robert W. Parlin .... President 1976-79
Patrick S. Roberts .... President 1979-84
Uwe Jacobsen .... President 1985-

PUBLIC EMPLOYEES BENEFIT SERVICES CORPORATION
John David Davenport .... Board Chairman & CEO 1973-76
                                                                    President & CEO 1976-82
Charles H. Wilkinson .... Board Chairman 1976-82
Jay Wilkinson .... President & CEO 1982-

SCOTTSDALE INSURANCE
Rolland L. Wiegers .... President 1982-94
Vickie F. Kartchner .... President 1994-

WAUSAU INSURANCE
Leon J. Weinberger .... President 1985-93
Galen R. Barnes .... President 1993-

WEST COAST LIFE INSURANCE COMPANY
Francis V. Keesling, Jr. .... President 1963-68
H. Curtis Reed .... President 1968-73
John E. Mellen .... President 1973-79
Robert N. Powell .... President 1980
John U. Metzger .... President 1980-

Appendix B

CHRONOLOGY

1919   Farmers seeking to get more for products, pay less for supplies, form Ohio Farm Bureau Federation (OFBF).

1925   OFBF wants lower-priced auto insurance for farmers. Ohio insurance commissioner says State Farm Mutual of Illinois doesn't meet requirements for out-of-state insurer. Executive secretary Murray D. Lincoln suggests OFBF start insurance company.

1926   Farm Bureau Mutual Automobile Insurance Company launched with $10,000 from OFBF bonds.

1928   Service expands beyond Ohio; five states added, two more to come in 1928. Sponsorship program established to develop cooperatives, insurance markets. Maryland Farm Bureau joins OFBF as second sponsor.

1934   Membership in Cooperative League of the USA sets stage for international cooperative leadership. Farm Bureau Mutual Fire Insurance Company started.

1935   Life Insurance Company of America (later Nationwide Life) acquired for $376,000.

1942   Health insurance added to product lines.

1946   Peoples Broadcasting Corporation (later Nationwide Communications) is first affiliated company.

1948   Peoples (later Nationwide) Development Company formed. Ohio insurance department requests that OFBF and insurance companies separate; Lincoln resigns from OFBF to lead insurance companies.

1949   Group insurance added to product lines.

1951   Decentralization prompts the opening of regional offices.

1952   Mutual fund management company acquired; six years later agents will sell mutual funds.

1955   Name change — to Nationwide Insurance. Nationwide Corporation activated as first "downstream" holding company of a U.S. mutual insurer.

1956   Nationwide Life reaches first billion dollars of life insurance in force.

1957   Oregon is first state market west of the Mississippi River. Nationwide General Insurance Company formed to pioneer merit-rated auto insurance.

1960   Nationwide first major insurer to endorse Medicare before passage of the law in 1965.

1962   Puerto Rico first expansion outside continental U.S. Ruralite Services joins Nationwide sponsors.

1963   Industry's first seat belt incentive is 50% extra medical benefits for Nationwide policyholders wearing belts when injured.

1964   Lincoln retires, succeeded as president by Bowman Doss. Neckura, West German casualty company, formed in joint venture with German retailing enterprise.

1966   Nationwide becomes Medicare claims administrator for Ohio and West Virginia.

1969   Doss retires. George H. Dunlap is first general chairman and chief executive officer. Dean W. Jeffers is president of insurance companies. Gates, McDonald & Company, industry leader in cost control services for risk management and unemployment insurance, is acquired.

1972   Dunlap retires, Jeffers is general chairman and chief executive officer. John E. Fisher is president of insurance companies, John L. Marakas president of Nationwide Corporation.

1974   Ground broken for One Nationwide Plaza; 40-story home office will anchor redevelopment of north downtown Columbus.

1976   Golden Anniversary — Nationwide has assets over $2.5 billion, 13,000 agents and employees serving over four million policyholders. First employees move into One Nationwide Plaza. Full ownership of Neckura acquired.

1977   Nationwide Life tops $10 billion of life insurance in force.

1979   Colonial Insurance Company of California acquired for nonstandard auto and motorcycle insurance. Nationwide Property and Casualty Insurance Company formed to serve more of the high quality auto insurance market. Nationwide designs

SPECTRUM, first variable annuity with multiple-funding options, no front-end sales charge.

1980 Bond and money market mutual funds join two Nationwide equity funds. A tax free fund will be added in 1986.

1981 Jeffers retires. Fisher is general chairman and chief executive officer. Paul A. Donald is president of property-casualty companies, Marakas of life companies and Nationwide Corporation. Two Nationwide Plaza office building completed.

1982 Public Employees Benefit Services Corporation (PEBSCO), leading administrator/marketer of deferred compensation plans for public employees, acquired. Scottsdale Insurance Company formed for excess and surplus lines. Farmland Insurance acquired from Farmland Industries which joins Nationwide sponsors.

1985 Wausau Insurance Companies affiliate; $250 million investment is largest in Nationwide history. Nationwide Communications buys eight radio stations, with eight already owned is an industry leader, along with TV and cable holdings.

1986 At 60, Nationwide is a $17 billion organization. Ground broken for Three Nationwide Plaza, coordinated office venture with the State of Ohio.

1988 Donald is assistant chief executive officer, D. Richard McFerson property-casualty president-elect.

1991 Financial Horizons Distributors Agency formed — annuities, mutual funds and life insurance for financial institutions' customers. NEA Valuebuilder Investor Services formed — tax deferred products for National Education Association members.

1992 Planning for Fisher's retirement, board names McFerson chief executive officer, property-casualty president. Pennsylvania Farmers Association (later Pennsylvania Farm Bureau) is company sponsor.

1993 McFerson unveils new Vision for the Nationwide Insurance Enterprise — will build on heritage, strengths. Southern States Cooperatives join sponsors.

1994 Nationwide Mutual sells $500 million of surplus notes — will supplement already strong property-casualty capital, support life growth. Harvest States Cooperatives becomes a company sponsor. Nationwide Communications sells TV, cable holdings to focus on radio. Fisher retires as general chairman. Nationwide is $42 billion enterprise; over 11 million policies serviced by 32,500 employees, full-time agents.

Appendix C

REFERENCE NOTES

The vast majority of the quotes for *On Your Side* came from three sources: Murray D. Lincoln's papers in the archives at Nationwide's headquarters in Columbus; interviews conducted primarily in the 1980s with more than a dozen directors, officers, consultants and employees, and a decade later several score of additional interviews with past and present directors, officers, agents and employees.

Louis V. Fabro, media relations director, and Karen Benedict, archivist, conducted most of the earlier interviews. The author interviewed each member of the larger and more recent group.

Footnotes to quotes obtained from these interviews have been omitted unless they clarify the voice for the reader. All other sources of quotes and information are referenced herein.

CHAPTER 1

[1] William Turner, *Ohio Farm Bureau Story 1919-1979*, p. 62.
[2] *Buckeye Farm News*, November 1980, p. 15.
[3] Page Smith, *Redeeming the Times* 8:14.
[4] Perry L. Green, unpublished *History of the Ohio Farm Bureau Federation*, p. 111.
[5] Ibid., p. 122.
[6] Ibid., p. 103.
[7] Ibid., p. 290.
[8] Michael E. Parrish, *Anxious Decades: America in Prosperity and Depression, 1920-1941*, p. 52.
[9] Warren Sloat, *1929: America Before the Crash*, p. 272.
[10] Murray D. Lincoln, *Vice President in Charge of Revolution*, p. 60.

[11]*Building Through Cooperative Action: The Story of the Ohio Farm Bureau*, p. 12.
[12]Ibid.
[13]Lincoln, p. 62.
[14]Ibid., pp. 64-65.
[15]Minutes of Nationwide Insurance board meeting, November 8, 1956.

CHAPTER 2

[1]Robert S. Lincoln, unpublished family history, January 1990.
[2]Murray D. Lincoln, *Vice President in Charge of Revolution*, p. 3.
[3]Ibid. p. 13.
[4]P. 14.
[5]Lincoln, p. 15.
[6]Ibid., pp. 22-23.
[7]Ibid., pp. 26-27.
[8]Perry L. Green, unpublished *History of the Ohio Farm Bureau Federation*, p. 287.
[9]Lincoln, p. 38.
[10]Interview with J. Richard Bull, July 12, 1993.
[11]Lincoln, p. 42.
[12]Ibid., p. 43.
[13]Anne H. Lincoln, interview March 1952.
[14]Lincoln, *Vice President*, p. 50.
[15]William Turner, *Ohio Farm Bureau Story 1919-1979*, pp. 42-43.
[16]Lincoln, p. 58.
[17]Anne H. Lincoln.

CHAPTER 3

[1]Frank Freidel and Alan Brinkley, *America in the Twentieth Century*, 5th ed., p. 171.
[2]Annual meeting minutes, Ohio Farm Bureau Federation, pp. 201-204.
[3]Executive committee minutes, Ohio Farm Bureau Federation.
[4]Board minutes, Ohio Farm Bureau Federation.
[5]George H. Dunlap, interview October 26, 1982.
[6]Murray D. Lincoln, *Vice President in Charge of Revolution*, p. 72.
[7]Executive Committee minutes, Ohio Farm Bureau Federation, November 11, 1925.
[8]Lincoln, talk to the boards, Nationwide Insurance Companies, November 8, 1956.
[9]Lincoln, president's report to the boards, Nationwide Insurance Companies, February 13, 1957.
[10]Ezra C. Anstaett, letter of understanding to G.J. Mecherle, Inc., December 11, 1926.
[11]Lincoln, president's report, February 13, 1957.
[12]Lincoln, address to the board, Farm Bureau Cooperative Association, February 11, 1947.
[13]Lincoln, *Vice President*, p. 75
[14]William Turner, *Ohio Farm Bureau Story 1919-1979*, p. 101.

[15]Lincoln, "Ezra Anstaett Is Leaving," Farm Bureau Auto Insurance, Bulletin No. 191, February 20, 1930, p. 2.

[16]Town & Village Insurance Service promotional flyer, *The Greatest Development in Automobile Insurance Practice*, 1928.

[17]Board minutes, Farm Bureau Mutual Automobile Insurance Company, March 30, 1931, pp. 160-161.

[18]Bowman Doss, address, "People Working Together," The Newcomen Society, Columbus, OH, May 1, 1968.

[19]Ibid.

CHAPTER 4

[1]*Variety*, October 30, 1929.

[2]Frank Freidel and Alan Brinkley, *America in the Twentieth Century*, 5th ed., p. 201.

[3]Murray D. Lincoln, *Vice President in Charge of Revolution*, p. 113.

[4]William Manchester, *The Glory and the Dream*, p. 36.

[5]D.M. Odaffer, letter to "M.D. Lincoln," January 12, 1934.

[6]William Turner, *The Ohio Farm Bureau Story 1919-1979*, p. 132.

[7]George Moss, *America in the Twentieth Century*, p. 153.

[8]Lincoln, p. 132.

[9]Ibid.

[10]Ibid., p. 133.

[11]Turner, p. 184.

[12]Ibid., p. 112.

[13]Ralph Jordan, interview August 29, 1983.

CHAPTER 5

[1]Murray D. Lincoln, speech to Nationwide Insurance employees at spring regional meeting, 1955.

[2]Perry L. Green, unpublished *The History of the Ohio Farm Bureau Federation*, p. 293.

[3]*New York World-Telegram & Sun*, April 9, 1963.

[4]Lincoln, *Vice President in Charge of Revolution*, pp. 328-329.

[5]Lincoln, speech to Nationwide Insurance employees at spring regional meeting, 1955.

[6]Ibid.

[7]Lincoln, *Vice President*, p. 185.

[8]"Four Veteran Ohio Farm Bureau Members Resign Following Dispute," International News Service, February 15, 1945.

[9]Bowman Doss, interview June 13, 1985.

[10]Lincoln, address to National Cooperative Congress, Deshler-Wallick Hotel, Columbus, September 9, 1946.

[11]Fred H. Posey, "Co-ops Map Plans with CIO to Run Industry and Agriculture," *Columbus Dispatch*, September 9, 1946, p. 1.

[12]Posey, "Co-Operative Society Proposed at Meeting," *Columbus Dispatch*, September 10, 1946.

[13]Lincoln, talk to the boards, Nationwide Insurance Companies, December 5, 1956.

[14]Lincoln, talk to the boards, Nationwide Insurance Companies, November 8, 1956.

[15]Lincoln, report to the boards, Farm Bureau Insurance Companies, July 1, 1947.

[16]p. 262.

[17]Ashley T. McCarter, retired senior vice president, Nationwide Insurance Companies, interview June 28, 1993.

[18]Steven P. Berger, interview August 16, 1993.

[19]Lincoln, report to the boards, Farm Bureau Insurance Companies, July 7, 1948.

[20]Lincoln, *Vice President*, p. 259.

[21]Lincoln, undated address to the board, 1951.

CHAPTER 6

[1]Minutes of a special meeting of the board, Farm Bureau Mutual Automobile Insurance Company, September 12, 1947.

[2]Murray D. Lincoln, report to the boards, Farm Bureau Insurance Companies, February 5, 1946, pp. 2-3.

[3]Lincoln, *Vice President in Charge of Revolution*, p. 221.

[4]Lincoln, speech to Nationwide Insurance employees at spring regional meeting, 1955.

[5]Lincoln, *Vice President*, p. 222.

[6]Ibid., p. 227.

[7]Ibid.

[8]Minutes of the board meeting, Farm Bureau Mutual Automobile Insurance Company, November 7, 1945, p. 890.

[9]Lincoln, board report February 5, 1946.

[10]Dunlap, interview November 11, 1982.

[11]Dr. Robert A. Rennie, interview February 24, 1982.

[12]Lincoln, report to the boards, Farm Bureau Insurance Companies, August 5, 1954.

CHAPTER 7

[1]Frank Freidel and Alan Brinkley, *America in the Twentieth Century*, p. 393.

[2]Murray D. Lincoln, remarks to the boards, Nationwide Insurance Companies, July 1, 1965.

[3]Paul Boardman, undated memorandum, "The Alliance Manufacturing Company," circa spring 1954.

[4]Bowman Doss, interview June 13, 1985.

[5]McKinsey & Company, "Organizing for National Expansion, Farm Bureau Insurance Companies," December 1, 1954.

[6]Doss, "Doss Makes Progress Report on New Plans," *The Dividend*, December 17, 1954, p. 1.

[7]Herbert E. Evans, memorandum to Murray D. Lincoln, "Two Organizational Suggestions," April 14, 1955.

[8]Dr. William Brown, interview December 10, 1984.

[9]Lincoln, President's Staff Conference, January 16, 1956.

[10]Louis E. Dolan, interview March 14, 1994.

[11]Dean W. Jeffers, interview August 28, 1981.

[12]Lincoln, *Vice President in Charge of Revolution*, p. 274.

[13]Lincoln, talk to the boards, Nationwide Insurance Companies, November 8, 1956.

[14]George H. Dunlap, remarks at a management meeting of the affiliated companies, February 18, 1970.

[15]"Nationwide and Mutual Funds: A 25th Anniversary Look Back," *Issues*, February 1982, Vol. 3, No. 2.

[16]"Ahead of His Time," *Forbes*, May 1, 1959.

[17]Larry Young, "Farm Bureau to Tie-in Mutual Fund-Life Sales," *The Journal of Commerce*, July 1, 1954.

[18]Jeffers, interviews August 28, 1981, and June 23, 1993.

[19]Lincoln, statement at an Ohio Department of Insurance hearing, Columbus, June 23, 1959.

[20]Dr. Robert A. Rennie, "Dual Licensing of Agents: Economic and Social Benefits," statement at an Ohio Department of Insurance hearing, Columbus, June 25, 1959.

[21]Gene Smith, "Mutual Funds: Dual Sales Weighed in Ohio," *The New York Times*, July 27, 1959.

[22]"Stock Issue Seen As Growth Step," *The Dividend*, April 4, 1956, p. 1.

[23]Bernard P. McMackin Jr., "National Casualty Experiments in Ohio with Writing Substandard Auto Risks," *National Underwriter*, July 11, 1957.

CHAPTER 8

[1]Murray D. Lincoln, report to the boards, Farm Bureau Insurance Companies, August 5, 1954.

[2]Lincoln, report to the boards, Farm Bureau Insurance Companies, July 7, 1948.

[3]Ibid.

[4]Lincoln, letter to employees, Nationwide Insurance Companies, March 30, 1956.

[5]Lincoln, report to the boards, Nationwide Insurance Companies, February 13, 1957.

[6]Lincoln, talk to the boards, Nationwide Insurance Companies, January 9, 1957.

[7]Ibid.

[8]Ibid.

[9]Lincoln, "Message from the President," Nationwide Corporation annual report, March 1, 1961.

[10]Levering Cartwright, "The Week in Insurance Stocks," *National Underwriter* - Life and Health edition, February 7, 1981.

[11]Lincoln, "To My Way of Thinking...We Can Win Economic Freedom," *Minutes*, December 1956, pp. 31-32.

[12]Vinton E. McVicker, "Nationwide Insurance Group Has Grown in 20 Years From a $10,000 Start to a Half-Billion Outfit," *The Wall Street Journal*, February 26, 1957.

[13]Jack M. Kaplan, personal letter to Lincoln, February 29, 1956.

[14]Lincoln, talk to the boards, Nationwide Insurance Companies, November 8, 1956.

[15]Lincoln, talk to executive session of the boards, Nationwide Insurance Companies,

March 22, 1957.

[16]Lincoln, report to the boards, Farm Bureau Insurance Companies, September 5, 1951.

[17]Ibid.

[18]Dean W. Jeffers, interview June 23, 1993.

[19]Ashley T. McCarter, interview June 28, 1993.

[20]Louis E. Dolan, interview March 14, 1994.

[21]Lincoln, talk to the boards, Nationwide Insurance Companies, March 13, 1957.

[22]Notes from executive session of the boards, Nationwide Insurance Companies, June 7, 1957.

[23]Ibid.

[24]Lincoln's notes from conversations with Roger M. Kyes in Detroit, May 19 and 20, 1958.

[25]P. Lee Thornbury, memorandum to Murray D. Lincoln re "Vorys vs. Nationwide Mutual Insurance Company, et al," August 22, 1961.

[26]Dolan.

[27]Mardo Williams, "Local Business Group Buys Control of Brunson Bank," *Columbus Dispatch*, March 13, 1964.

CHAPTER 9

[1]Murray D. Lincoln, "Message from the President," 1963 annual report, Nationwide Corporation, March 2, 1964.

[2]Robert S. Allen, "Business Bombshell," Hall Syndicate column, October 4, 1949.

[3]Lincoln, letter to John A. Hartford, October 5, 1949.

[4]John A. Hartford, letter to Lincoln, October 19, 1949.

[5]Lincoln, draft of report, January 28, 1964.

[6]Lincoln, letter to Allan P. Kirby, June 30, 1960.

[7]Grady Clark, letter to Lincoln, August 18, 1961.

[8]Lincoln, president's report to the board, Nationwide Corporation, July 10, 1963.

[9]Lincoln, memorandum "To All Members of the Nationwide Sales Organization," January 8, 1962.

[10]Howard K. Smith, personal letter to "Mr. Murray Lincoln," November 24, 1962.

[11]"MDL Affirms No Censorship Pact with Smith and ABC," *The Dividend*, November 15, 1962, pp. 1 and 4.

[12]Calvin Kytle, memorandum re "Howard K. Smith Program," March 5, 1963.

[13]Lincoln, memorandum, May 13, 1960.

[14]Lawrence M. Hughes, "The Co-operatives' Lincoln - More Marketing 'Revolutions,'" *Sales Management*, June 1960.

[15]Lincoln, draft of report to the board, Nationwide Corporation, December 26, 1963.

CHAPTER 10

[1]Murray D. Lincoln, *Ohio Farm Bureau News*, 1954.

[2]Lincoln, letter dated March 23, 1964.

[3]Seved Apelqvist, "Co-operation Among Insurance Co-operatives," International

Co-operative Insurance Conference, Vienna, September 1-2, 1966.
[4]Peter Neckermann, interview August 24, 1993.
[5]Robert M. Culp, interview July 6, 1993.

CHAPTER 11

[1]Murray D. Lincoln, draft of president's remarks to the boards, Nationwide Insurance Companies, December 20, 1963.
[2]Calvin Kytle, confidential memorandum to Murray D. Lincoln, January 2, 1964.
[3]Louis E. Dolan, interview March 14, 1994.
[4]Bowman Doss, interview June 13, 1985.
[5]Doss, unpublished autobiography.
[6]Lincoln, statement given to the boards, Nationwide Insurance Companies, April 2, 1964.
[7]Columbus *Citizen-Journal*, April 3, 1964, p. 1.
[8]Dolan.
[9]Annual meeting minutes, Nationwide Corporation, April 28, 1964, p. 400.
[10]J. Richard Bull, interview July 12, 1993.
[11]Lincoln, memorandum to the boards, Nationwide Insurance Companies, July 1, 1965.

CHAPTER 12

[1]Robert W. Heffner, vice president, insurance expansion, and J.R. Koenig, vice president, zone manager, memorandum to Ashley T. McCarter, vice president, field operations, re "New States Study," September 27, 1963.
[2]Bowman Doss, "Report on the Companies' Operating and Administrative Problems," confidential memorandum to the boards, Nationwide Insurance Companies, October 7, 1964.
[3]Doss, memorandum from the president's office, October 16, 1964.
[4]Doss, "Timely Today," *Challenger*, January 1954. Vol. 13, No. 5, pp. 16-21.
[5]"New Man in the Insurance Business: 'I enjoy making deals,' says Lou Dolan, successor-apparent to Murray Lincoln at Nationwide Corp. He sure does," *Forbes*, September 15, 1964, pp. 44 and 47.
[6]Louis V. Fabro, memorandum to all Nationwide vice presidents, September 16, 1964.
[7]"West Coast Life Still May Merge: Study Under Way," San Francisco *News-Call Bulletin*, June 17, 1965.
[8]Doss, "People Working Together," an address to The Newcomen Society, Sheraton-Columbus Hotel, May 1, 1968.
[9]Doss, "Doss Appeals for Rededication to Bright Future for Companies," *Challenger*, May 1965, Vol. 22, No. 9.
[10]Doss, "A Progress Report in Respect to the Companies' Operating and Administrative Problems," report the boards of the Nationwide Insurance Companies, October 6, 1965.

[11]Doss, "Message from the President," 1964 Nationwide Insurance annual report, March 1, 1965.

[12]Doss, "On the Move Again," President's Dinner Meeting address, October 28, 1966.

[13]Ibid.

[14]Bob Krause, "The Ballroom Swings as Nationwiders 'Live Again,'" *The Dividend*, February 15, 1968, Vol. 18, No. 10, p. 1.

[15]Frank B. Sollars, interview August 12, 1993.

[16]Doss, notes from an unpublished autobiography.

[17]Dean W. Jeffers, "Jeffers Pledges Dedication to Presidential Task," *The Dividend*, April 9, 1969, Vol. 19, No. 14.

CHAPTER 13

[1]Ralph Jordan, interview August 29, 1983.

[2]"Nationwide Resumes Sales of Auto to New Customers," *Challenger*, February 1971.

[3]"Facing Those Riskier Risks," *Journal of American Insurance*, January-February 1971.

[4]"Jeffers Announces 50 Percent Rate Increase for Powerful Cars," *The Dividend*, October 9, 1969, p.1.

[5]Dean W. Jeffers and George H. Dunlap, 1970 Nationwide Insurance annual report, April 1971.

[6]"Record Operating Gain is Reported for Nationwide Mutual During 1971," *Challenger*, February 1972.

[7]Ronald E. Ledwell, "Nationwide Corporation," *Dow Digest*, December 1972, pp. 56-57.

[8]John L. Marakas, "The Executive Corner," *The Wall Street Transcript*, June 10, 1974, p. 37,202.

[9]Galen Van Meter, "Suggestions for the Transfer of Certain Assets," November 27, 1962.

[10]Peter D. Franklin, "Nationwide to Go Private," *Columbus Dispatch*, November 4, 1982, p. A10.

CHAPTER 14

[1]Bill D. Wymore, memorandum to Lee Weinberger, April 20, 1988.

CHAPTER 15

[1]Robert W. Gunderson, *The Wausau Story*, p. 154.

[2]Clyde F. Schlueter, address to The Newcomen Society, "The Wausau Story," Milwaukee, WI, May 8, 1974.

[3]Ibid.

[4]Ibid.

[5]John E. Fisher, speech "Realities About the Insurance Industry — An International Business," Columbus Council on World Affairs, April 23, 1986.

[6]John A. Schoneman, "1980 Report to Policyholders," Wausau Insurance Companies, p. 14.

[7]Gunderson, p. 148.

[8]Lowell H. Tornow, interview August 2, 1993.

[9]Judy Wenzel, "Wausau's Woes," *Milwaukee Journal*, June 2, 1985, pp. 1,6,7.

[10]Steve Weiner, "Wausau Chief Quits Abruptly, Citing '84 Loss," *The Wall Street Journal*, June 6, 1985, p. 44.

[11]Bill D. Wymore, interview August 2, 1993.

[12]Judy Greenwald, "Wausau to Meet with M&M about Memo on Insurer's Health," *Business Insurance,* June 17, 1985, pp. 2 and 34.

[13]Peter F. Frenzer, memorandum to the Nationwide Bond and Investment Committee, "Recommendation for Investment and Plan of Affiliation," November 6, 1985.

CHAPTER 16

[1]Hoyt Johnson, "What a Story!", *Scottsdale Scene Magazine*, May/June 1991.

[2]Patrick L. Doyle, interview September 15, 1993.

[3]D. Richard McFerson, interview October 20, 1993.

[4]"PBC Grosses One Million Dollars In Browns Football Team Sale," *The Dividend,* March 30, 1961.

[5]Evelyn Keseg, interview May 16, 1985.

[6]Dean W. Jeffers, minutes of Chairman's Council, December 5, 1977.

[7]Barnet D. Wolf, "Nationwide to Sell Its 3 TV Stations," *Columbus Dispatch*, April 23, 1994.

[8]"Why We Acquired Farmland's Insurance Operations," *Issues*, September 1982, Vol. 3, No. 9, p. 3.

[9]"Gates McDonald Projects New Look," *Issues,* September 1992, Vol. 13, No. 5, pp. 3 and 4.

[10]John D. Hicks, *The American Nation*, 2nd ed., p. 406.

[11]GatesMcDonald *Insights*, 60th anniversary edition, 1989.

[12]*Issues.*

[13]Ibid.

CHAPTER 17

[1]Dean W. Jeffers, address "The Nationwide Story, Volume II," The Newcomen Society, Columbus, May 6, 1981.

[2]Edward F. Wagner, "The Involved Companies," *New York Times* advertising supplement, October 29, 1972.

[3]Ibid.

[4]Gerald D. Keim, "Corporate Grassroots Programs in the 1980s," *California Management Review,* 1987, Vol. 28, No. 1.

CHAPTER 18

[1]D. Richard McFerson, memorandum "Image 2000 Report" to Robert Quinn, February 11, 1980.

[2]McFerson, "President and CEO McFerson Responds to Questions About His Vision for a Changing Nationwide Insurance Enterprise," *The Nationwide Dividend,* December 16, 1993, p. 2.

[3]Ibid.

[4]"McFerson: Ongoing Changes Spur Business Success," *Issues,* July 1993, Vol. 14, No. 4, p. 2.

[5]McFerson, "Nationwide Heritage Provides Foundation for Our Vision," *The Nationwide Dividend,* December 16, 1993, p. 4.

Appendix
D

INDEX

on your side

Designed by William Shillington and Mark Mills
in the Office of Public Relations and Customer Relations,
Nationwide Insurance Enterprise.
The book was set in Adobe Garamond and printed
on Cougar Natural Opaque paper by Weyerhaeuser.

Printing and binding provided by
The Emerson Press, Inc.
and
Quebecor Printing (USA).